CORRIDORS

CORRIDORS

Passages of Modernity

ROGER LUCKHURST

REAKTION BOOKS

Published by Reaktion Books Ltd
Unit 32, Waterside
44–48 Wharf Road
London N1 7UX, UK

www.reaktionbooks.co.uk

First published 2019

Printed and bound in Great Britain by
T.J. International Limited, Padstow, Cornwall

A catalogue record for this book is available from the British Library

ISBN 978 1 78914 053 8

Contents

Untitled Corridor Project

You may remember it differently but
all I see is one long corridor
hot-wired to the nervous system
I feel the change in pressure on my face

a corporate corridor
vacuum cleaners sashaying in wide arcs
a ship's corridor
portholes reflected like a row of buttons
        on the floor

a hotel corridor
where fear feels like a solid thing
and music leaks from the ceiling

upgrading to an airport corridor
a shadowless hospital corridor
with an ending phoned-in by the gods

I suspect the scenery is changed behind me
that I walk in an endless loop
a recession of dead spaces

note the identifying thread in the carpet
that print repeated on the wall

                                just in case
I carry an ampoule of poison into the hall

Chris Greenhalgh

One need not be a chamber to be haunted,
One need not be a house;
The brain has corridors surpassing
Material place.

Emily Dickinson

Introduction

Every workday morning I step out of the door of my somewhat battered post-war duplex onto the 60-metre (200 ft) concrete deck of my housing block and walk to the end staircase. I take the London Underground for a couple of stops, through Farringdon to King's Cross, the oldest stretch of track in the network, first opened in 1863. Since 2010 the Circle Line (although it no longer circles) has been upgraded to connected corridor carriages, so at quiet times you get a snaking sightline down the whole train. I leave King's Cross through the Euston Road exit: since the arrival of the Eurostar terminus, the lower level has been transformed into a shopping arcade. My office in Gordon Square, in disreputable Bloomsbury, is in the row of Georgian town houses once owned by Virginia Woolf and her sister Vanessa Bell, and later by Maynard Keynes. These houses, rented by the University of London, used to be a warren of backstairs and convoluted passages. To get between the houses sometimes involved descending to the basement or up to the garrets in the loft to move across the load-bearing walls. A refit has now punched lateral corridors through the building, imposing some degree of logic, although they twist and turn, still mark the boundaries of the separate houses, and it is common to find lost souls wandering the hallways bewildered by the elusive room-numbering system.

This is a journey dominated by corridors, that quintessentially modern space. There is a complex history in this short journey – moving

Access deck of the Golden Lane estate, London, built 1957–62.

from that clouded dream of Modernist collective housing, of shared decks and communal living, through a Victorian transport corridor on a corridor train first introduced, with much fanfare, in the 1890s, getting off through a shopping arcade that was a wholly new kind of commercial space in the 1810s, to a university that in its idealist, expansionist phase in the twentieth century saw the corridor as a model of enlightened, circulating knowledge, a place of exchange where the disciplines would flow together.

Yet, to be honest, these spaces are merely *passages*, volumes to pass through on the way to somewhere else. These are the parts of the journey most likely to be done on autopilot, the minutes and hours vanishing into routine habit. Dead time and dead space.

Architectural history tends to agree. 'Corridor' entered the English language in the early eighteenth century, yet as late as 1978 Robin Evans declared that 'the history of the corridor . . . has yet to be written.' Paul Olivier, in the exhaustive *Encyclopedia of Vernacular Architecture*, remarks in a brief entry that 'The word "corridor" is among the rarest in the books on vernacular architecture, reflecting both the neglect that they have received, and their passing function.' When the French experimental writer Georges Perec decided that he would write about the everyday modern spaces to which we ordinarily pay no attention and retain no memory, his first instances are 'towns . . . or the corridors of the Paris Métro, or a public park'. Corridors recur throughout the foreword to his *Species of Spaces*, but perhaps symptomatically Perec then fails to write another word about them, as if they remain invisible even to the master of the forgotten and overlooked.[1]

Why this disregard? Most office jobs are now located in open-plan offices, which emerged in the 1950s as a model of post-war modernization and efficiency. Many office workers now live in spaces where the internal walls, so loved in domestic settings by the Victorians, have been knocked down and the interiors opened up. The middle classes read lifestyle magazines that have been selling a vision of wall-free, corridorless loft living since the drive to recapitalize old inner-city industrial spaces in the 1980s. This open plan is not only for hipsters and gentrifiers. We do not wait for hospital appointments in corridors in new hospitals any more, but sit in vast, open glass atria. Every winter, when the British health service comes under intense pressure, the worst hospital nightmare is to be stranded in an in-between place: 'Stroke victim spent 54 hours in corridor.'[2] This is an *anti-corridic* world.

Corridors are now regarded as infrastructure, the underpinning service elements of the world that are too big, or buried, or boring, to deserve comment. Infrastructure 'seldom sustains mindful attention, manifesting instead the stuff of an unremarked substrate simply servicing the basics of everyday life'.[3] Drains, cable pipes, vents, service roads, electrical substations – and corridors. It is engineers, not architects, who pore over schematics of large-scale trade and transport corridors, or plan ecological corridors – a metaphorical extension that seemed to arrive in the 1960s just as domesticated corridors were disappearing. It is engineers, not architects, who ensure compliance with health and safety rules, for instance that Fire Exit corridors hidden away in the shameful back-room quarters of modern buildings conform to International Building Codes. These define an exit corridor as a continuous and unobstructed path of egress from any occupied portion of a building to a public way. They must meet the minimum width restrictions, which remains roughly two shoulder-widths wide, one for the column of evacuees to exit, one for the column of fire service personnel to enter. Surely these are technical matters for the engineer, not the architect, so that the corridor becomes what Stephan Trüby has called an un-architecture.

If you buy any popular architectural guide, such as *How to Read Houses* or *How to Read a Building*, the corridor will not feature in it. Gaston Bachelard's *The Poetics of Space* famously explores 'the power of attraction of all the domains of intimacy' in the home, but only passingly mentions 'nooks and corridors'.[4] We want to know about the resonance of rooms, not the passages between them. Doorways and thresholds have rich literature and history dedicated to their profound symbolic resonances: from the earliest cultural traces, 'the idea of passage and transition functioned as a key paradigm for the discovery and acquisition of new knowledge,' Daniel Jütte explains in his marvellous survey of the door-as-symbol, *The Strait Gate*.[5] Is there an equivalent for the corridor? Not really.

Yet at the same time as this disappearing act, I found that I was seeing corridors everywhere in cinema, on TV, in computer games. Whenever I explained to someone that I was writing a cultural history of the corridor, nearly everyone's first reference point was Stanley Kubrick's film *The Shining* (1980), where we watch the young boy

Danny hurtle through the labyrinths of the Overlook Hotel on his tricycle, drawing impossible figures as he loops through those confounding spaces. These short scenes stick in the mind because viewers had literally never seen anything like this before. Kubrick took the relatively new invention of the Steadicam and turned it upside down, so that it rested close to the floor where the angle made the corridor a looming, terrifying space revealed in the frictionless glide of what we know is a malignant, inhuman gaze stalking the young boy.

The Shining revealed something about the emotional latency of corridors: a simple lesson in the social construction of space. Before *The*

Danny riding his tricycle through the Overlook Hotel, from Stanley Kubrick's *The Shining* (1980).

Shining, the haunted house had been about the verticality of staircases, attics and basements, the house as a stratified metaphor of the conscious and unconscious mind (think of *Psycho*, the detective climbing the steps to his doom, while Norman's mother rots in the basement and his victims sink into the lower depths of the swamp beyond the motel). After *The Shining*, however, dread lurked in the unhistoried horizontal horror of corridors, in the anonymous modernity of hotel vistas and the bland hallways of public institutions.

This corridor trick has been repeated in a thousand horror films and computer games, where the corridor plan becomes an uninterrupted, unfolding space that at once limits the action but multiplies the threats of menace from off-screen space as the camera moves forward. The earliest video games in the 1970s were based on mazes or labyrinths, and famous breakthrough computer games of the 1990s such as *Doom* or the first version of *Resident Evil* mainly involved running about in corridors. Any glimpse at contemporary film or TV will reveal cameras intent on corridor spaces, from the CCTV fixed on the void of the landing space beyond the bedroom door in *Paranormal Activity* (2007), to the exuberant swoops through the passages of the haunted house, the asylum or the hotel in the *American Horror Story* TV franchise, or the soulless scientific lab-mazes of secret military-industrial complexes that form the principal spaces of the *Resident Evil* series, or *Stranger Things* or *Westworld*. There is a whole subgenre of 'corridor as gauntlet', where our heroes have to fight from one end of a corridor to another through impossible numbers of violent antagonists, from *Hard Boiled* and *Oldboy* via *World War Z* or *The Raid* to Netflix's *Daredevil*. Perhaps the most influential horror novel of recent times has been Mark Z. Danielewski's *The House of Leaves* (2000), which concerns the appearance of an impossible corridor, resolutely empty yet utterly terrifying, in the small domestic house of the Navidson family.

The interesting questions then become: why and when did the corridor start to be associated with fear? Or, if not fear (not every corridor promises spooky twins, hordes of ninjas or a gauntlet of zombies, after all), then the tone of those quieter unnerved emotions of anxiety, eeriness or dread? In 1968 a group of community planners and architects declared that 'long corridors with many rooms off them are dysfunctional; people dislike them; they represent bureaucracy and monotony.' They designed from the premise that 'long corridors set the scene for everything bad about modern architecture.'[6] Was this a turning point, when it was felt that there was something destructive about the large-scale corridor plan in public buildings or social housing, a Kafkaesque annihilation of the self in the plunging single-point perspective of the institutional corridor? At about the same time, the oppressive instrumental rationality of modern bureaucracy was represented by the office corridor in Jean-Luc Godard's science-fiction-of-the-present *Alphaville* (1965).

In a slightly different way, the architects Joshua Cameroff and Ker-Shing Ong suggest a kind of dialectic between structure and infrastructure, open visible design and closed-off, invisible function, in modern architecture:

> Modern buildings, like modern subjects, thus came to contain unspeakable cavities. Channeled winds, mobile waste, captive lightning – all of these are smuggled into the walls of the home and the office. Those who work in design and construction are familiar with these obscure and recessive spaces, how they contradict the resolved bourgeois exterior. Simply put, they are a mess. In order to sustain this disappearing act, the modern partition is conceived as a complex assembly of membranes, organized around a vacancy. Again, this is quite recent. The walls of the pre-modern building had no unseemly interior.[7]

The answer, they might suggest, is that just as the corridor ostensibly seems to vanish in modern design, it rears back up as a kind of return of the repressed, inevitably tinged with horror. The gleaming white cube still needs its sewage outlets, its back-room service corridors, its fire exits.

But there is a longer and more complex genealogy to the strange emotional tenor of corridors, and this book is an effort to trace this history from the first appearance of the corridor in Western architecture to its strange afterlife as simultaneously disregarded infrastructure or overextended metaphor. This is a cultural history rather than a strict architectural one, moving across sources from the built environment, spatial theory, public policy, fiction, painting and varieties of screens, to capture the shifting resonances of the corridor.

The corridor emerges with the Enlightenment as a newly rational proposal for the distribution of private and public space, and I want to argue that its development and changing meanings offers a striking account of the trajectory of modernity itself. The handful of histories available often regards the corridor as a device of class distinction and social separation, particularly in the bourgeois home of Protestant northern Europe, and particularly in the nineteenth century. Symptomatically enough, when Windsor Castle was rebuilt for George IV from 1824 by Jeffry Wyatville, the new distribution centred on the 168-metre-long (550-ft) Grand Corridor, which divided staterooms, guest rooms and private family quarters. Robert Kerr, whose book *The Gentleman's House* became the touchstone for Victorian mansion-building in the 1860s, was entirely obsessed with corridors as devices to secure the middle-class private life and separate family from servants. He returns compulsively to the corridor because it is a fraught and liminal space of passage, a place where social divides are asserted but might collapse at any moment.

However, it is also important to remember that the new-fangled corridor was also thoroughly imbued with ideas of rational reform and social improvement as soon as it emerged. Indeed, it was considered so transformational a space that the corridor was intrinsic to many utopian conceptions of public spaces for well over a century, from Charles Fourier's phalanstery, which housed people along a gallery that promised infinite unalienated happiness and sexual possibility in 1807, to the socialist town planners of post-1945 England, who built around the communal corridor as the structure that might redefine selfhood itself, just as prison reformers, asylum builders and Soviet collectivists had believed before them. The curdling of that utopian prospect after the 1960s is what has at once eclipsed the corridor and yet ensured its persistence in the cultural imagination as a space of either monotonous bureaucratic uniformity or of Gothic unease and dread.

This, in capsule, is the story that I want to tell. Recovering this history has allowed me to see the bland, overlooked volumes of everyday life, the *infrastructural stuff* we spend so much time just passing through, really for the first time. I hope to pass this act of re-vision on to you and make you think about these apparently dead, transitional spaces in a new kind of way. So let's start with first things first: the arrival of the corridor.

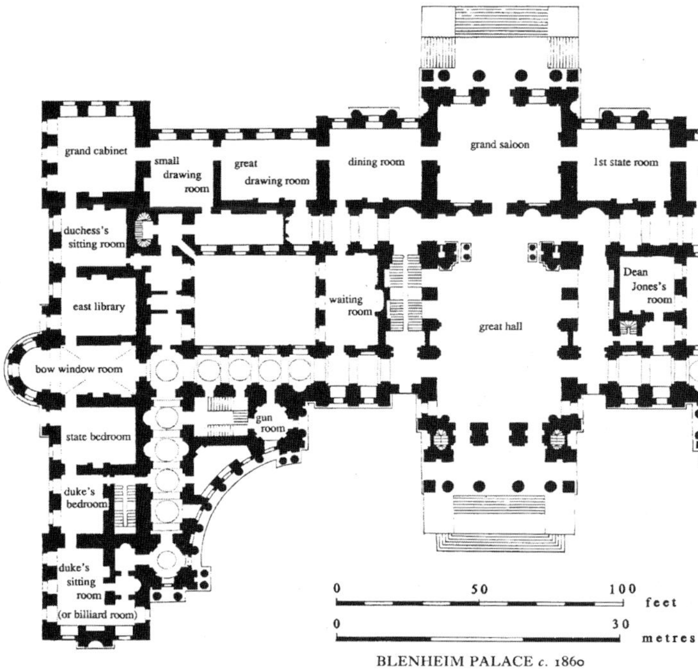

The floor plan of Blenheim Palace, c. 1860.

1

Origins

In 1716 the architect Sir John Vanbrugh wrote to the Duchess of Marlborough to explain aspects of his design for Blenheim Palace, over which she had expressed many doubts: 'The word Corridor, Madam, is foreign, and signifies in plain English, no more than a passage.' She remained sceptical about this detail, but Vanbrugh bragged to another friend that Castle Howard, his first Baroque triumph (which had been started in 1699), had surely proved the worth of his innovative design.

> For my Lord Carlisle was pretty much under the same Apprehensions with her, about long passages, High Rooms, etc. But he finds what I told him to be true. That those Passages would be so far from gathering & drawing wind as he fancied, that a Candle wou'd not flare in them of this he has lately had the proof, by bitter stormy nights in which not one Candle wanted to be put into a Lanthorn, not even in the Hall.[1]

In both houses Vanbrugh designed very dramatic entrances with sweeping staircases, but strikingly pushed access to the wings behind them, distributing the saloon and main public rooms along a long, lateral corridor. This had the deliberate effect of extending the already imposing mass of the building, and internally created a recessive effect. 'Vanbrugh used the corridors to great effect', Charles

Saumarez Smith judges: 'they permitted independent access to the cabinets at either end of the arcade . . . and they created an extended and architecturally impressive vista.'[12]

The word 'corridoors' only began to appear on architectural plans, as in Colen Campbell's survey of grand buildings, *Vitruvius Britannicus*, in 1715. This technical term was rarely used over the next century, however, and it only entered everyday language in the 1820s (Byron's 1814 poem *The Corsair* – 'He pass'd the portal, cross'd the corridor/And reach'd the chamber' – is the first literary instance).

Quite how Vanbrugh, a former trader with the East India Company, soldier and playwright, received the commissions to build these houses remains unclear. He was a member of the aristocratic Kit-Cat Club in London, whose membership included his two clients, Charles Howard, third Earl of Carlisle, and John Churchill, the war hero and first Duke of Marlborough, for whom Blenheim was built. Aristocrats enjoyed Vanbrugh's conversational wit, yet he had no prior architectural experience. Vanbrugh worked on both of these grand projects with the professional architect Nicholas Hawksmoor, who was key to completing both designs (he continued with Blenheim after Vanbrugh had been fired from the project).

Perhaps Vanbrugh's lack of deference to architectural norms in England left him open to new influences. He had travelled in India, been imprisoned by the French in Paris at a time when the city was largely closed to English travellers, and had learnt about spectacular theatrical space when writing comedies for the Drury Lane theatre in the 1690s. This interest later led to designing the Queen's Theatre in the Haymarket. His patron at Castle Howard had also spent three years travelling in Italy, absorbing influences.

Yet modern aristocratic houses across Europe tended in the seventeenth century to announce their grandness not with corridors but receding vistas of rooms that opened onto each other through a procession of aligned doorways. This arrangement was known as an *enfilade*, as in the royal apartments at the Palace of Versailles (1682).

These might have had narrow passageways hidden alongside, but those parallel structures were only for use by servants. Vanbrugh moved the passageway from the hidden margin to become a central part of the design of the house.

The word 'corridor' derives from the Italian verb *currere*, to run, and thus shares the same root as *courier*. The messenger who speeds along was a *corridore* in Italian. *Corridoio* was first used in the fourteenth century as an architectural term to describe the unobstructed path built immediately behind defensive fortifications to ensure that messages could be conveyed quickly to the commanders of defence forces. These developed over the centuries into military structures like the covered way that afforded, according to one 1830 definition, 'a safe communication around all the works, facilitates sallies and retreats, and the reception of auxiliaries . . . and its parapet protects the fortifications in its rear'.[3] *Corridoio* could also be used to describe secret passages in and out of palaces, such as the one built in 1565 for the Medicis over the Arno river in Florence to connect the Palazzo Pitti and the Palazzo Vecchio.

The corridor then shifts to become an internal architectural device in ducal palaces in Italy. Francesco Borromini built one in his redesign of the Palazzo Spada in Rome in 1653, the famous Galleria Prospettica that used a trick of forced perspective to extend a short colonnade in the courtyard into the optical illusion of a much deeper receding arcade. The first plans to be marked with a *coritore* leading straight through the building date from 1644.[4]

This direct new route through the palazzo was designed to provide the fastest passage to the cabinet of the ruler, avoiding cluttered manoeuvring through successive rooms. It was a way to avoid the lobby, too, that anteroom to power associated with rituals of gossip and the longueurs of waiting for an audience. Although the phrase 'corridors of power' was not coined until the 1960s, from the beginning a corridor thus announced a certain importance of the resident, a need for connection to networks of information. Across Europe,

Renaissance kings and aristocrats used architecture as an articulation of their political power. If 'political rule is a spatial reality', then the corridor is an embodied metaphor of communication and mediation, designed to transport bodies and circulate information at speed.[5]

This makes some sense of the gesture made by the corridors at Castle Howard and Blenheim Palace, since both were intended as expressions of the political power of their owners. Charles Howard inherited his title and twice served as First Lord of the Treasury in crucial administrations that consolidated Britain's imperial ambitions. Blenheim was built on land donated by Queen Anne to John Churchill, the soldier who had led the British forces to victory over the French at the Battle of Blenheim in 1704, which effectively secured Britain's dominance in Europe as an imperial power. The palace for the newly ennobled Duke of Marlborough was to be paid for by the public purse, although, this being England, the Treasury soon began to drag its heels on payment for Blenheim, particularly after the political climate shifted against the Whigs in the years after the commission.

In fact, Vanbrugh's houses became emblems of the English Baroque that quickly fell out of fashion for their overwrought style. Robert Adams decried buildings 'crowded with barbarisms and absurdities', a mark that Neoclassicism had begun its long tenure as the architectural norm for civic and political buildings.[6] Vanbrugh's houses did not find favour again until a revival of interest in the 1890s.

Vanbrugh is one of the key moments marking the arrival of the *tangential corridor* in British architecture, a new kind of distribution of rooms opened into along a central axis. Still, I need to step back for a while to give some account of the prehistory of this space. Confusingly, architectural historians sometimes retroactively apply the term 'corridor' to plans of buildings from eras when no such structure existed. While there is possibly nothing worse than the prospect of pedantry about how to classify different genres of passageway, it is necessary to sketch out a quick genealogy of this space to get a grip on the distinction between some adjacent or overlapping terms and to convey a sense of the symbolic importance of what might be called more generally *corridic* spaces.

Before the Corridor: The Ancient World

Ancient antecedents are best divided into religious, civic and domestic forms. Many ancient temple structures can be described as being organized along *transversal* corridor plans. As Stephan Trüby helpfully explains:

> In most temple and palace architecture, the main tower or building is located in the centre of a void surrounded by courtyard-corridor type buildings. Constructed as a complex and not as a single interior space, individual buildings are connected by diverse types of corridors such as courtyard corridors, roofed walkways, sky-bridges and perimeter corridors – all of them wrapping or penetrating a void: this is the transversal corridor, a line that can cut through a system of lines (or spaces).[7]

The angle and alignment of these transversal pathways often had astronomical import given the worship of heavenly bodies in many cultures, a mapping of birth and death in the trajectory of the Sun or Moon. Egyptian and Greek temples were simple rectangular enclosures, sanctuaries for a sacred sculpture of the god. Yet the approach to this space was complex, constituting a series of symbolic transitions from the mundane to the sacred, a procession of increasingly restricted pathways. At the temple complex of Edfu in Upper Egypt, for example, the supplicant passed through an avenue of sphinxes, then entered a peristylar forecourt, open to the sky but laterally restricted, then into a roofed portico, before crossing a threshold into an anteroom, and finally facing the last threshold of the inner sanctuary. This *cella* or sanctum was, R. D. Martienssen says, 'dark, narrow and low, completely insulated from the outside world, and only approachable through a succession of ever greater restricting volumes: a cell which, within the limits imposed by human size, reflects a complete antithesis to the light and free space of the outer world'.[8] The architecture becomes what Mircea Eliade calls 'vehicles of passage' or 'images of an opening' between heaven and earth, the sacred and the profane.[9]

Mystery cults in Greece and Rome typically exploited these successively restrictive spaces to create a path of disorientation, anticipation, fear and wonder, before the culminating unveiling of the god. Precisely what went on in these rituals was secret and passed on only between initiates. Plutarch's essay on the Isis cult speaks vaguely of 'walking in circles, some frightening paths in the darkness that lead nowhere . . . And some wonderful light comes to meet you . . . with sounds, and dances, and solemn sacred words.' The sequence was a passing from the darkness into the light, a ritual unveiling of the embodied god.

Another version of this ritual space was the labyrinth. There are two famous ancient examples of these. The first was the Egyptian structure built at Medinet el-Fayum during the reign of pharaoh Amenemhet III (1839–1791 BCE). Long lost until the traces were rediscovered in the late nineteenth century, this place was described by the Greek traveller Herodotus in 440 BCE in very evocative terms as a vast complex of over 3,000 rooms that dwarfed the pyramids in their ingenuity and scope. Herodotus exclaimed: 'The baffling and intricate passages from room to room and from court to court were an endless wonder to me, as we passed from a courtyard into rooms, from rooms into galleries, from galleries into more rooms, and from there into more courtyards.'[10] He was not allowed to see the lower level, which was underground, and which he speculated was a sacred necropolis for the rulers of the region. Four centuries later the Greek geographer Strabo also travelled there and described 'long and numerous covered ways with winding communicating passages, so that no stranger could find his own way into the courts or out of them without a guide'.[11]

The more influential example was the labyrinth at Knossos on Crete. This Minoan structure (destroyed by fire in 1380 BCE) became wrapped in Greek legends and myths about the vengeful King Minos, who commands his engineer Daedalus to build a labyrinth in which is imprisoned the Minotaur, a half-man, half-bull. The monster devours the sacrifice of Athenian youths and maidens sent every nine years as tribute, until Theseus slays the monster and finds his way out of the labyrinth by following the thread of Ariadne, the daughter of Minos. As Ovid retells a version of the story in the *Metamorphoses*, one translation reads:

> The structure was designed by Daedalus,
> That famous architect. Appearances
> Were all confused; he led the eye astray
> By a mazy multitude of winding ways . . .
> So Daedalus in countless corridors
> Built bafflement, and hardly could himself
> Make his way out, so puzzling was the maze.[12]

This version smuggles in the modern corridor to translate the Latin '*innumeras errore vias*' (countless false roads, or ways), but it is very suggestive of how we now consistently associate large corridor complexes with the ancient labyrinth. Perhaps this is because Sir Arthur Evans, who excavated the ruins at Knossos from 1900, was convinced that he was uncovering the palace of a king and rebuilt portions of the complex with reinforced concrete, giving names such as 'The Corridor of the Procession' to embed his speculative guesses about the function of the architectural spaces he was uncovering. The Knossos visited now is a 'delirious' interpretation of the ancient past constructed in the modern era by 'the temple builders of an age of concrete'.[13] Evans had already used labyrinth motifs throughout the corridors of the rambling house he had built at Youlbury in Oxfordshire in the 1890s.

The symbol of the maze or labyrinth is found in many of the earliest human cultures and has been interpreted as the journey into the land of the dead, or as the tortuous path of initiation: 'the aspirant trod the winding paths of an intricate maze that signified our mortal life.'[14] The symbol is also sometimes thought to be a trap designed to prevent malign spirits or demons from finding their way, which is why they are often drawn at doorways or thresholds. Turf mazes for ritual dances survived in England into the nineteenth century, and the menacing resonances of the tall hedge maze, designed to confound with its dead ends and multicursal branching pathways, is evoked in modern horror again in Stephen King's *The Shining* as a clear adjunct to the corridors of the Overlook Hotel. It has become a metaphor for psychic convolutions of mental confusion, but this is underpinned by millennia of powerful associations. Beneath the corridor there lies the mythic resonances of the labyrinth.

Ancient initiation rites were therefore literalized as a series of passages and movements across thresholds. Often the doorway was the bearer of the heaviest symbolic load. Pylons marked the entry to sacred space in many ancient cultures, the sanctified zone the Greeks called the *temenos*. This symbolic threshold continued in the Christian tradition. 'I am the door,' Jesus sermonizes in the New Testament, and Augustine later elaborated: 'It is through the door of the church that we enter paradise.'[15] Early Medieval churches had already begun to expand and complicate entrances to increase this transitory zone between the profane and the sacred with the construction of steps, porches, archways and entrance halls (or narthexes) and the development of a number of rituals held on the threshold of church doorways.

In classical Greece, temple sanctuaries themselves remained simple cells, however elaborated the anterooms, doorways and porch structures became. Steps always lifted up a base for the temple's construction, but Doric temples became peripteral structures, surrounded on all four sides by a colonnade. It was the exterior that was important, not the interior. Altars stood outside, the ritual sacrifices framed by the temple behind. It was in the movement of processions along ritual pathways, crossing a series of marked thresholds, as along the Panathenaic Way towards the Acropolis in Athens, where belief was enacted.

In the loosest sense, these symbolic pathways towards the sanctuary might be called *corridic*. They are transversal in the sense that they point at something, aiming to deliver the body of the initiate or just the gaze of the spectator to one place and one place only: the threshold of the sacred interior. Those looking for recurrent archetypes in the human psyche might, I suppose, align the modern corridor with these ancient symbolic pathways of life and death, although modern corridors are meant to operate tangentially, multiplying destinations rather than restricting them to one. Even so, as we will discover, those who have had Near-Death Experiences frequently report travelling along a corridor towards an intense light at the far end, rather like Greek or Roman initiates slowly moving towards their encounter with the face of god.

One way of defining the sacred path or delineating sacred spaces in ancient Greece was the development of long, narrow-columned structures called stoa. These were free-standing colonnades, typically columned and open on one side and solid at the back. They were used to provide shade for audiences watching processions or for framing temple sanctuaries, as with the examples at Olympia or Delos. The colonnades had grown to impressive lengths by the fourth century BCE – the stoa of Philip II at Megalopolis was 150 metres (500 ft) long – and sometimes used a second row of interior columns to increase the width, which turned them into major independent buildings. As frames for sacred spaces, you can get a strong idea of their effect from the vast elliptical colonnades that frame the piazza in front of St Peter's basilica in Rome, built by Bernini with massive Baroque columns in the seventeenth century.

In classical Greece these narrow colonnades were also gradually adopted for use in the secular, civic city. Below the sacred rock of the

Acropolis in Athens, the chaotic city at the foot of the mountain was slowly shaped into a meaningful public sphere, the Agora, over the centuries by a succession of large stoa that marked out a civic square. The stoa turned a confusing ad hoc space into one with sharper definition and greater monumentality. The ruins of the Agora are now dominated by the reconstruction of the later Stoa of Attalos, gifted to Athens by Attalos II of Pergamon (r. 159–138 BCE) and rebuilt in the 1950s to house a museum. The Stoa of Attalos is just under 120 metres (395 ft) long and 20 metres (65 ft) wide, of two storeys, with a double colonnade that allowed the rear to be filled in with 21 shops on each floor. The stoa was a promenade and a marketplace, a space that later merged with Syrian influences to become a forerunner of the enclosed Oriental bazaar. It was also a place for informal public debate: the Stoic philosophers were so named for their philosophy of the stoa. This, therefore, was one of the key spatial forms intrinsically linked to the expression of classical democracy.

Other civic buildings, particularly governing council houses (such as the Bouleuterion in the Athenian Agora), were more clearly delineated from sacred architecture in their design. The Greeks built debating chambers with tiered seating inside boxier structures. Clear sight lines required fewer internal columns, although Greek architects never quite solved the problem of how to support large roof spans without them. The tiers of seats were often stabilized with an internal support wall that created a narrow vestibule space inside the building. Some historians term this a corridor. It was a space 'used by small groups for caucusing, without interfering with the deliberations of the council as a whole' – in other words, the forerunner of the parliamentary 'lobby'.[16] The most elaborate council house structure was found at Miletos, which could seat 1,200 under one of the largest unsupported roof spans in ancient Greece, to which was added a forecourt, colonnaded on three sides, and a Corinthian propylon entryway.

Stoa of Attalos, in the ancient Agora of Athens, originally built c. 150 BCE.

In the end, secular buildings often borrowed imposing anticipatory corridic structures from temple complexes.

In contrast, Roman architects began to use roof trusses and other devices, and in imperial Roman buildings the expression of religious and civic power was signalled by the vastness of the span of domes and basilicas. Romans also built long, narrow structures with barrel-vaulted roofs that helped carry the weight of the floors of grand civic buildings above. This foundational cellar or storage space was called a *cryptoporticus*, another very corridic structure. In early modern Europe, borrowing from the Roman model, the expression of power in palaces was articulated through the vast unsupported spans and complicated roof ribbings of their ceremonial public halls, designed to dwarf the visitor with imposing size. Any corridor-like interior divides would have detracted from this visible announcement of strength.

When we shift to domestic architecture, and despite the confusing use of 'corridor' by some architectural historians, it is strictly accurate to say that the Greek house contained no corridors. Emphasis on the public expression of citizenship in classical Greece often meant simple private houses, presenting a plain, unadorned exterior, particularly in densely populated city-states. The grand houses later built for nobles on the fringes of the city or as retreats coalesced around the peristyle format. This had come from public banqueting buildings, which often had rooms for diners set back behind colonnades. As described by Vitruvius, the Greek house had a very small entranceway (called the *thyroron*). This was often just large enough to house a room for the *ianitor*, the entrance guard. This then opened directly onto a rectangular peristyle, a four-sided court, colonnaded on three or four sides and open to the air at the centre, which then allowed for circulation to separate rooms all accessed from the central court. Larger houses sometimes had a second peristyle that allowed for separation of family and servants and a clearer demarcation of the male and female domains. Even the most extensive palaces tended to follow the model of the enclosed peristyle, repeating it on a grander scale, as in the palace at the early Macedonian capital of Aigai (now Vergina), which extends nearly 9,300 square metres (100,000 sq. ft) in a vast rectangle.

The ideal Roman villa, although in practice built in many various ways, developed this plan a little more. The Roman Vitruvius was clearly dismayed at Greek entrances marked by 'passages of scanty width'. In a culture that built archways to commemorate military victories and worshipped the god Janus, also known as the Doorkeeper, Roman entrances were very important. Beyond the porch and main door was a vestibule, representing the proper passage from public to private domain, opening onto a small entrance hall called the *fauces,* sometimes referred to as the 'front passage' or even a 'corridor' in later discussions.[17] This series of thresholds opened then onto a preparatory rectangular atrium. This was open to the air above, with a matching pool of water below, and lined with small rooms or *cubicula.* The atrium in turn led through to the main colonnaded peristyle courtyard at the core of the house, allowing for access to further rooms, including the dining room, the *andron* (the male retreat) and the *lararium*, which housed the altar to the gods and the familial dead. The peristyle served complex overlapping functions, existing, like the later corridor, somewhere between a public and private space. Yvon Thébert notes that in later Roman imperial architecture, privacy was managed by beginning to half-wall some of the interior colonnades, and to increase the number of interior doors or hangings at thresholds.[18]

Clive Knights rather exuberantly calls such a model Roman house, as found for instance in Pompeii, a 'perforated vessel', 'a nebula of thresholds, a coming together of empierced layerings and interstitial domains inhabited by gods and humans'.[19] Elsewhere, further from the imperial centre, local variations, of which there are a great deal, meant the occasional emergence of extended passageways to reach the main part of the house, often forced by lack of space or local terrain, and these begin to take on the look of axial corridors, with rooms coming off on both sides. Experts call these variations rare and 'idiosyncratic', however.[20] It is still safe to say, though, that Greek and Roman domestic architecture was not formed around the distributive tangential corridor.

Cloisters and Galleries: Pre-corridic Medievalism

The most relevant religious structure to evolve in the passage from late antiquity to early Christian Europe was the formation of the *claustrum* or cloister. The *claustrum*, meaning 'enclosure', was a large square yard surrounded by galleried porches nearly always attached to the southern flank of a church. This created a sacred enclosure in which monks, separated from the secular world, pursued the bulk of their existence.

The origin of the cloister remains disputed. Early Christian communities came together to provide support for devotees who found the solitary life of the hermit difficult to sustain alone. The first cenobitic communities were organized by Pachomius (292–346) in Egypt. Individual scattered huts were arranged into 'ribbons of contiguous cells', perhaps on the model of housing for ancient Egyptian workers.[21] The communities were walled to signal a withdrawal from everyday life into ascetic contemplation. Pachomius set up an important community at Tabennesi in the ruins of an old sanctuary of Isis, which grew to include over 2,000 members, and this required a series of formal rules to regulate the religious and communal life there – the beginning of monasticism. As this model spread, there is evidence that monasteries were founded in the spaces of late Roman villas, where the peristyle could be adapted as the core of the enclosed community. At Lorsch, for instance, a monastery was built in the 760s on the model of the Roman villa.

It was St Benedict of Nursia (480–543) who established a whole chain of communities that became the standard European model of the monastery. The Benedictine Rule was formalized into chapters, the sixty-sixth of which insisted on an enclosure 'so that the monks may not be compelled to wander outside it, for that is not expedient for their souls'.[22] Benedict used the term *claustrum* to encompass the whole site, but this was gradually narrowed to identify only the square with covered walkways at the core of monastic life.

The blueprint for the monastery design was the famous Plan of St Gall, an architectural plan written on calfskin vellum and composed either in 817 as a monastic ideal or later, in 830, as the St Gall complex was being built.[23] The spatial distribution on the plan did become a norm for monasteries across Europe. After St Gall, a two-storey cloister was nearly always attached to the south side of the nave of a church, the entry point for monks to pass inside the sacred space. On the opposite side of the square, furthest away, were the kitchen and communal refectories for the monks (communal eating being a key Benedictine Rule). At right angles to the church on the east side were the communal dormitories, with a warming room below. Night steps often led directly from the dormitory into the church, so that the monks had a shortcut for offices to be said at midnight and pre-dawn. On the west side, the Plan of St Gall identifies storage for food and drink, for the materials produced by the land worked beyond the enclosed part of the monastery. This fourth side had variable functions in different monasteries down the centuries.

The cloister was a transitional space, the inner enclosure of the community but one that always mixed sacred and profane functions. The four arcaded walkways have been schematically linked to distinct operations: the liturgical on the north, since this was the direct link to the church itself, the domestic to the south, labour to the west, and discipline to the east, as here in addition to the dormitory was the chapter house, the place where administrative and legal matters and questions of punishment in the community were decided.[24]

The architecture of the cloister shifted in the medieval period, particularly after the Benedictine Rule was challenged by different

orders breaking away. The Carthusian order, established in eleventh-century France, turned away from elements of communal living to return to a more eremitical life of individual seclusion. Consequently the cloister became a service passage along which individual cells for monks were arranged, with hatches built into the doorways for food and waste to be passed without direct contact. Carthusians also buried their dead in the central garth of the cloister, the better to contemplate mortality.

The trace of one cell remains in the surviving wing of the cloister at the Charterhouse monastery complex in London, established in the fourteenth century to pray for the souls of the vast numbers killed by the Black Death. This is a good example of the constant repurposing of cloisters. Following the Dissolution of the monasteries, this portion of the cloister was preserved as an arcaded walkway to the Duke of Norfolk's indoor tennis court, a pointedly secular change of function. When Charterhouse became a school, the Norfolk Cloister was pressed into service as a corridor and a place for ball games. It is part of the mythology of Charterhouse that the narrow dimensions of the walkway were the reason an offside rule was invented for football.[25]

In contrast to the strict seclusion of the Carthusians, the Cistercian order emphasized the humility of their community through everyday labour on the land alongside other workers, and this openness led to large numbers joining the order. This resulted in complex, sprawling monasteries with cloisters that were much more open to movement between religious and lay members of the community. The Cistercian cloister was less a cordoned-off space marked by clear thresholds, and more a set of pathways for circulation between spaces with very mixed functions. At sites like Rievaulx Abbey in Yorkshire, the cloisters were extended and expanded along the east and west sides; the communal dormitories, one historian suggests, must have created 'a spectacular vista'.[26]

Surviving cloister of the 14th-century Charterhouse monastery in London, which later became a school corridor and site of origin for the offside rule.

I have spent some time on cloisters because their association with Catholicism and enclosure long continued to haunt the post-Reformation Protestant imagination. Monastic ruins are central to Gothic literature and art in the eighteenth century, and as we shall see ancient cloisters and passages converted into modern corridors remain one of the *genius loci* for the sighting of ghosts, the stubborn traces of the past that resist the passing of time but return in these suitably interstitial spaces. The phantom steps of the dispossessed monks in alleys and hallways measure out their perverse cenobitic seclusion. Yet their spectral return and the common tales of monks issuing curses on their Protestant usurpers as their homes were destroyed are the traces of guilt at the often violent dispossession that imbues the surviving architectural spaces of monastic life. In the foundational Gothic romance, Horace Walpole's *The Castle of Otranto* (1764), crypts, dungeons and secret passageways riddle the castle with uncanny porosity. And, memorably, it is in the gallery where an ancestral portrait is seen to sigh in moral outrage at the usurper of the house's rightful lineage, and step out of the frame to stomp off in high spectral dudgeon.

The much more secular space of the *gallery* is another type of covered circulation space associated with the early modern period, usually external to the rooms of a building, and which (like the peristyle or the cloister) is partially open on one side, with pillars and a guardrail. They are often on upper levels, and are used either to provide access to rooms or can serve distinct functions, such as stages to provide entertainments for the hall below (hence the minstrel gallery). Vanbrugh used galleries over the atrium spaces of Castle Howard and Blenheim precisely for this theatrical effect. The development of the gallery as a distinct space for the display of artworks comes in the late sixteenth century. The origin of this structure is unclear, owing something to Germanic traditions of large halls, but also to the Italian *loggia*; the *Oxford English Dictionary* dates its arrival in English to 1500, but it was used fairly interchangeably with 'corridor' in the eighteenth and nineteenth centuries before the common use of the corridor had quite settled down. The gallery, however, had a different set of functions from the modern corridor that had first appeared in seventeenth-century palazzos.

Private Perspectives: *View of a Corridor*, 1662

The Italianate mansion built at Dyrham Park for William Blathwayt between 1692 and 1704 holds a surprise at the end of a vista of aligned doorways. The succession of rooms seems to continue further than it actually does because a trick painting, *View of a Corridor* by the famous Dutch artist Samuel van Hoogstraten (1627–1678), has been hung to deceive the eye. This picture was completed by van Hoogstraten in 1662 during his first year in London seeking new commissions. It was painted for the grand house of the Secretary of War, Thomas Povey, in Lincoln's Inn. He had hung it in a way to amuse his guests by tricking them, however momentarily. Samuel Pepys recorded in his diary in May 1664 that Povey 'opened the closet door and there I saw that there is nothing but only a plain picture hung upon the wall'.[27] Pepys thought Povey's house had the finest interiors that he had ever seen. The painting was purchased by his nephew, William Blathwayt, when the interiors of Dyrham Park were decorated in fashionable Dutch style.

The title of the painting is inaccurately translated as 'View of a Corridor', which does not quite make sense of the space depicted. A better translation would be 'Perspective from a Threshold'. It is a typical genre painting of Dutch art, which took a significant turn to the study of interiors in the mid-seventeenth century. Although considered a lower art than that of history or landscape painting, the luminous Dutch interiors painted in large numbers in the 1650s reflected the domestic world of the mercantile classes, who were noted as avid buyers of these relatively cheap artworks. The masters of this form – Gerrit Dou, Nicolaes Maes, Pieter de Hooch and Samuel van

Hoogstraten – were long regarded as realists recording authentic domestic spaces with a documentary eye. Only later was there a recovery of the enigmatic, allegorical qualities of these interiors, a mysterious interplay of open and closed meanings. Typically, views are framed by doorways, showing scenes in further rooms or merely tempting glimpses of other possibilities unfolding beyond the door frame. There are often scenes within scenes, frames within frames, paintings within paintings, complex vistas and vignettes that can play around with foreground and background and hint at risqué possibility. For instance, van Hoogstraten's *Interior Viewed through a Doorway* is known familiarly as *The Slippers* because the painting depicts a woman's shoes flung off at the threshold of a boudoir, perhaps projecting sexual promise that lies just out of sight.

View of a Corridor is included in this history for two reasons. The first is technical. As its Dutch title suggests, van Hoogstraten uses the succession of rooms and the patterning of flagstones on the passage to create the optical illusion of a recessive perspective, a depth perpendicular to the flat picture plane. Pepys reacted to it primarily as a 'perspective piece' rather than a painting, and van Hoogstraten also experimented with perspective boxes, models with multiple apertures for viewing *trompe l'oeil* effects of depth in lovingly detailed miniatures of architectural spaces. His *Perspective Box of a Dutch Interior* (1657–61) is one of the few of these objects that survives. The painter was of a generation that transposed scientific research in optics on the propagation of light into art, securing the modern conventions of unified pictorial space that had been not been used in earlier art. Indeed, early technical illustrations of how to draw receding perspective often used chequerboard floors to demonstrate this device, so *View of a Corridor* is almost a formal exercise in how to construct this space in paint. Receding vistas in Dutch art were so familiar by the 1650s that they became known as *doorsiens* (or 'see-throughs'), 'a versatile

Samuel van Hoogstraten, *View of a Corridor*, 1662, oil on canvas.

compositional device that creates dramatic spatial recession'.[28] Van Hoogstraten's own manual on painting, published in 1678, argued that 'a vista provides substance and grace, in which the eye delights and playfully sails.'[29] Plunging perspective gives layering and depth, an entrance into the painting for the eye.

Just as the passageway or the recessive vista gives depth to Dutch art in the seventeenth century, the corridor in painting, photography and cinema later becomes a privileged device for providing a central convergence to an image, a single perspective or *vanishing point* (a term first used in English in 1715 in a treatise on linear perspective). Repeatedly, images of corridors lead the eye down the converging lines of the walls towards a point of disappearance. This was something, for instance, that Stanley Kubrick used compulsively in his films, a device that sucks the viewer into the frame. The genre paintings of Dutch interiors are the first modern art form to do this.

The second point is more historical. These paintings of interiors are a record not just of specific Dutch domestic spaces, but are an important indicator of the transformation of the idea of the private life *as such* across seventeenth-century Europe. The paintings consistently tease with vistas that open from semi-public hallways or alleyways into more private spaces. We glimpse liaisons in back rooms, through windows or doors, families that are locked in private discussions, women dangerously eavesdropping on staircases, or receiving letters at doorways, or reading private letters closeted away, whatever secrets the writing reveals forever tilted away from our line of sight. In the monumental survey *A History of Private Life*, published under the aegis of the French historian Philippe Ariès, these early Dutch interiors are used as symptoms of a shift from a world where the only inhabited space was communal to one where there are increasing possibilities to conduct a private life. There was consequently a change in domestic architecture that produced different kinds of spaces of retreat. Orest Ranum tracks the rise of these 'refuges of intimacy' after the medieval period, where there were only fugitive nooks and crannies of solitude, and no real concept of privacy. There was the emergence of small walled gardens for private reflection, the *camera* (where family papers and wealth is locked away), the *ruelle* (a private space that emerges between the bed and the wall furthest from the door), the male *studiolo* or *cabinet*, where men could retreat from family life to 'shutte up our selves' (as it was put in 1592), and the female equivalent, the *boudoir*.[30]

These requirements increased the need for new kinds of spaces of circulation between rooms. 'Private stairways, halls, corridors, and vestibules were soon provided to allow rooms to be entered without the need to pass through other rooms,' Roger Chartier notes.[31] In England, the Smythson family of architects began experimenting with galleries and corridors in the late sixteenth century to ease movement around grand houses.[32] In Holland, architects like Philips Vingboons (1607–1675) developed walkways and inner courtyards that moved the kitchen and the servants away from the main house to improve family privacy and separated out entrances to rooms. One of the most famous paintings of this period, *The Courtyard of a House in Delft* (1658) by Pieter de Hooch, offers a classic *doorsien* of a receding perspective that splits the servants in the courtyard from the woman occupying the passageway of the house in the distance. The inside and the outside, the new house and the ramshackle courtyard, the masters and the servants, are at once proximate yet entirely separated. It is a lovely detail that the plaque above the entrance to the passageway of the house is a memorial stone taken from the Hieronymusdale cloister in Delft. The house's modernity is marked by what it repurposes from the past (much of the city of Delft was destroyed in a fire in 1536). It is the private home that is now the sacralized space.[33]

As the mercantile classes increased in wealth in Holland, there was a redesign of the entranceway to houses, which had previously been very open in plan. Now they were organized on the ground floor around a *voorhuis*, or what Simon Stevin in 1590 called the *voorsael*:

> Anyone entering the *voorsael* should not have to pass through any of the other four rooms, but instead through a *voorsael* into each of them. For the *voorsael* serves as the common place for the whole household, as well as for strangers coming inside to speak to anyone in the house . . . The *voorsael* should be placed . . . so that one can freely go through it into each room.[34]

In these developments we are getting close to the emergence of the corridor as a space that secures a new kind of privacy for the affluent mercantile family. The artists that depict the interlocking space of these rooms assert the importance of transformation of the domestic scene in this new genre. Some historians speculate that the sovereign significance of the home had much to do with the political disturbances in the Dutch state in the mid-seventeenth century. But at the same time that these family portraits announce a new social and economic power in the household, the playful use of space and perspective in some of the interiors they depict hint at the potential subversions introduced when private spaces multiply inside the home. The corridor differentiates, separates and divides the bourgeois house, but it also unnervingly makes linking things together much easier: genders and classes, family and strangers, mix. When the corridor was established in English domestic architecture by Robert Kerr's publication of *The English Gentleman's Home* in 1864, it was finally consolidated in what has been called 'the birthplace of privacy', a spatial form that was shaped entirely by northern Protestant conceptions of the private self and its dispensations.[35]

If this seems to be a late date, it is worth recalling Orest Ranum's comment that

> Despite the installation of innumerable hallways, doors, antechambers, and partitions in old buildings, there may have been little increase in privacy before 1860. The wealthy naturally increased the amount of private space available to them, but for the rest of

Pieter de Hooch, *The Courtyard of a House in Delft*, 1658, oil on canvas.

the population . . . the idea of privacy did not extend beyond the bedroom, and perhaps not beyond the bed curtains.[36]

For all this long prehistory, this confirms my sense that the corridor is a distinctly modern architectural space. I don't want to leave the impression, however, that this is a steady historical movement from the open stoa of the Greek marketplace, through the enclosure of the medieval cloister, to the private distributions of the Victorian bourgeois home. The corridor always hinges on being both public and private, open and closed. Indeed, in turning to the eighteenth-century plans for buildings that start to place the corridor as the defining device for distributing interior space, it is openness that first appeals. We are led into the promise of modernity by a utopia of corridors.

2

The Utopia of Corridors, I: Charles Fourier's Phalanstery

'Architecture writes history,' declared the French utopian socialist Victor Considerant in the revolutionary year of 1848. Considerant believed that the ideal society was fostered through the ideal architectural milieu, and that this social transformation, on the edge of which Europe seemed to be trembling, would occur in a building that he called the *phalanstère* (the phalanstery or phalanx, from the Greek for a tightly organized body of soldiers banded together).[1] This building was at the core of the utopian thought of his mentor, the eccentric writer Charles Fourier (1772–1837), but it was Considerant who issued the architectural plan of this glorious phalanstery, fixing it in the utopian imagination. This is where the modern utopia would be housed.

In the model phalanx precisely 1,620 people would live in harmony, since the space reconfigured all prior forms of family and social ties. It did so because it was built around a street-gallery that ran along the entire second floor, linking living rooms, large and small social halls, and canteens together, but also connecting to noisier workshops, kitchens and nurseries placed further away but still linked in one long unbroken spine through the building. As Fourier himself explained:

> The Phalanx has no outside streets or open road-ways exposed to the elements. All the portions of the central edifice can be

> traversed by means of a wide gallery which runs along the second floor of the whole building. At each extremity of this spacious corridor there are elevated passages which connect to all the parts of the Phalanx and the adjoining buildings. Thus everything is linked by a series of passage-ways which are sheltered, elegant, and comfortable . . . These sheltered passage-ways are particularly necessary in view of the fact that there is a great deal of movement in Harmony.[2]

This street-gallery – the modern tangential corridor – would conduct a whole new rhythm of transformed social being. It was, in a phrase picked out by Walter Benjamin, 'the hall of universal linkage', a machine for processing and transforming human beings.[3] Hygienic, comfortable, flooded with light, aired in the summer and heated in the winter, the street-gallery turned those who suffered the miserable economic inequalities of market capitalism and the dangerous social instabilities of post-revolutionary France into a complementary association of loved-up utopian citizens.

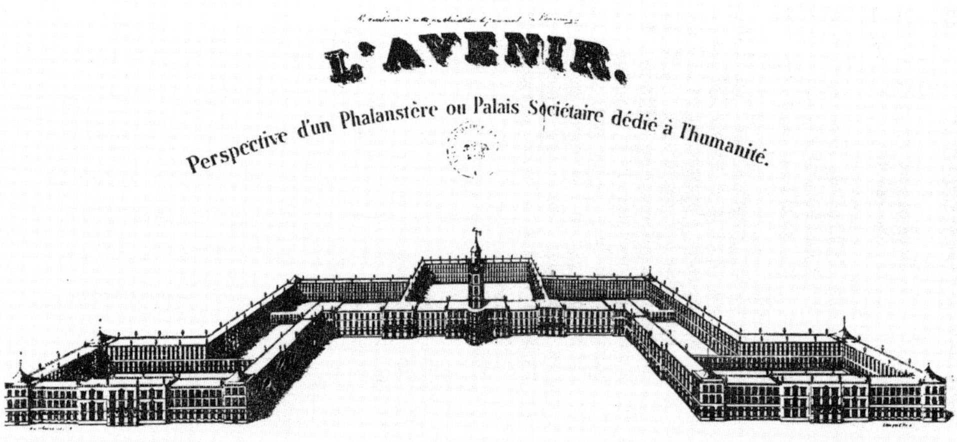

Victor Considerant, *The Future: Perspective of a Phalanstery*, c. 1840. This became the iconic image of Fourier's vision of a 'phalanx'.

In a typically overheated rhetorical flourish, Fourier declared that once anyone had 'seen the street-galleries of a Phalanx, he will look upon the most elegant civilized palace as a place of exile, a residence worthy of the fools who, after 3,000 years of architectural studies, have not yet learned how to build themselves healthy and comfortable lodgings.' It would take just one model phalanx to be built and within two years the whole wretched phase of civilization would be overthrown and its living arrangements transformed.

Once Fourier issued his detailed prospectus in 1808, which sold only twenty copies, he spent the next thirty years calmly waiting for a rich benefactor to knock on his door and realize his dream. He always made sure to be in for callers at noon, but also sent out his proposals to the French government, the American Consul in Paris and the Tsar. Though the call never came, to his initial astonishment and then growing bitterness, the Fourierist movement that Considerant and others established after his death had a profound influence on the meaning of these new architectural spaces for over 150 years, long into the twentieth century. Welcome to the utopia of corridors.

Galleried Utopias: Thomas More to Claude-Nicolas Ledoux

Writers of utopia have always been curiously precise about the architectural plans of their blueprints, perhaps because buildings are so much easier to sketch out and manage than pesky people. It seems intrinsic to utopian thought that the proper physical structure will regulate erring humanity. Since Thomas More's inaugural *Utopia* (published in Latin in 1516), the ambition to rethink community and commonality in an estranged 'nowhere' has favoured visions of collective living. Thomas More borrows a lot from classical sources: his island has 54 cities, all identical, at regulated distances from each other, walled, and built on the Roman square grid. It is in the capital Amaurotum (an orderly version of London) that More describes what the housing might look like:

> The buildings, which are far from mean, are set together in a long row, continuous through the block and faced by a corresponding one. The house fronts of the respective blocks are divided by an avenue of twenty feet broad . . . Every house has not only a door into the street but a back door into the garden. What is more, folding doors, easily opened by hand and then closing of themselves, give admission to anyone. As a result, nothing is private property anywhere.

The logic of the description is plain: it is the concrete design of these three-storey stone buildings that secures the abstract principle of commonality, where 'nothing is private property' and there is 'no lurking hole, no secret meeting place'.[4] More's humanism inheres in the architecture.

More's four-square communal city-state seems to echo the structure of the New Jerusalem and could be seen as a monastic cloister writ large, while also alluding to Plato's fourth-century BCE *Republic*, in which the Guardians abolished money and private property so that 'none shall possess a dwelling-house or store-house to which all have not the right of entry', and which also insisted on communal eating on the model of encamped soldiers rather than monks.[5] In Plato's later dialogue, the *Laws*, the ideal city-state Magnesia was a perfectly circular walled city restricted to 5,040 families, divided into twelve equal radial sections, the number chosen for its endlessly divisible permutations that ensure equity of distribution. The houses in Magnesia are uniform in structure, but little further detail is provided.

Ideal cities of the Renaissance fused the Christian heavenly city with Platonic ideals, and they dream themselves into being through the architecture of their times. Just as More seems to use the cloister, Tommaso Campanella's *City of the Sun* (1602) combines the perfection of the circle with the movement provided by the gallery or arcade. His city has seven circular concentric walls, each inner wall lined by 'large palaces . . . in such a manner as to appear all one palace'. The description continues: 'Arches run on a level with the middle height of the palaces, and are continued round the whole ring. There are galleries for promenading upon these arches, which are supported from beneath by thick and well-shaped columns, enclosing arcades like peristyles, or cloisters of an abbey.' The walls are painted with different categories of knowledge, turning a promenade into a form of encyclopaedic education. At the centre of these concentric circles, the temple is also raised up on columns with 'galleries for walking'.[6]

Retreat or monastic enclosure remains the model for the men of science lodged together in Salomon's House in Francis Bacon's *New Atlantis* (1627). The cloisters of Margaret Cavendish's vast palace at the centre of the island of Paradise in *The Blazing World* (1666) are further hidden from the world within a labyrinth of rocks and tides no stranger can navigate. In contrast, the urban utopias of the eighteenth century are less often closed in on themselves and increasingly concerned with earthly rather than divine politics. These plans seek to manage the circulation of the innumerable masses collecting in chaotic and overwhelmed modern cities, to reassert rational order. Where the English sensibility resisted Christopher Wren's grand plan after the Fire of London (largely for its disruption of property ownership and value), the Enlightenment in Paris was actively realized in radical interventions into the urban fabric, such as the laying out of the Place de la Concorde in 1755. This was a period of grand designs for the whole city, as in Pierre Patte's General Plan of 1765, or the proposals of Marie-Joseph Peyre in the 1770s. Abbé Morrelly argued that the new place of the sciences in society put More's *Utopia* within reach and that clean, rational urban lines could replace 'labyrinths of crooked, winding streets'.[7] The thirty years before the Revolution were awash with similar urban fantasias.

One of the most significant architects of this period was Claude-Nicolas Ledoux, who is sometimes seen as a forerunner of Modernist functionalism in his use of space and the severe symmetries of his Neoclassical and Baroque designs. Ledoux worked on grand houses and projects for aristocratic clients who were at the centre of the *ancien régime*, built prisons and factories, including the Royal Saltworks at Arc-et-Senans, and designed the hated wall around Paris from 1784 to 1787, the Ferme générale that had 45 tollhouses built to collect city taxes. He was also thought to be involved in the design of Masonic Lodges, dozens of which sprang up in Paris in this period, buildings shot through with occult ritual significance. It was hardly surprising, then, that Ledoux fell from grace during the Revolution, and many of his tollhouses were put to the flame by the revolutionary crowd.

While in prison between 1789 and 1793, Ledoux started sketching out plans for his ideal city of Chaux, a utopian settlement that he imagined as an elaboration to his Saltworks factory. The first plan was a large square, but with diagonal corridors across the inner courtyard that made for rigid geometrical symmetry. The second plan organized the buildings in a grand elliptical circle as utopian tradition demanded. These buildings 'were to be the instruments of reform and happiness for the region's rough but natural population of peasants, workers, and farmers'.[8] Every workplace, public building and private residence for different classes of worker was built to maximize health and productivity and was carefully integrated into an overall design. The structures were distinct yet interlinked with networks of avenues, pathways and galleries. His later designs included plans for communal dwellings. One, called the Cénobie, the House of Communal Life (after the 'cenobitic' community of a monastery), has been described as 'a unified dwelling with common facilities in a central pavilion joined by covered galleries to sixteen single-family apartments'.[9] It was meant as a sylvan retreat for recovery from overstimulation and so was designed to isolate rather than bring together.

For all its utopian thrust, Ledoux was neither a revolutionary nor an egalitarian. The designs he published in his 1804 *L'Architecture* were intended to reinforce natural hierarchy and social distinctions. Ledoux's explanations of his ideal city were symptomatically obscure, probably designed to evade further censure.

Fourier's Architecture of Association

Charles Fourier was no Jacobin either, and his dream of the phalanstery came as a direct answer to the instability of Revolutionary times. Born in 1772, the son of a modest cloth merchant from Lyons, Fourier had just inherited a modest sum from his father when the Revolution broke out. The town of Lyons at first resisted the fervour that spread from Paris. When Lyons fell to the Revolutionaries, however, Fourier was nearly included in the mass executions conducted there and he only survived by giving up his entire wealth to the new state. He was forced into the army for a miserable stint, then spent many years as a travelling salesman in the cloth trade, loathing the work he was forced to do. He later lived as a garret savant in Paris on a tiny annuity left him by his mother, plotting the transformation of the world. The only time he got close to official interest in his practical plans for social transformation was in the last years of the unstable Bourbon regency. There was some interest from the Ministry of Public Works, but the violent revolution in 1830 intervened and swept away all his contacts in government. Fourier's ideas were a product of revolutionary times, but they were also doomed by them.

He experienced two revelations in Paris when he travelled there in the 1790s. The first involved an apple, on sale for 14 sous, which was roughly one hundred times its value in the markets back home. From this basic lesson in the variability of market price, Fourier condemned not only the evils of mercantile capitalism but 3,000 years of Western Civilization *tout court*. He would overthrow a system of cruel inequality with one based on loving association and a perfect harmony of life and work. Newton had discovered the force of gravity from the fall of one apple; Fourier discovered the force of association from his.

The second revelation was the grandiosity and transformative potential of the capital's architecture. Fourier was remembered carefully assessing the grand buildings of Paris, sometimes obsessively measuring particular details with the length of his cane. 'He never walked in the street, or entered a public building, nor even a private house, without remarking the peculiarities of distribution,' one memoir recalled.[10] His phalanstery borrowed from the vast extended galleries of the Palais du Louvre (opened as a public museum by the Revolutionary authorities in 1793) and from the arcades that lined the edges of the Place de la Concorde, but principally from the four-storey, quadrangular Palais Royal. Before it was demolished and replaced by the iron and steel of the Galerie d'Orléans, the Palais had long ground-floor arcades where an extremely varied crowd would swirl and mix together in cafés, shops and the notorious gambling dens. In addition, it had leaky wooden galleries through the spacious gardens that Balzac called 'one of the most famous sights of Paris'. 'The Galleries,' Balzac wrote in *Lost Illusions* (1837–43), 'parallel passages about twelve feet in height, were formed by a triple row of shops. The centre row, giving back and front upon the Galleries, was filled with the fetid atmosphere of the place, and derived a dubious daylight through the invariably dirty windows of the roof.'[11] The place was full of booksellers, milliners, ventriloquists and hucksters, theatregoers, gamblers and businessmen, and was a haunt of prostitutes at night. The Stone Galleries were the parade for the most expensive women, the Wooden Galleries for the common streetwalkers, but all were part of an extravagant nightly spectacle. The Palais was a place of wealthy promenade and abject poverty, rag-pickers selling junk for loose change while aristocrats gambled away fortunes at the tables. For twenty years the Stock Exchange stood opposite the galleries on the ground floor of the Palais, making it the leading place of commercial and political intrigue between the revolutions of 1789 and 1830.

Fourier delighted in the Palais Royal: the poet Heinrich Heine recalled often seeing this prophet dawdling among the columns there. It would have reminded Fourier of his childhood among the silk merchants of Lyons, where the old town is famously riddled with narrow, covered passageways and covered routes through the buildings, shortcuts between workshop and market built by silk traders. Hundreds of these distinctive *traboules* (a contraction of the Latin *transambulare*, 'to pass through'), some incorporating elaborate staircases and tunnels, still survive. The Palais Royal in Paris of the early nineteenth century combined this with chaotic social mixing, like the Greek agora or the Arabian bazaar, whereas the iron and glass arcades that followed in the post-revolutionary era focused on the containment of urban energies and class demarcation.

Fourier's utopia of corridors thus began its life trying to bottle something of the spontaneity of these urban galleries. But it is also important to understand just how strange Fourier's philosophy of association was in order to grasp the transformative ambitions that he gave to the street-galleries of his phalanstery.

Fourier's traumatic experiences with social turmoil and alienated labour were resolved by his discovery of the principles of 'universal harmony', first proclaimed in a public letter in 1803 and then at great length in his *Theory of Four Movements* in 1808. For Fourier, humans were defined by their passions, and he held that all social organizations in history hitherto, from the savage and barbaric to the civilized, had only compelled people to live in miserable alienation from the true expression of their desire. With typical Enlightenment rigour, Fourier identified twelve 'passional types': the five luxurious senses, four 'group' passions (honour, friendship, spiritual love and family), and three 'serial' passions as yet unknown because blocked by current social formations (one for intrigue, a 'butterfly' passion that flitted around seeking variety, and finally a combinatory passion that creatively combined all the other passions). Delirious mathematics enabled Fourier to calculate every possible permutation, which produced exactly 810 passional types. A phalanx, like Noah's ark, required two of each, hence the ideal number of 1,620. This implied fixity in passional type, although the theory encouraged a butterfly flitting between different kinds of desirous being, and later Fourier argued that an individual human could cycle through every possible combination (even if this might take several lifetimes).

In the phalanstery there were further taxonomic divisions by age, organized into an 'ascending' wing, from babies, cherubs and seraphs towards puberty, then a 'descending' wing from adolescents and adventurers down to the reverend, the venerable and the patriarchs. This schema tended to prioritize the sexually mature, pushing noisy children to the ends of the corridors to give their elders some peace. Work activities were strictly limited by time and inclination, grouped together in 'series' but with frequent changes of kinds of work to escape the crushing threat of boredom. This was never an intrinsically egalitarian or classless reorganization, since each person was valued according to his or her different abilities and passions. But this was hardly an economic theory; it was primarily a social and sexual schema. It was the blissful fantasy of a lonely travelling salesman who lived an austere and, as far as we know, entirely celibate life. As Roland Barthes put it, Fourier offered 'orgasm by number, by classification', 'a vast madness which does not end, but which permutates', rather like the sexual mathematics of his contemporary, the Marquis de Sade.[12]

The street-gallery was at the centre of the phalanstery because it facilitated this constant movement of combination and recombination. It was an embodiment of the flitting nature of human desire. The openness of these wide communal galleries, speeding the movement to social halls and communal rooms, the constant sense of festival, the displacement of pre-sexual children and post-sexual elders from the centre of the building down along the corridor, were all integral to the architecture. The utopia that this new corridor brings is realized through a space intended to dismantle all prior social relations, most particularly the bourgeois family, folded in on itself behind closed doors. In utopia, the corridor always promises radical social reassemblage.

Fourier was utterly convinced of the merits of this arrangement and believed that within a few years of the establishment of a model phalanstery, if only such a project could find a financier, the whole world would experience a revolutionary conversion to its principles and embrace it. In 1832 there was a brief flutter of excitement when a group of his followers began to raise subscriptions for a trial phalanstery and even began to clear land in preparation for building at Condé-sur-Vesgre, but the project collapsed within eighteen months, never gaining enough funds or members. This heaped more ridicule on Fourier and his adherents.

Fourier retreated further into a reclusive life in Paris and concentrated on elaborating his bizarre cosmological speculations. He offered science-fictional journeys through the solar system, imagining the harmonious worlds of other planets, even the delirious copulation of astral bodies. He had long been mocked for his assertions that harmony would extend to the climate of Earth itself, moderating extremes of temperature, so desalinating the sea and changing its taste into a lovely, drinkable lemonade that would assist far-flung travel and bring the Earth further into blissful union. Now this extended to the solar system. Utopia indeed.

Fourier had experienced much ridicule for this and many other details since his first announcements in 1803. He had come to the attention of the Napoleonic police and the judiciary, but they had decided that he was mostly harmless. Later the hard-headed German communists Friedrich Engels and Karl Marx used Fourier as the absurd representative of unrealizable 'utopian socialism', the better to ground their own gritty version of 'scientific socialism'. 'The more completely [their plans] were worked out in detail,' Engels said, 'the more they could not avoid drifting off into pure phantasies.'[13] Remarkably, though, the idea of communal living in vast phalansteries very nearly made it into the final draft of the 1848 Communist Manifesto, with the promise of 'the construction, on state-owned lands, of large communal palaces designed to bridge the gap between city and country'.[14] Fourier was still lauded as one of the ancestors of the Bolshevik Revolution in Moscow in 1917, and the idea of transformative collective architecture has haunted communism since Fourier's first proposal.

The longevity of Fourier's influence was partly because his short book *The New Industrial World*, published in 1827, left out most of the weird sex stuff and offered itself as an answer to the problem of labour in the nineteenth century. His ideas were also translated into less eccentric and meaningful practical plans of action by his followers Victor Considerant in France and Albert Brisbane in America. These were to offer the pursuit of practical corridic utopias for a millennial era, but mainly after Fourier had died in 1837. Without Fourier, in fact, Fourierism became a very successful movement in the 1840s.

The Phalanxes of Robert Owen and the Associationists

Before we examine the actual outcomes of Fourierism, though, it is worth remembering that Fourier was not a lone figure in considering the utopian potential of architecture to transform human character. His most significant contemporary in Britain was the wealthy industrialist Robert Owen, who had set up a model textile factory at New Lanark in Scotland in 1799. The housing, schools and institutions he established around the factory became famous examples of industrial reform in the early years of atrocious conditions for mass industrial labour. New Lanark was set up as an entirely capitalist exercise, but his social and labour reforms constantly provoked Owen's co-owners because these principles so clearly interfered with their extraction of profit. In 1813, Owen published *A New View of Society*, which turned New Lanark into a full-scale social experiment. Owen believed that environment was entirely responsible for the shaping of character and that beyond improvement of factory conditions he could now mould his workers through early education (between the ages of five and fourteen), and through collective social institutions and new kinds of living arrangements. Industrialists had paid lots of attention to the mechanical devices of the factory, Owen said, but these ideas would redress the balance and address the efficiency of the 'living machinery' of his complex.[15] In 1816, the year he was forced to buy out the other owners of New Lanark, Owen set up his Institution for the Formation of Character. At the dedication speech, he told the assembled villagers that the institute would shortly abolish all poverty, crime and misery, and that communalism would provide an environment of 'more permanent happiness than can be given to any individual under the principles which have hitherto regulated society'.[16]

There were several communal ideas at New Lanark, including a 'large house' built to accommodate and educate up to five hundred 'charity' children from the area who also worked in the factory. But soon Owen's imagination extended to visions of a total institution that would fulfil his mechanistic vision of social improvement. He began thinking about constructing a giant Parallelogram, a vast four-sided building where learning, labour and leisure would create a society without conflict and dissolve the vicious character engendered by competitive mercantile capitalism. The philanthropic industrialist had started on his journey towards cooperative socialism.

Fourier was a classic poor garret dreamer, but Owen was an extremely wealthy man. Like many utopians before him, Owen decided that this experiment needed to start from scratch in an unsullied Eden – and in 1824 he travelled to the young republic of America. He was interested in the Shaker villages, a sect of strict religious observers of 'Bible communism' but also canny merchants who had established a successful economic model and a stable community. The building and design of New Lebanon and other Shaker settlements were consciously intent on 'redesigning the entire architecture of social relations'.[17] In this case, Shakers built on the premise of strict division of the sexes and obsessively doubled doorways, entrances, halls and dormitories in mirroring symmetries. Owen then travelled to the village of Harmonie in Indiana, which was the settlement of another religious sect run by a German immigrant, George Rapp. After some negotiation, Rapp sold the entire village and the neighbouring farmland to Owen for $125,000. This was to be New Harmony, right at the centre of the American republic.

Owen travelled on to Washington and in March 1825, upon the invitation of President Monroe and President-elect John Quincy Adams, he presented his utopian ideas in two addresses to the full House of Representatives. The buildings of New Harmony were only temporary, transitional spaces. What would replace it was a vast Parallelogram, presented in a model and later sketched by the British architect Thomas Stedman Whitwell. As Owen explained to the American government:

> The model represents a square of buildings, each side of which is 1,000 feet in length, and each side contains every domestic arrangement that can be required for 5,000 persons. The square is also intended to contain a complete school, academy, and university, and it will comprise the first combination of circumstances which has yet been formed to do anything like justice to the physical and mental powers of any human being.[18]

He explained that communal functions would exist in four buildings within the square and at the corner junctions, with 'private dwellings' on the first and second floor and dormitories on the third floor for the unmarried. 'There is communication under cover', Owen further explained, 'from each dwelling to every other, and to all the public rooms, throughout the whole extent of the square.'[19] The core principles of 'a system of union and co-operation' would again be embodied in a corridic structure that owed much to More's quadrangular city of Amaurotum. This was the fullest application of Owen's 'science of the influence of circumstances', the building 'a new machine for performing in a superior manner all the purposes of human life'.[20]

The 'preliminary society' established at New Harmony proved chaotic. For all his careful theoretical elaboration, Owen seemed

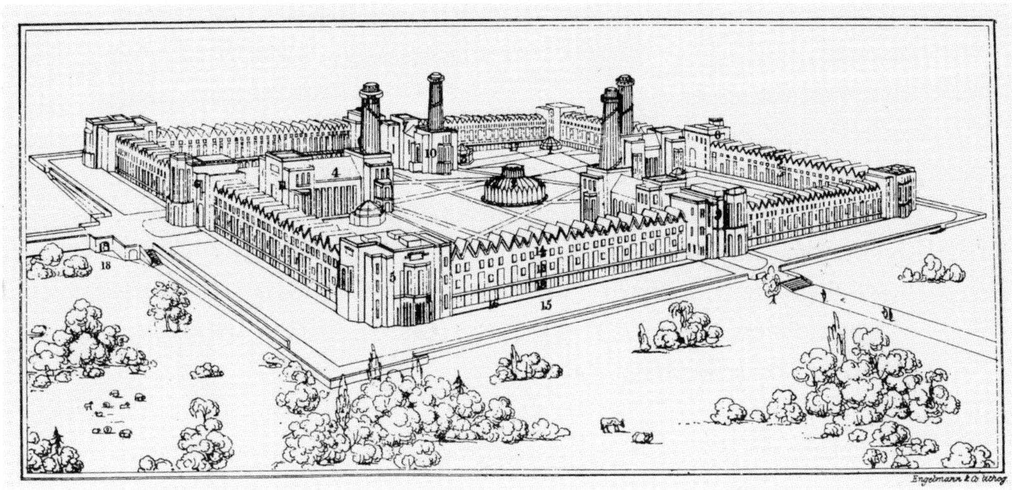

The architect Stedman Whitwell's image of the communal buildings for the New Harmony settlement in Indiana, drawn for Robert Owen in 1824.

uninterested in practical details. He established no criteria for entry, little contractual detail for membership of the community, and left the day-to-day running principally to his young sons William and Robert Dale Owen. Owen himself was often away and, despite little progress, declared after a year that they were close to the end of the Preliminary phase and on the threshold of the millennial Community of Equality. Owen, following Francis Bacon's *New Atlantis,* also famously brought a boatload of scientists and savants in January 1826 to establish New Harmony as a centre of learning. He persuaded the educationalist William Maclure to invest a further $100,000 in the project. Although these arrivals only caused further friction between the community of labourers, those struggling to farm, and this new class of savants, this scientific ambition had lasting results (Robert Dale Owen was later instrumental in setting up the Smithsonian Institute, for instance).

Robert Owen had spent the equivalent of 80 per cent of his vast fortune very quickly on keeping New Harmony afloat. Facing a poor harvest and full economic collapse, his sons declared the experiment a failure by March 1827, dissolving all agreements. Owen returned to Britain in June 1827, never to return to New Harmony. As one historian judges: 'The distance between model and drawings and the concrete village of co-operation was a long one. Words and pictures proved much easier to produce than the real phalanstery.'[21]

Owen also sold New Lanark that year and spent the last thirty years of his life as a social and political theorist and agitator, mainly in London. After Spiritualism emerged as a movement in New York State in 1848 and spread around the world, Owen became one of the most prominent converts. This is not so surprising, since Spiritualism in its radical proletarian form was close to utopian socialism, its visions of the afterlife resolutely communitarian: 'You could look forward to your own arrival *in* socialism after your physical death irrespective of whether you saw the arrival *of* socialism on this earth as imminent.'[22]

When Fourier died in October 1837, his leading follower in Paris, Victor Considerant, declared at his graveside: 'To us, his disciples, we have only to raise a monument to his memory: that monument is a phalanx.'[23] In contrast to his reclusive and paranoid master, Considerant was an able public speaker, agitator and campaigner, streamlining a doctrine of Fourierism that bracketed the master's praise for free love and his eccentric cosmic speculation. He pushed a communalist programme through the newspapers he established, *La Phalanstère* and *La Phalange*, and in his influential summary of the doctrine, *Social Destiny* (1840). The phalanstery remained at the centre of Considerant's socialist thought, and in *Description du Phalanstère* he held to the central insight that the architectural milieu would determine the formation of the 'sociétaire intégrale'. His vision was for a phalanstery of about 2,000 people living in a single structure, roughly four hundred families making up a hive of life, love and industry. He was, however, cautious about realizing this project too soon and while publicly committed to the experiment at Condé-sur-Vesgre (labouring on the site through the summer of 1833), he privately thought French society not yet ready for utopia. He was proved right by its rapid collapse. In the 1840s Considerant's own socialism drifted further from Fourier's beliefs and his willingness to escape narrow doctrinalism made him an important figure in the revolutionary turmoil in Paris in 1848. It was his subsequent exile from France after the failure of the Revolution that led to his eventual decision to join a phalanx in the wilds of Texas in 1855.

Considerant wrote in *Great West* (1853): 'On our globe, America is at present the Country of Realization. Its spirit is that of diversity, of movement and enterprise, the love of inventions, of experiments, of adventures.'[24] As with Owen, so Considerant also thought that America was the utopian *tabula rasa*. By this point Fourierists pushed for utopian colonies outside France to be established by joint-stock investment schemes that would raise their own capital and share the profits, and through the Colonization Society in Paris a tract of land was purchased 5 kilometres (3 mi.) south of a tiny settlement in Texas called Dallas, which then stood unknown on the very edge of the republic. The phalanx of La Réunion never attracted more than 350 people, and again struggled with finances and even subsistence-level farming. More significantly, the commune voted down the idea of communal living in the very first months, deciding that they would associate together only in labour, not in life. They voted to build small family log cabins, explicitly, they declared, 'so as to escape in our private lives all notion of communism'.[25] Of course, this was for Considerant the end of any chance for architecture and milieu to transform the disastrous history of the private life through the dream of corridic communalism. The failure of La Réunion from this early rejection of foundational principle until its final collapse and sale in 1859 was a bitter blow to Considerant, who abandoned practical politics and retreated to his own family plot in Texas for nearly a decade before he returned to France and picked up the cudgels again.

Considerant was in America not just because it housed religious millennialists and Owenite dreamers, but because Fourier's ideas had been transplanted there in the 1840s by the tireless Fourierist proselytizer Albert Brisbane. Brisbane, the son of a wealthy New York landowner who inherited a large fortune, had travelled to Europe as a young man in 1828 eagerly in search of enlightenment. His first plan was to go to Berlin and study with the philosopher G.W.F. Hegel. Unfortunately Hegel turned out to be a tedious and uninspiring lecturer (probably something you could have guessed from his prose style). Brisbane, hungry for an ideal, soon drifted from Berlin, did the Grand Tour to Italy and Turkey, and ended up in Paris, where he mixed with the idealistic followers of the French utopian economist Henri de Saint-Simon. Soon he found his way to Fourier's door in the rue Richelieu in 1832. Brisbane became a convert overnight and paid Fourier handsomely to be his tutor for two years. He later recalled that in those years he never once saw Fourier smile.

On Brisbane's return to America in 1834 he tidied up Fourier's digressive style, cleaned up the sexual unorthodoxies about marriage

The North American Phalanx, Monmouth County, New Jersey, built in 1843. The main building stood until 1972, when it was destroyed by fire.

North American Phalanx.

and free love, and published two summaries of the doctrine, *Social Destiny of Man* and *A Concise Exposition of the Practical Part of Fourier's Sound Science,* which became the key texts of the American wing of Fourierists. They gathered under the banner of Associationism.

This was not just a theoretical movement. Brisbane converted the New York journalist Horace Greeley, who promoted Associationism through the major journal the *New York Tribune.* Together they soon had enough interest to set up the model North American Phalanx in New Jersey in 1841, and the building was put up in 1843. After that, there were another thirty or so attempts to build phalanxes across the country on Associationist principles.

Brisbane always kept architecture at the core of his phalansterian vision. As he explained in *Social Destiny* in a chapter called 'Defects of System of Separate or Isolated Households', associations worked best with communes of about 2,000 people. Brisbane declared:

> The cabin, the cottage or the dwelling house of civilization, with its monotony, with the daily repetition of its petty and harassing cares ... debilitates the energy of the soul. We must drag man out of this cramped sphere, out of civilization; we must found Association, we must build a Palace for a Phalanx of two thousand beings.[26]

He argued for 'a large and elegant Edifice', but in a departure from the long history of quadrangular shape, the cloistered structure from Thomas More to Robert Owen, argued that 'the square must be avoided; the edifice should be composed of a centre, wings, and sub-wings, so as to prevent uniformity of any kind.' And in this crucial passage, Brisbane continued:

> Up to the present time, there has been no Unity in the architecture of man; he has erected isolated buildings for special purposes which bear the impress, with a few exceptions, of his incoherent social existence and the perversion of his passions. In the dwelling-house, we find depicted the selfishness and circumscribed spirit of the isolated family ...
>
> Association will have ITS ARCHITECTURE, and it will be an architecture of combination and unity. When we are associated and united, one vast and elegant edifice will replace hundreds of the isolated and miserable constructions of civilization ... From a perfect knowledge of human nature, can we not deduce the construction of an edifice perfectly suited to it?[27]

The journals of the Associationist movement followed through with precise architectural discussions. *The Phalanx* addressed 'The Edifice – Mode of Living' in 1844, reassuring readers that 'private apartments will be separated by division walls, and the domestic circle will be no more intruded upon than in any other situation.' At the same time, though:

> The doors will open upon a large covered corridor or inclosed plaza, from eighteen to twenty-four feet wide, which will wind around one entire side of the Edifice. This covered corridor will form the means of communication between all parts of the building, and the inhabitants can at all times go through it to the workshops, placed in one wing of the building, to the dining halls, the lecture rooms, the library, to concerts, the exchange, &c. &c., and visit each other without exposure to the inclemency of the weather or sudden fluctuations of temperature.[28]

This was the type of building that was constructed, in varying sizes, in many of the American communities that followed Brisbane's principles. They combined Fourier's grand dream of the palace with the vernacular American architecture of long cabins, whose rooms were accessed by 'plazas' or 'piazzas' (northeastern terms for a colonnade or enclosed walkway). The North American Phalanx was set up in 1841 by enthusiastic converts to American Associationism in Monmouth County, New Jersey, on 240 hectares (600 ac.) with a phalanx at the centre. Initially it had sixty members who had put in $7,000 each (both Brisbane and Horace Greeley feared this would not reach the critical mass for success). It started out with a small wooden structure with twelve suites for family units, but they built successively larger temporary structures, all on the way towards Brisbane and Greeley's plan for a Grand Unitary Edifice to house 2,000. When the famous landscape architect Frederick Law Olmsted visited in 1852, he described a farm, mill and a phalanx for 150 people, further connected by covered walkways to communal wash-houses, kitchens and dining rooms. 'The united household (and semi-conglomeration) of families works better than I was willing to believe possible,' he declared, and although he would never choose to live there, he thought it offered a better education to a young man than Harvard or Yale.[29]

The influence of this model phalanx prompted other experiments. 'Ceresco', the Wisconsin Phalanx, was set up in 1844 and remained one of the strictest adherents to Fourierist principles. The community demanded collective living of its members and constructed a 'common house', known as the Long House, which was over 60 metres (200 ft) long and housed thirty families. The founder, Warren Chase, explained that 'We have organized groups and series in a simple manner, and thus far everything goes admirably . . . We keep in harmony of feelings and concert of action.'[30] The commune was dissolved by 1849, however, as the original members drifted away and the community proved reluctant to recruit replacements.

At the famous Brook Farm experiment, established in 1841 by George Ripley (and later fictionalized by Nathaniel Hawthorne in *The Blithedale Romance*), the community mixed Transcendentalist principles with more Fourierist notions. In 1844 they ended up building one of the largest phalanxes. The three-storey structure was nearly 60 metres (200 ft) long, with single rooms in the attics, family units on the floors below, and lecture rooms and halls in the basement, the entirety of it 'connected by piazzas that ran the whole length of the building'.[31] A catastrophic fire destroyed the building just as it was being completed. Interestingly, the letters of Marianne Dwight, a Brook Farm member and ardent Associationist, recorded 'a feeling of relief' that this experimental building had failed, 'that building so foolishly undertaken, so poorly built and planned, and which again and again some of us thought and said we should rejoice to see blown away or burned down'.[32] However, since the building was uninsured and the farm was already beset by creditors, the $7,000 sunk into the phalanx building effectively meant the financial ruin of the whole experiment. The North American Phalanx was also ended by a fire in the mill in 1856, but it had survived thirteen years through the profits on its farming, making it one of the longest-lasting phalansteries.

One of the most enduring phalanx buildings emerged from a splinter group that left the North American Phalanx and established the Raritan Bay Union in New Jersey in 1853. It was led by Marcus

Spring, who was alarmed by godless Fourierism and preferred a more avowedly Christian ethos. He spent $40,000 of his own money building a stone phalanx that housed forty families but restricted the communalism to a large shared dining hall. (Spring, however, made sure to build himself a conventional separate house for his family to live alone in next door.) Thoreau lectured there, calling it a 'queer place', but it was known as a centre for anti-slavery intellectuals and campaigners. Since it was built of stone, instead of the more usual wooden clapboards, the structure survived the dissolution of the commune in about 1859, later becoming a school and a hotel – suitably corridic institutions – before falling into ruin.[33]

Plans for phalanxes had accelerated in the late 1840s, with collective fundraising projects like the Phalansterian Realization Fund Society (established by Horace Greeley) or the Philadelphia Unitary Building Association. The latter, headed by the prominent Philadelphian artist John Sartain, issued a model Constitution but also a lithograph of their ideal edifice with an elegant three-tiered columniated facade and an interior that emphasized 'social circulation spaces' and 'galleries of association'.

Symptomatically, cooperative communities often voted down plans for communal living as too radical in the reordering of social relations. The first attempt to build a communal phalanx for farm workers in Russia was said to have been burnt down by the workers housed in it. The French Owenite Étienne Cabet – who coined the term *communisme*, wrote *Voyage to Icaria* in 1840 inspired by reading Thomas More's *Utopia* in exile in London, and then travelled to America to found a real 'Icaria', first in Texas and then in Illinois – was expelled by his own community for his diktats on the conduct of everyday life and his bans on alcohol and tobacco. The enforcement of silence in workshops was the last straw. Cabet had planned Icaria extensively, with gridded cities, family homes with terraces onto the streets and porticos on slender columns on every pavement. People, once again, screwed up the neatness of this architectural vision.[34]

The two most successful long-term communities to emerge from these utopian ideas survived because they were smaller in ambition and scale and found ways of integrating into the surrounding capitalist economy rather than setting themselves up in implacable opposition. In France, the industrialist Jean-Baptiste Godin built a model factory and housing complex at Guise, based on a mix of ideas from Robert Owen and Charles Fourier. He started on his phalanx, which he called a *familistère*, in 1859, but built slowly, constructing one wing first, then the central court several years later with the last wing completed only in 1879. It was termed a 'united dwelling' and housed about 1,200 people with communal access on three floors from a glass-covered central court.

> Three continuous balconies go round the four sides of the interior of the court. These balconies are nearly four feet wide, and as they are free from divisions one can walk right round them; they give access to all the homes, and each is in fact a kind of suspended street. Staircases at the corners of the building lead to the balconies, and allow free circulation in every direction. Large passages on each floor put the central court in connection with the two wings.[35]

There were no interior corridors, but each two-room unit had double aspects, one into the central court, the other out onto the open country beyond. Communal shops, washrooms, a school, theatre and health centre were located nearby. After the main block opened, and workers populated it rapidly, Godin built another housing block for six hundred workers. An illustrated pamphlet from the Labour Co-partnership Association in 1903 lavishly praised this model of collective life and labour, although it was evidently a hopeless compromise with the 'civilization' Fourier steadfastly condemned.

The other success, in America, was considerably weirder than Guise. The Oneida Community was founded by the preacher John Humphrey Noyes in 1834 after a spiritual revelation. He abandoned his respectable seminary training at Yale to preach the Perfectionist heresy, holding that humanity was perfectible rather than intrinsically sinful and fallen because Christ's Second Coming had already happened and the kingdom of heaven was now realizable on earth. The community followed a familiar form of 'Bible communism', where all property was shared and communal life and worship was integral to practice. Notoriously, though, Noyes further interpreted the mystical marriage of heaven and earth to be best achieved through multiplying sexual unions among his followers.

In 1846 Noyes introduced the practice of 'complex marriage', in which multiple partners could be agreed if all parties (and the wider community) consented. It was clearly influenced by Fourier's ideas, proving that the bowdlerization of Associationism in America did not entirely suppress this aspect of achieving harmony. The scandal in this small community became public knowledge in 1847 and Noyes was forced to move the community across a state line to avoid arrest for adultery. They settled in the remote Oneida Creek in upstate New York to build their utopia.

The Oneida Community lasted as a religious community until it was formally dissolved in 1881. By that time they had institutionalized the dissolution of the traditional nuclear family by dissolving 'married' quarters and separating children from their mothers at two years old. Children were housed collectively, and at thirteen were initiated into the community's sexual economy. Unsurprisingly, perhaps, Noyes himself volunteered to take on this solemn task for all the girls. From 1868 the community also experimented with 'human stirpiculture', the attempt to improve the racial stock of the community by selective breeding, the quicker to bring perfectibility to pass. 'Stirpiculture' was Noyes's coinage as the more familiar word, eugenics (invented by Darwin's cousin Francis Galton), had not quite yet entered the language.

Oneida survived because soon after they had moved to their remote settlement they acquired a very lucrative patent on a design of animal trap. Later they developed as a silversmith business (which still exists). 'In order to subdue the world to Christ,' Noyes said, 'we must carry religion into money-making.'[36] This holy marriage with capitalism helped them avoid the precarious subsistence communism that led to the failure of many other phalanxes.

This surplus also allowed Oneida to realize their philosophy in architectural form. There were four successive waves of building at Oneida, and this programme of concretizing utopia again illustrates how the corridor remained central to communalism. They replaced the extant farmhouse and other outbuildings with a single communal Mansion House, completed in 1852. This structure conceived of community in terms of a single dining room and parlour for compulsory evening group assemblies. These were linked by an external piazza or covered walkway. 'The Court' was a central hallway that was functionally underdetermined yet located at the centre of circulation paths, maximizing social encounters. The real innovation was the scandalous Tent Room, a series of double compartments for sexual coupling, divided by heavy curtains suspended on wires that could be quickly rearranged in different formations and obviously intended to break down the closed family unit. Elsewhere, however, fixed double rooms retained a more conservative conception of the marriage bed, suggesting a community in transition towards acceptance of a more complex marriage.

The New Mansion House, built in 1859, was a much larger structure than the original core building, testifying to the growing numbers in the community. It was also more radical in using the space to imprint ideology on behaviour. The central 'parlour' needed to accommodate several hundred, resulting in smaller offshoots, although this caused worry about fragmenting association. Each adult could retreat to a single room, many of which were laid out along corridors on one side, opening onto larger communal spaces across the hall. To get to a bedroom, members of the community had to traverse Hamilton's Avenue (named after the architect), which forced individuals to pass through the sitting rooms at the intersection of the corridors and other collective workspaces. This was all designed to maximize interaction and to discourage the formation of antisocial couples or subgroups. Those who refused to participate in the wider sexual economy of the community were placed on a dark double corridor on the top floor, with no through passage: a deliberate spatial dead end or ghetto and symbol of their internal exile. A major wing was added in 1869 to house the school, and the last project, a north wing, was started in 1877. This last building was the first not to be designed by Noyes or his close circle. It was inevitably more conventional, with hotel-like double-loaded corridors to the bedrooms with almost no public spaces built in to break the flow. There was no sense of investment in using architectural space to generate movement, circulation or passional attraction. It remained unfinished before Oneida elected to dissolve itself as a religious community; the core ideology was clearly beginning to fade.[37]

The dreams of these street-galleries and corridors of the phalansterians, even though many of these utopias came to bitter ends in economic collapse, conflagration or irreconcilable differences, remained a powerful underpinning idea in public architecture long into the twentieth century. The Oneida Community's entrepreneurial direction hints at the commercial dreamworlds that stole some of Fourier's sparkly stardust for their immersive corridic spaces – and I will look at these in Chapter Four. The most obvious debt to Fourier's ideas, however, lay in ideas of social housing, schemes that often explicitly echoed the Fourierist ideal.

3

The Utopia of Corridors, II: Social Housing from Petrograd to the Barbican

In his dramatic month-by-month account of 1917, the year of the Russian Revolution, China Miéville constantly evokes 'an unease, an uncoiling in government corridors' as the Bolsheviks push for an end to all compromise with the machinery of government. The October Revolution that brought Lenin's faction to power in Russia in 1917 was a victory, Miéville says, of the 'corridor-squatters' that eventually overran the Winter Palace.[1] It might seem an odd way to focus such transformative events, but architectural form was a key element in thinking about the shape of the Union of Soviet Socialist Republics.

The Soviet Social Condenser

After victory in the Civil War that followed (1918–21), the USSR was awash with utopian projects throughout the 1920s. In the fervour to transform every aspect of life, grand projects for industrialization were combined with dreams of new transport networks, new cities, new buildings. 'The imperceptible, ant-like piling up of quarters and streets, brick by brick, from generation to generation, will give way to titanic constructions,' Leon Trotsky, in his *Literature and Revolution* (1923), promised. 'In this struggle, architecture will again be filled with the spirit of mass feelings and moods', he continued, assuring that 'Man will learn . . . how to build people's palaces on the peaks of Mont Blanc and at the bottom of the Atlantic.'[2] This architectural dreaming had long been part of Bolshevism. In Alexander Bogdanov's Bolshevik utopia *Red Star*, first published in 1905, the year of revolutionary failure, the fully communist Russian colony on Mars is a settlement of vast collective houses, transparent glass factories, museums and hospitals.

The echo of Fourier's phalanstery in these Bolshevik visions was deliberate. At least ten new translated editions of Fourier's work were published in the Soviet Union in the decade after the Revolution. Just as they had in America, Fourier's ideas reached Russia in the 1840s, through the advocacy of Mikhail Petrashevsky and his circle in St Petersburg. (It was involvement in this group that led to Dostoevsky's sentence to death by the Tsarist regime in 1849, a judgement then commuted to prison time as he awaited the firing squad.) A trial phalanx had been built to house peasant workers, but the experiment ended when the peasants burnt it down. The post-Revolutionary housing crisis demanded a mass building programme for basic shelter, and this was also seized as a chance, following the ideas of Fourier as much as Marx and Engels, to dismantle the structure of private ownership of the family home with all its petit-bourgeois trappings. Instead, collectivized environments would promote what was called the *novyi byt*, a new kind of everyday life. The Revolution would be properly lived only by overthrowing old spatial habits and norms. Communal life would be the chrysalis for the birth of communism's 'new man'. Fourier's street-galleries remained central to this utopian vision in the heady first decade of the Revolution before Stalin's repression began.

Housing was nationalized by Lenin in 1919. On the model of the workers' soviets or councils, many large buildings became communes managed by local Housing Committees for the people. Briefly, rent was abolished, but economic crisis meant that this could not last for long. The shortage of housing stock after years of war was chronic, but even so the Commissariat of Health set a 'sanitary norm' of 8.25 square metres (88 sq. ft) per person (increased to 9 square metres (97 sq. ft) in 1926, which remained the Soviet norm in theory, if not in practice). The assumption in this abstract figure was the provision of space rather than four walls and a door. Indeed, the drive was to minimize the private room and emphasize instead communal kitchens, dining rooms, bathrooms, toilets and laundries, and otherwise prioritize all aspects of the properly socialized life. This was proclaimed as a liberation of women from domestic servitude – an important element of Bolshevik ideology – and a freeing of the general population into social being. In 1930 V. Kuzmin wrote in his essay 'The Problems of the Scientific Organization of Life' that collectivism would be best realized 'through the mechanism of common space and passageways to encourage interaction'.[3] The corridor was placed in the service of the revolution in its role as a *s*ocial condenser.

The idea of the 'social condenser' was coined by the technophiliac Bolsheviks in an echo of the function of the electrical condenser – a place to store revolutionary energies and build capacity. Social condensers were intended to use architectural space 'to turn the self-centred individual of capitalist society into a whole man, the informed militant of socialist society in which the interest of each merged with the interests of all'.[4] Initially this aim was pursued through public buildings like Palaces of Culture and Workers' Clubs built for specific trade unions or collectives for after-work education, meetings, theatre and cinema performances and social events. The idea was that the club, a traditional form of association under the Tsars, would now serve as what the revolutionary architect El Lissitzky called 'social power plants', or 'a workshop for the transformation of man'.[5]

There were several remarkable Workers' Clubs constructed in Moscow in the 1920s, five by the Constructivist architect Konstantin Mel'nikov, all materialist responses to specific sites and social groupings, and all of which emphasized dynamic movement and circulation, with multifunctional spaces and moveable partition walls that could transform the interior space and invent new collectivities at a moment's notice. Many of these clubs have survived beyond the Soviet Union, even if their dynamic public spaces have been left somewhat stranded by the rise of Russian gangster capitalism. When the architectural critic Owen Hatherley toured them twenty years after the end of the USSR, he remarked: 'It is hard not to imagine that Soviet architects were thinking of Fourier in the early 1920s when they devised the "social condensers".'[6]

Konstantin Mel'nikov brought Soviet Constructivism to international attention with his design for the Soviet Pavilion at the Paris Exposition of 1925, a dynamic glass and concrete structure pushed into dramatic asymmetry by the explosive forces it held in fragile balance, and sliced diagonally in half by an open concrete staircase and corridor under a soaring cantilevered roof.[7]

But the key architectural theorist of the Constructivists was Moisei Ginzburg, who published the manifesto *Style and Epoch* in 1924 and was the founding member of the OSA Group, the Organization of Contemporary Architects, which produced some of the most utopian projects and proposals for building in the Soviet Union between 1925 and 1932, the point at which it was dissolved by Stalinist decree.[8] In *Style and Epoch*, Ginzburg set out to address 'the basic task confronting modernity: . . . workers' housing and the house of work'. The 'spirit of collectivism' had to supersede the sentimentalism of the old structures of house and cottage for a new form that he modelled on the factory. In a striking section, he argued that the factory was dominated by the 'prevalence of horizontal forces', the dynamism of the machines on the production line, and so the architecture of modernity needed to convey not just the 'vigorous daring of the vertical' but a 'boundless' horizontality too, giving impetus to a corridic thrust in monumental buildings.[9]

The logic of building for the communist epoch was most fully realized by Ginzburg and the OSA in the idea of the *dom kommuna*, the communal house. The communal house was the most avowedly Fourierist and utopian conception to emerge from this experimental period. In 1918 the architect B. Venderov designed a small-scale phalanstery for 38 families, and in 1921 the phalanstery designed by the Soviet architects Tsverkoi and D. P. Buryshkin won an architectural prize for proletarian housing in Petrograd. Neither of these was built, but the plans got grander and grander. The economist Leonid Sabsovich, who served on the central GOSPLAN, the Commission for a General Plan (which orchestrated the Soviet command economy), issued a series of proposals in *Socialist Cities* and *The USSR in Ten Years* that promised a complete rational redistribution of the total population of the Soviet Union to evenly sized small-scale cities with 'housing combines' each for 2,000 or 3,000 citizens. This plan followed Marx's anticipation of the dissolution of the boundary between the country and the city. A second edition of Sabsovich's plan had to be retitled *The USSR in Fifteen Years*, the arrival at utopia slightly delayed as the republic crashed against harsh economic realities.

Sabsovich envisaged that these Soviet phalanxes, rather like the monastery, would have very small single cells for each worker, perhaps as little as 5 square metres (54 sq. ft), placed in ribbons along corridors. As he explained:

> These houses should not have separate apartments with kitchens, pantries, etc. for individual domestic use, since all of the workers' everyday needs will be completely socialized. In addition, they should not include space for private family life, because the idea of family, as we now know it, will no longer exist. In place of the closed, isolated family unit we will have the 'collective family' of workers, in which isolation will have no place.[10]

Soviet projections often suggested that children would need to be housed and educated in separate phalanxes, just as some Associationists had proposed in the 1840s. This responded to the Bolshevik aim to liberate women from servitude, but was also intended to generate proper Soviet citizens. 'We must rescue children from the harmful influence of family life,' Lenin's close ally Zlata Lilina argued: 'We must nationalize them.'[11] Plans were drawn up for children's settlements of about 800 to 1,000 children, who would live and be schooled collectively. (In Bogdanov's *Red Star*, the children on Mars live in a separate colony in large communal two-storey houses.) The architects Barshch and Vladimirov issued a design for a phalanx of a thousand adults in a narrow block housed along communal corridors, with pre-schoolers and older kids situated in separate blocks at right angles that were linked by walkways. This was offered in the service of revolutionary 'de-familization'.[12] However, in the same year as this proposal, 1929, the official Party line turned decisively against collective childcare and these early radical plans were dropped.

The new state did build numerous cities from scratch around vast new factories in the push to increase industrial capacity and production, such as the large-scale complex at Magnitogorsk. But Sabsovich's plans also proved too radical for the Party under Stalin (Sabsovich was censured by name for his 'infantile' utopianism in 1930). Alongside the Constructivist Workers' Clubs, however, there

The Constructivist Narkomfin building, Moscow, 1928. This block of flats is an example of Soviet-era collective living.

were several experimental communal houses that were actually realized at this time. The most famous was the Narkomfin building in Moscow, designed by Moisei Ginzburg and Ignaty Milinis and built between 1928 and 1932.

The main building of the Narkomfin complex, a narrow five-storey block with dramatic lines of continuous concrete balconies, housed the employees of the Commissariat for Finance in 54 units of two standardized types entered on two corridors on the second and fifth floor. Ginzburg had been commissioned in 1928 to create standardized housing types by the central building committee 'to establish the norms for all subsequent state housing for the entire Russian Republic', and the Narkomfin trialled the 'F-type' and the larger 'K-type' in this main building.[13] There was a covered walkway bridge that connected this block to the separated communal services – kitchen, dining room, gymnasium and library. The laundry was another separate block, and there was a plan to build a separate crèche, either to liberate women into working during the day or more radically to fulfil the proper disaggregation of the bourgeois family. This crèche, however, fell by the wayside with the change of official Party policy, and a second large housing block meant to complete the complex was also abandoned.

Ginzburg was explicit in his writing that 'the well-lit access corridor could become a sort of forum, a setting for the development of purely collective functions and social exchanges.' He proclaimed that this complex of

> one-room type F apartments is a new organism that will lead us toward a socially superior mode of life – the communal life. The presence of a horizontal artery – the external corridor – makes it possible to link such units organically with a communal dining room and kitchen, recreation room, baths, and so on.[14]

This is rhetoric familiar from the Fourierist street-gallery.

The Narkomfin was only ever intended as a 'transitional' block on the way towards full socialist living (the single cells were mixed with larger family K-type units, for instance), but this kind of solution to housing fell out of favour before it was completed. Over the years, internal walls were punched through, illegal hotplates were smuggled into rooms to create improvised private kitchens, and the roof was dominated by a structure that became the private penthouse for a leading party apparatchik. The Narkomfin fell into gentle ruination in later decades as a mark of official disapproval.

Actual realizations of the *dom kommuna* were extremely rare. There had been suspicions of avant-garde 'Westernism' or formalism in Constructivist OSA housing plans as early as 1927, but the first official censure of these was delivered by communiqué in 1930, and this was followed by the Central Committee's abolition of all architectural associations in April 1932. There was now only one Union of Soviet Architects and the adoption of one official style, the blocky classicism of Socialist Realism, a style that is full of grand archways, processional routes, passageways and grand corridors, which was aimed, Owen Hatherley comments, 'at instilling the feeling that you are always about to *arrive at something*'.[15] To survive, Ginzburg denounced communalism and retreated to the technical exploration of prefabricated construction for mass housing.

While the Bolsheviks' architectural utopias had embraced Fourierist communal life, from early on a writer like Yevgeny Zamyatin saw the potential for oppressive conformity coiled within these post-Revolutionary designs. In his famous dystopia *We* (published in English before Russian, in 1924), the communal glass living units and factories of the twenty-sixth-century OneState erase all individual names and identities, and ensure that the millions act according to a single timetable. This fragmented, poetic account includes nightmare visions of corridors with 'lightbulbs on the curved vaults [that] made an endless, twinkling, swaying dotted line', a Logical Labyrinth from which there is no escape.[16] The limitless, faceless corridor is one of the foundational images of envisioning a totalitarian condition, the individual swallowed up by the larger structures of the state.

Given the desperate pressure to house the population after the Civil War, the common housing solution in the early years of the Soviet Republic tended to be to commandeer old buildings. The state evicted bourgeois and aristocratic owners, priests and any members of the Tsarist police or bureaucracy, and carved up this recovered space into provisional family units, often using very basic wooden partitions. Within these improvised solutions there were some spontaneous experiments in radical communal living in the 1920s, perhaps more than five hundred communes that pooled all property and income (a handful also experimented with abolishing monogamy). However, after the Party rejection of communalism, most of the population came to live in *zhilischchnye kooperativi*, 'housing cooperatives' that limited collectivism to laundries, bathrooms and the shared space of corridors. These were social condensers of very different moods and affects after the suppression of the Bolsheviks and the rise of Stalin.

Svetlana Boym's memoir about growing up in this kind of cooperative in St Petersburg, *Common Places*, was written shortly after the collapse of the Soviet Union and is an evocative account of the distance between a long-gone Bolshevik utopia and post-Stalinist reality. These repurposed buildings, she recalled, meant 'creating strange spaces, long corridors, and so-called black entrances through labyrinthine inner courtyards'. To enter her building 'requires a long "rite of passage": in and out through a dark hallway with ruined mosaics and pieces of beer bottles and across the interior yards full of communal trash'. The interior corridor, the central thoroughfare distributing the living units of such block-communes, dominates her memories and her dreams. She thinks of this corridor space as 'everywhere in daily life and nowhere in its official representation':

> The hallway occupies a special place in Soviet mythical topography; it is a space of transition, a space of fear, the dark limit of the house

> ... The hallways are usually inhabited by old drunks, local fools, youth gangs, and teenagers in love. Here all sorts of unofficial initiations take place ... As you enter the communal corridor you hear the flutter of slippers and the squeaking of the floors and many pairs of eyes scrutinizing you through half-opened doors.

The plywood partition walls were thin enough to abolish any notion of privacy, but no longer in the service of an idealized collective, more in the spirit of the fearful pressure to conform by constant surveillance from neighbours suspicious of any deviation from the perceived norm. In a more reflective passage, Boym suggests that in the Soviet Union 'there was no interface between public and private, no space of conventional socialization, the space that is governed neither by official decorum ... nor by the unwritten rules of intimacy. The space between is the space of alienation – the Soviet zone.'[17] Joseph Brodsky also recalls a 'horizontal stripe at eye level, running unfailingly across the whole country, like the line of an infinite common denominator: in halls, hospitals, factories, prisons, corridors of communal apartments ... [as] maddening as it was omnipresent'.[18]

This communal corridor space is a continual feature of the art installations of Ilya and Emilia Kabakov that came right at the end of the Soviet era. In *Incident in the Corridor near the Kitchen* (1989), a short stub of an angled corridor is full of pots, pans and other kitchen utensils hanging on wires, as if fixed at the moment of explosion. In *Labyrinth (My Mother's Album)* (1990), Ilya Kabakov constructed a 49-metre-long (160-ft) shabby corridor that twists and turns, the ceiling held up by improvised wooden struts, the floor scattered with rubble, doors opening into dirty cabinets. Along the walls are 76 framed sections of the account of his mother's life, born in 1902 and thus living through the entire span of the Soviet experience. As Kabakov explains:

> When I think about that world in which my mother's life passed, about the condensed image of it, what arises in my imagination

> is a long and semi-dark corridor which is twisted like a labyrinth, where behind each new turn, behind each bend, there is not a bright exit glimmering in the distance, but just the same grubby floor, the same gray, dusty, poorly painted walls illuminated by weak, 40-watt light bulbs.[19]

These accounts suggest a momentary instant of avant-garde possibility in the Soviet Union around the ideas of the Constructivists that barely lasted five years before suppression. Yet the ideal of mass communal housing for the twentieth century, the possibility to finally realize the Fourierist dream, did not end in the harsh economic priorities of the first Soviet Five-year Plan. In fact the ideas of Ginzburg and the OSA were already in dialogue with one of the most influential architects of the Modernist era, Le Corbusier, a man who would finally build his own Fourierist 'social condenser' in Marseilles in 1952.

Le Corbusier's *Rues Intérieures*

The Swiss architect Charles-Édouard Jeanneret (1887–1965), who branded himself 'Le Corbusier' in 1920, became interested in the problem of mass housing during the First World War and researched techniques of prefabricating concrete elements to reduce costs and increase the speed of construction, merging architecture and engineering. After building in a regional Arts and Crafts style for his first projects, he claimed to have had a revelation upon seeing the Carthusian monastery at Galluzzo (or Val d'Ema) near Florence in 1907, its elegant quadrilateral cloister and cells the model of the harmonious balance of individual and collective, earthly and spiritual, life. Although Le Corbusier's Modernist/Internationalist Style is associated

Ilya Kabakov, *Labyrinth* (*My Mother's Album*), 1990, large-scale immersive corridor installation that twists and turns, disorienting the visitor.

with unadorned concrete, the free plan and open spaces, the cloistral and corridic kept returning in his designs.

After 1920, when Le Corbusier began the avant-garde Modernist journal *L'Esprit nouveau* with the painter Amedée Ozenfant, these researches were combined with an interest in grand schemes for the wholesale transformation of cities. The plan for the Contemporary City in 1922 wiped the medieval labyrinths of Paris off the map for clean, symmetrical grids of wide boulevards lined by 'vertical garden cities', cruciform skyscrapers marching across the page in geometric heaven. He embraced the vertiginous speed and creative destruction of the machine age and the house, as the slogan went, was reconceived as a machine for living in. In 1923 Le Corbusier's key manifesto *Vers une architecture* (translated as *Towards a New Architecture*) ended with sections on 'Mass-production Housing' and 'Architecture or Revolution'. The book finished with the peroration: 'It is a question of building which is at the root of the social unrest of today; architecture or revolution.' Le Corbusier was insistent that a 'great epoch has begun', which required that 'we eliminate from our hearts and minds all dead concepts in regard to the houses' and build instead 'a new state of mind of living in mass-production houses'. Given the resistance to this stream of avant-garde provocations, however, he was fully aware that 'The right state of mind does not exist' – not yet, anyway.[20] It was going to be necessary to build that consciousness.

Perhaps the shape of this ambition was why Trotsky was an admirer of the writing in *L'Esprit nouveau*. The last pages of Trotsky's own *Literature and Revolution* burst with utopian architectural imaginings, as we have seen. Certainly the Russian Constructivists responded to Le Corbusier's proposals, and in 1928 the Swiss provocateur was invited to submit designs for a Soviet architectural competition. This resulted in the construction of his winning design with Nikolai Kolli for Moscow's Tsentrosoyuz building (the Central Union of Consumer Cooperatives), a large office for 3,500 workers that was finished in 1933 (and which still stands). After winning the competition, Le Corbusier travelled to Moscow in 1929, where he lectured on urbanism and presented his large-scale Moscow Plan. The Narkomfin design then under construction also showed the influence of Le Corbusier and he discussed its construction with Ginzburg, since both were pioneers in standardization, prefabrication and massification of concrete blocks.

With the tide already turning against communal experiments and avant-gardism, however, Le Corbusier found himself denounced in the press by Moisei Ginzburg and El Lissitzky as an 'absolute individualist' with an intrinsically 'antisocial nature . . . that separates him from the expectations of the great mass of people'.[21] Although Le Corbusier was often accused by detractors of Bolshevik tendencies (particularly after his formation of CIAM, the Congrès Internationaux d'Architecture Moderne in 1928), these accusations made by the Soviets were actually fair enough. In his 'Reply to Moscow', published as part of *The Radiant City* in 1933, Le Corbusier claimed that all of his building and city plans were premised on individual liberty: 'Where the planning of collective life threatens to demolish the liberty of the individual, we must respect it.' His foundational architectural premise was the individual cell and the 'basic human need' of 'personal solitude. When the door is shut I can freely enter my own world.'[22] He knew this was anathema to the Bolsheviks, who called him 'morbid'. In turn, he denounced the 'de-urbanization' tendencies of the first Soviet Five-year Plan, the proposal to disperse the population to smaller-density cities of no more than 50,000 people. Le Corbusier took this as a personal affront to his own vision of superdensity in cities. In the 1930s he would drift towards a more technocratic and avowedly elitist vision of top-down city planning, an anticipation of his brief association with the Vichy regime under German Occupation in 1941. Le Corbusier always claimed his architecture was biological rather than ideological, finding *natural*, *essential* and *universal* laws, a surefire way of falling victim to the shifting tides of politics.

The Radiant City contains Le Corbusier's most important reflections on ideas of circulation and movement from the largest scale city plan to the question of standardized uniform housing. It was here that he sketched out his hugely influential ideas on high-density high-rises separated entirely from now redundant notions of the street. Traffic, work and living would be thoroughly disarticulated. Industry would be stretched along ribbon developments alongside super-highways with immense, ever-flowing cloverleaf junctions. In city centres, housing blocks would be set in parklands, with each block lifted up on pilotis and apartments distributed along elevated walkways, since the necessity of orientation by street was now abolished. At the heart of these standardized housing blocks were the *rues intérieures*, which he formulated directly in relation to the Soviet Union:

> The interior street has existed in embryonic form in two or three apartment houses built last year in Moscow. It was considered undesirable to continue its application, because children made a deafening racket in the corridors and the neighbours could see directly into the apartments opening onto the corridors. Certain circles in Moscow, subdued by this failure, are thinking of abandoning the principle of the interior street and coming back to that of the separate stairway for every two apartments. The time of decision has come; let's remain calm, let's react against panic: so the interior street did not work in Moscow. I say: let's not give up the principle of the interior street, but instead, let's try to create a new organ which is the interior street . . . How can we organize the interior street? That is what we must work out: *we must create that organ.*[23]

The interior corridor, picked up from Fourier and trialled in the USSR, was revised again in Le Corbusier's post-Soviet manifesto as one of the key transformative spatial devices for his model of both the Radiant City and its necessarily reprogrammed citizens. It took another twenty years for the architect to realize a vision with the interior street at its heart, but when l'Unité d'habitation de grandeur conforme (the Standard Size Housing Block) opened on the outskirts of Marseilles in October 1952, it had a huge influence on the forms of post-war social housing that were subsequently built across Europe.

There are signs all along the wide boulevard heading out of the historic centre of Marseilles that direct you to *la Ville radieuse*, so the taxis find this 'no-place' utopia considerably easier to locate than Thomas More's island. When you clear the vast tracts of indifferent later housing blocks that surround it and see the Unité unencumbered for the first time, it is breathtaking – a vast, uniform concrete block with bold coloured panels, 168 metres (550 ft) long but only 24 metres (80 ft) wide. It rises seventeen floors but the whole bulk is somehow jauntily lifted above the ground on angled concrete struts. From the roofline jut expressive forms like funnels that reinforce the sense of a luxury ocean liner mysteriously beached a long way from the harbour, as if you are living inside J. G. Ballard's *The Drought*. Close-up, the concrete is not smooth, but rough edged, deliberately bearing all the artisanal imperfections of its pouring. This is *béton brut*, rough concrete: one of the origins of what soon came to be called New Brutalism.

In the spirit of communalism, the public areas of the building are easy to access. Halfway up the building are the communal services along a double-height glass atrium (shops, laundry, a bar and restaurant, the hotel, and the shell of a once radical ideal of post-war convenience, a supermarket, now closed). The concrete roof deck, accessible to all, is a blinding wonderland in the sun of abstract concrete blocks, making up a crèche, a paddling pool, a stage and backdrop for theatre, a wall-garden that provides some shade, and surrounded by a running track, all with views that stretch one way to the sea, the other to the mountains. Jonathan Meades, the architectural critic and ardent advocate of Brutalism, lives in the building and considers the roof 'a transcendent work' that has the true force of art. Nicholas Webber is no less hyperbolic: he calls it 'a turning point in the history of how human beings live'.[24]

Much of the technical architectural interest is focused on the modular system Le Corbusier used to construct the duplex apartments, the 23 variants slotted into the structural grid like bottles into a rack. It meant that every apartment had a double-height window at one end, to flood it with light. Yet the real secret of the building lies in the seven floors where interior streets provide access to the apartments. Outside, there is the blazing sun and the continuous noise of heavy traffic. Inside, these double-loaded corridors are cool, quiet and dim like a church, the coloured glass panels around the apartment doors providing, as one guidebook puts it, 'an extraordinary and mysterious symphony of colours' that dance across the floor in the dappled shadows.[25] The corridor is the 'counterpoint to the revelatory lightness of the individual apartments'.[26]

'THIS IS NOT AN ESCAPE INTO UTOPIA', Le Corbusier had sloganized in *The Radiant City*. At that time he wanted to be careful to distance himself from the lunatic dreams of the Bolsheviks. And yet in his small book on l'Unité twenty years later, discussing the organization of communal services in the building, he declared 'we can have Utopia tomorrow.'[27] L'Unité d'habitation has 337 apartments, and was designed for 1,600 residents. Yet again Fourier's magic number for the ideal phalanx pops up. L'Unité is meant to be Utopia realized, or at least a fragment of it, the first experiment in a scheme to be rolled out on a grand scale.

Le Corbusier was commissioned to build the experimental block by the French Minister of Reconstruction in 1945. The port of Marseilles had been fiercely bombed during the war, and a project to reconstruct the housing of the poor working areas of the city was urgent. Typically, Le Corbusier planned a whole cluster of these standard blocks, eight Unités to house 20,000 people displaced from the city. This single, experimental building, a long way from the old port, was the only one that was built and this was in the teeth of a

Interior corridor in Le Corbusier's l'Unité d'habitation, Marseille, 1952.

relentless campaign to block its construction. There were a number of procedural attempts to declare that the planned block breached structural or hygiene regulations. The president of the Ordre des médecins de la Seine authoritatively declared that the building 'would favour the outbreak of mental diseases', and some called it la Maison du fada, the Loony Bin.[28] Having been denounced as a prospective slum, when a model apartment was opened in the shell of the building in 1949 it was declared unnecessarily luxurious.

When the building finally opened in 1952, Le Corbusier was defiant. In his inaugural speech he observed that already, spontaneously, those tenants who lived there 'rapidly formed an association, as a real vertical community without any political affiliation, to defend its interests and to develop its human values'. This was a self-generated board that would look after the 'practical, moral and other management of this Unité . . . in an atmosphere of great mutual understanding'.[29] It was the communal spaces of the building, its interior streets and roof deck, that had resulted in this spontaneous appearance of Associationism up in the clear blue skies of the Riviera.

All the same, Le Corbusier could never quite shake the paternalistic control of being the master planner of his utopia. His statements about the spontaneous communalism were often leavened with ominously dictatorial comments. 'There can be no individual liberty without external order,' he proclaimed. 'That order may be freely consented to, but it is none the less a discipline. Discipline has much to give.' He might have appealed to a language of biology and harmony, but his buildings also demanded of its resident a 'know-how of dwelling'; they would need to learn a 'new code of manners and customs for the tribe'.[30] As always, as in Zamyatin's *We*, a potential dystopia could be found coiled inside utopia in such ominous assertions.

Le Corbusier had the fervent hope that his modular design for the Radiant City would spread across the city, and then France, and then beyond, along the transport corridors he envisaged that could infinitely extend this web. In fact only four more Unités were built, in Nantes, Berlin, Briey-en-Forêt and Firminy Vert (the last of these was finished in 1968, after his death). Unlike Marseilles, though, Le Corbusier never had the same freedom from regulation and constraint, and he was forced to make many compromises to the conception – so much so that he disowned the building in Berlin.

Strangely enough, one of the fullest adoptions of Le Corbusier's ideas came in Britain, where the same urgent impetus to rebuild catastrophic housing stocks after 1945 was pushed by a combination of a socialist national government, communist town planners, private building companies seeking contracts for modular prefabricated building systems, and architects enamoured of International Modernism. In Britain, the *rue intérieure* lived on for another three decades as the utopian 'street in the sky' at the heart of post-war planning.

British Post-war Housing: Streets in the Sky

The devastating war in the air over Britain meant that government agencies started presenting plans for reconstruction as early as 1942. *The County of London Plan*, written by Patrick Abercrombie and J. H. Forshaw in 1943, proved very influential in acknowledging the 'unprecedented' disaster of the Blitz but also that the devastation presented the first opportunity since the Great Fire of 1666 to rethink the city significantly.[31] Evacuated populations could remain dispersed, redistributed in wholly new towns, to allow a managed plan for London as a patchwork of smaller precincts, centred around schools. The corrosive problem of through-traffic from growing car use could be expelled by creating a series of concentric ring roads at ever-greater distances from the centre. This separation of different kinds of circulation was to become a post-war planning norm. For housing, the English would have to overcome their suspicion of the continental apartment block, but Abercrombie always envisaged mixed developments of traditional family houses and smaller flats for younger urban workers. To accelerate reconstruction, Abercrombie argued for concentrated development areas: for example, sections of the East End, badly damaged by dockland bombing and requiring major slum clearance anyway, while the South Bank, opposite the Houses of Parliament, could house a major cultural centre (this became the space for the Royal Festival Hall, completed in 1951 in time for the Festival of Britain). Abercrombie also drew up plans for the rebuilding of devastated cities like Plymouth and Coventry, in a series of published designs and reports at the end of the war. Le Corbusier's master plans for cities were once condemned as megalomaniacal; now they were an urgent necessity.

The reputation of post-war planning has veered wildly since 1945, obviously because it was always intrinsically political. It was the architectural embodiment of the principles of the new welfare settlement outlined by William Beveridge, implemented by the Labour government. Under Clement Attlee's premiership between 1945 and 1951, the London County Council planning department was full of avowed socialists and communists, such as Arthur Ling, the senior planning officer who published the admiring pamphlet *Planning and Building in the USSR* in 1943, and who had been studying the grand Soviet works in Moscow at the outbreak of the war. Ling later helped bring CIAM to England in 1947. There were a number of exiles of European Modernism in England for the duration of the war, and many architects who were advocates of ideas that derived from Constructivism, Bauhaus or Le Corbusier. This spirit of utopian modernity crested with the Scandinavian Modernist vision of the Festival of Britain in 1951, centred on the South Bank site, a summer celebration amid the ruins, visited by more than eight million people and full of rickety and eccentric futuristic visions hidden under the flying saucer of the Dome of Discovery and other exotic pavilions built on shoestring budgets. The Festival included an allied 'Living Architecture Exhibition', featuring the model of an integrated housing estate, managed street market and shopping centre located in Poplar, an area of the East End almost entirely erased by the bombing.

Even if the Festival of Britain site was dismantled by the incoming Conservative government in 1951, determined to erase an emblem of socialist populism, there was still a broad consensus about the need for large-scale house building and town planning that lasted another twenty years. It was the Tory Harold Macmillan who, as housing minister in 1953, oversaw the building of the largest number of council houses in Britain in any single year. Major municipal building projects and estates continued to be built into the mid-1970s. At this point a critique of social housing was beginning to emerge from the New Right as a result of the economic and political crises of the late 1960s and '70s. High rises, concrete slab blocks, municipal shopping centres, prefab secondary modern schools and large-scale town developments became the embodiments of the failures of socialist or Keynesian planned economies. Post-war 'concretopia' curdled into dystopias of crime and deprivation, illustrated by the street gangs of *A Clockwork Orange* (the ultraviolence filmed in the 1971 film adaptation by Stanley Kubrick in the new estates south of the Thames at Thamesmead) or the sociopathic behaviour in J. G. Ballard's equivocal satire *High-rise* (1975). Many significant post-war landmarks of architectural Modernism have now been wiped off the map by this profound shift of political climate, often in a spirit of open political vengeance. The fate of more than thirty major buildings are recorded in Owen Hopkins's book *Lost Futures: The Disappearing Architecture of Post-war Britain*, a title indicative of a notable wave of melancholic memorials to a vanishing utopian architecture now refashioned as retro-futurist 'mid-century modern' style.[32]

Post-war plans did not offer monolithic solutions and planners were factionalized. Old school socialists appealed to the anti-urban spirit of John Ruskin, William Morris and Ebenezer Howard and pushed for de-centralization. The New Towns Act (1946) brought Crawley, Harlow, Hemel Hempstead and Stevenage into being on the model of the 'garden city' movement. Ian Nairn trenchantly denounced this tactic of suburban dispersal as the abominable creation of 'subtopia' in 1955, a monolithic sameness that was creeping across Britain along new arterial roads from Southampton to Carlisle, oozing 'like a gaseous pink marshmallow'.[33]

Meanwhile, those planners enamoured of Swedish welfarist solutions to housing – important since the model blocks shown at the Stockholm Expo in 1930 – were the 'soft' modernists. It was this group that brought the tower block to England. The first 'point block' was called 'The Lawns' and built in Harlow New Town by Frederick Gibberd in time for the Festival of Britain in 1951. In the point block, the flats were accessed off a central core of lifts and stairs, the vertical stacking eliminating the need for corridors. As an experimental block, 'The Lawns' was much visited by designers from around the world (including the Soviet Union), and got the seal of approval from the Bauhaus Modernist Walter Gropius. An array of point blocks was then built as part of the Alton East development in Wimbledon, in a mixed development with lower blocks. The blocks were set on the edge of the site in landscaped parklands, much as Le Corbusier had advocated for the Radiant City. This development was also widely admired at the time, embraced as a suitably English compromise of modernity in a bucolic setting. It was even called 'picturesque'. As a result, point blocks began to spread across the country as an ideal replacement for monotonous streets of slum houses. Continued pressure to build in bulk and use cost-cutting 'system building' with prefabricated elements meant that later estates, particularly in industrial working-class cities like Hull, Liverpool and Glasgow, became relentlessly uniform and high-density. The partial collapse of the Ronan Point tower in 1968, which killed four people, is typically held as the end of the affair with the tower block, leading to later wholesale demolitions of high-rise developments.

Yet it was the buildings of the other faction of post-war architects and planners, the younger generation of 'hard' modernists, that later became the main focus of opprobrium about the failures of post-war architecture and planning. Alison and Peter Smithson's famous steel and concrete Hunstanton School building (1950–54) was indebted to the strict functionalism of the Modernist Mies van der Rohe, embraced the rough poetry of Le Corbusier's *béton brut*, and was defiantly avant-garde and urban. They finished their training in Newcastle in the late 1940s, away from the metropolitan centre, before setting up their own practice. It was the Smithsons' work in the 1950s that became associated with the term 'New Brutalism', a slogan given some meaning as a movement by their friend and ally, the architectural critic Reyner Banham in 1966. New Brutalism overlapped with the proto-Pop Artists Richard Hamilton, Eduardo Paolozzi and Nigel Henderson. The Smithsons themselves defined New Brutalism somewhat gnomically as 'a crystallisation of an attitude to purity of structure; services that speak of their own disciplines'.[34]

What the Smithsons emphasized was not the vertical but the horizontal. Hunstanton School presented a low-slung concrete, glass and steel extension that screamed its contrast from any natural landscape. This horizontal extension was further emphasized in their radical proposals for the 1952 competition to build a model estate at Golden Lane in the bomb-devastated Barbican area north of St Paul's in the old City of London. Although never built, the Smithson proposal had a significant impact as a statement of avant-garde intent. What they offered was a single continuous narrow block that zigzagged above the existing bomb site in defiance of the existing street plan and local scales. This piece of 'connective urban form' raised pedestrians onto continuous concrete decks. As they stated in their narrative accompanying the entry:

> Our aim is to create a true street-in-the-air, each 'street' having a large number of people dependent on it for access . . . Each part of each street-in-the-air will have sufficient people accessed from it for it become a social entity and be within reach of a much larger number at the same level.[35]

A later commentary added that this proposal was 'a diagram of city elements with an angular pedestrian linkage as "streets-in-the-air" that built towards the association of dwellings at high densities in cities, allowing sweeter, more agreeably differentiated patterns of vehicle and leisure movement on the freed ground'.[36]

They were of the firm belief that the decks could recreate the unpredictable life of the inner city street, that they would be genuine places rather than simply functional tangential corridors servicing flats. The plans were presented in dramatic collages, designs overlaid on photographs of the site, schematics of the street decks populated by cut-outs of Marilyn Monroe and Joe DiMaggio. These were architectural plans as proto-Pop Art, provocations to prevailing taste. Equally provocative was their London Roads Study of 1959, which imagined a raised motorway network beetling across the ruined city beneath and lined by continuous 'route buildings', 'linear megastructures'.[37]

The Smithsons eventually realized some of these ideas in the immense buildings of Robin Hood Gardens in the East End (1966–72), two gigantic angled slab blocks that presided over the entry to London from the east and the Blackwall Tunnel from the south like vast military emplacements. The blocks defied their immediate environment, huffily turning their back on it. All entry to the flats was from their continuous street-in-the-sky decks, corridors that look like castle wall walks. The Smithsons called this project 'building for the socialist dream', although adding with typical ornery resistance that this meant 'something different from simply complying with a programme written by the socialist state'.[38] The scale of this corridic horizontality surely aimed to reconfigure the subjectivity of those who lived in it, just as much as Fourier or the Soviets had hoped to do with their phalansteries.

But such an overtly political project, resting on the edges of the hyper-capitalist 'enterprise zone' of Canary Wharf with its thrusting macho high-finance verticals, was long cherished as a target for demolition. Studied neglect by the local council and a campaign that almost inevitably included the local Labour MP consistently sought to pull it down. Despite a resurgence of interest in post-war Brutalism and more concerted attempts to preserve mid-century buildings, Robin Hood Gardens was demolished in the winter of 2017.[39]

One of the key actual uses of streets-in-the-sky was in the Park Hill estate, which looms over the railway station when you arrive in Sheffield. The design for Park Hill was presented by two young architects, Jack Lynn and Ivor Smith, in 1961, soon after they had been taught by Peter Smithson at the Architectural Association in London. The interconnected housing blocks swarm across the side of the steep hill, the concrete walkways allowing access and horizontal passage through the whole estate in emulation of the Smithsons' idea of branching decks or 'street-twigs'. The reception of the building was

Robin Hood Gardens, Poplar, London. This Brutalist London council estate, opened by Alison and Peter Smithson in 1972, was demolished in 2017.

Park Hill estate, Sheffield, designed by Jack Lynn and Ivor Smith, 1961.

positive in the late 1960s, one reporter praising the idea of 'a sort of street in mid-air, with front doors opening on to it, where children can play and their parents are thrown together as much as they were along old terrace streets on the ground'.[40] Within ten years, however, these walkways were considered a social disaster and this too was allowed to fall into disrepair. A private regeneration plan has restored one of the principal blocks, but others remain in shuttered limbo, their streets in the sky boarded up.

The Smithsons declared that their streets-in-the-sky would be 'places and not corridors or balconies'. Yet their ideas are plainly a transposition of Le Corbusier's *rue intérieure* from l'Unité in Marseilles, as they themselves acknowledged. Le Corbusier's building exerted a powerful influence over British architecture and the housing department of the London County Council (LCC) even before it was completed. The *Architectural Review* published a symposium of reactions to the still incomplete building in 1951, and Le Corbusier was in London to receive the RIBA Gold Medal for l'Unité in 1953.[41] One of the younger, 'hard' modernists there, John Partridge, confessed that 'For us, a trip to the Unité d'Habitation in Marseille was almost mandatory' and he returned 'in total awe of the great master'.[42] The first British attempt to build in the Unité style in the LCC was the slab block in Bentham Road in Hackney (built 1956–9), which shifted Le Corbusier's double-loaded interior corridor to run as a single-loaded deck along the whole length of the exterior, a neat solution for the dingy British weather.

Six-storey slab blocks, built with narrow, functional service decks, rather than the wider corridors envisaged by Fourier or Le Corbusier, became one of the key designs for post-war social housing. One of the most consistent and striking uses of this horizontal design was in the practice of Chamberlin, Powell and Bon (CP&B). They formed following their successful proposal for the Golden Lane Estate in London (built 1957–62). Unlike the Brutalist Smithson single structure proposed for the site, CP&B built a mixed array of slab blocks, arranged in loose squares or cloisters around sunken gardens (the remains of the basements of the bombed-out factories that had stood there). There was also a single tower block, briefly the tallest residential block in England when it opened in 1959, at sixteen storeys. They used brick and bold glass panels in bright primary colours, this splash of Mediterranean verve directly evoking the Unité in Marseilles almost as much as the concrete decks built to access the maisonettes in the blocks. Later additions to the Golden Lane site shifted to more severe concrete forms: Crescent House, the building that curves with the bend of the road at the western edge of the estate, is a complex structure built around an interior corridor-like courtyard through the centre of the building, open to the sky to allow for more light. The estate included a community centre, playground and swimming pool, the last adding flashes of water glimpsed through a colonnade of slender white concrete columns. Golden Lane is soft-edged, impure and quirky: the tower block wears a jaunty concrete hat to hide the lift works and there is a mysterious circular bastion in one of the gardens that serves no apparent purpose. This is not a strict, ideological Modernism, yet it contains all the elements of not just Le Corbusier's ideal community, but the collectivizing functions of a Soviet 'social condenser'. Eventually reaching 1,400 apartments, Golden Lane is larger than Fourier's phalanstery, but shared some of its transformative hopes. No wonder the City of London, in hock to profiteering building corporations, treats the place with such open contempt.

Golden Lane was a small model estate. The team at CP&B then won the commission to build the much larger Barbican complex, just a stone's throw away, and perhaps the most famous exercise in concrete Brutalism in London. The housing blocks, entirely isolated from road traffic and street plan, were in vast horizontal slabs raised up on access decks, connected by streets-in-the-sky walkways, ranged around a concrete central lake. A narrow walkway transects the lake above, providing an urban vista for pedestrians that enthusiasts are willing to call 'sublime'.[43] The lake fronts on to the multi-levelled arts centre (a late, immensely complex addition to the plans). All of this is presided over by three 41-storey tower blocks, their stark angled concrete balconies making arresting spinal column silhouettes. By the time the arts complex opened in 1982, it was at the height of the New Right counter-reaction to post-war dreams and the place was mocked as an unusable labyrinth, perversely designed to disorient individual agency, symbolizing everything that was wrong with large-scale planning. A yellow line was drawn on the floor to lead hapless visitors from the Barbican tube station to the arts centre, like

Ariadne's thread. The complex featured as the perfect place to lose a tail in the otherwise impeccably anti-Thatcherite TV drama *Edge of Darkness* (1985, dir. Martin Campbell). Yet real estate value has silenced most critics: with the highest per-capita income population in Britain, this mid-century modern estate is now an international investment opportunity. Wealth is what preserves the Barbican as surely as poverty condemns Robin Hood Gardens.

The Barbican's streets-in-the-sky were meant to connect to a much larger City of London network of elevated walkways. This was part of the planning orthodoxy of separating pedestrians from traffic, to liberate walkers from what was condemned in the 1950s as 'the muddled and obsolete corridor street'.[44] After lots of initial resistance, there was by 1965 a plan for 48 kilometres (30 mi.) of connected 'pedways' to be raised up on podiums, as the traffic thundered below, linking public and private buildings seamlessly through the City. Of course, political interests and private developments resisted this subsumption into a grid of planned collective walkways, particularly after the deregulation of the planning process in the mid-1980s. Priapic verticality returned, contemptuous of the municipal horizontal. You can still walk along stubs of this planned street-in-the-sky, but many routes end abruptly, sawn off by new developments, or are just left hanging.

In the 1960s the wildest architectural dreams included proposals like Geoffrey Jellicoe's Motopia (1961), a plan for an infinitely extendable city of a continuous grid of five-storey slab blocks, with flats off decks and corridors, the whole raised up on pilotis like the Unité, so that pedestrians could walk beneath while all the traffic travelled across the flat roofs above, in a vision of perfectly unencumbered circulation.[45] Eight years later Alan Boutwell and Mike Mitchell proposed the *Continuous City for 1,000,000 Human Beings* that was meant to stretch in a narrow single-slab block all the way across America in a straight line from New York to San Francisco. This speculative thinking overlapped with what Reyner Banham called the craze for megastructures, vast integrated complexes 'in which all the functions of the city are housed' in one gigantic form.[46] The megastructures that were built emphasized the horizontal separation and vertical layering of railways, motorways, shopping centres, pedestrian walkways and ribbons of housing along decks and corridors.

In this category Banham discussed the Brutalist Cumbernauld town centre (1963–7), built outside Glasgow, which was soon considered a wind-blasted concrete planning disaster and has now largely been demolished and replaced. The stub of the Brunswick Centre in London (1967–72) is significant as another model of horizontal separation in its twin lines of concrete terraced blocks facing each other across a narrow pedestrian shopping centre, with all cars parked beneath the superstructure. The designers had plans to extend this building much further north, ploughing through more of the then disregarded early Victorian squares of Bloomsbury. Horizontal forms are in principle infinitely extendable, of course. Banham also points to the Byker Wall housing development in Newcastle (1969–82) as a megastructure, a continuous, undulating wall of housing units, originally built as a kind of baffle against a motorway that, in the end, was never built. Even as these megastructures were struggling to be completed, Banham was sensing an end of them in the mid-1970s, attuned as ever to a tectonic shift of politics and taste. His subtitle for *Megastructure*, 'Urban Futures of the Recent Past', precisely evokes a sense of utopia being cancelled even as mayors were cutting ribbons at grand municipal openings.

It is impossible to write about the utopian project of post-war social housing without knowing that this was starting to curdle into the emblem of dystopia by the early 1970s. The language of the attack on these architectural forms has remained remarkably consistent for nearly fifty years. The architect and writer Charles Jencks polemically located the end of Modernism as 15 July 1972, at exactly 3.32 p.m., when the first blocks of the notorious Pruitt-Igoe estate in St Louis were blown up.[47] The estate had been designed by the Modernist architect Minoru Yamasaki and was a complex of 33 identical eleven-storey blocks, each built around communal walkways and facilities set back from the streets in landscaped parkland. Completed in 1954, just two years after Le Corbusier's Unité, it was intended as a racially integrated estate, but chronic underfunding left it a poor black community, the buildings under-populated, the services underfunded, the underlit parks places for violent crime. In 1965, just before the rent strikes and protests of a radicalized African American community escalated the difficulties there, *Architectural Forum* had analysed Pruitt-Igoe as 'the case history of a failure'. The estate was systematically demolished between 1973 and 1976.

In 1972 the American writer Oscar Newman published *Defensible Space*, based on his research of the 169 public housing projects in New York City. In alarming terms, he spoke about 'a breakdown of the social mechanisms that once kept crime in check'.[48] This book had a major impact in the UK too, where Newman appeared in several TV documentaries about British estates. His polemic against social housing was almost entirely focused on the corridors and walkways of these estates.

> In a high-rise, double-loaded corridor apartment tower, the only defensible space is the interior of the apartment itself; everything else is a 'no-man's-land', neither public nor private. The lobby, stairs, elevator, and corridors are open and accessible to everyone. But unlike the well-peopled and continually surveyed public streets, these interior areas are sparsely used and impossible to survey; they become a nether world of fear and crime.[49]

Insistently, Newman blamed architectural design, the danger of communal spaces, rather than economic deprivation for the failure of estates. His concept of private 'defensible space' also needed little translation into the English common-law assertion that 'an Englishman's home is his castle'. Ten years later, as council-house building was brought to an end and the stock made available for private purchase, the researcher Alice Coleman bolstered this profound ideological shift in *Utopia on Trial,* which denounced 'the great utopian blunder' of post-war housing policy and again blamed the 'design determinism' of large-scale housing and 'the bureaucratic hand' of council planning departments for social and economic disaster.[50] Like Newman, Coleman also concentrated on corridor spaces. 'Residents are keenly aware of corridor problems, which received more mentions than even the more publicized size factors. Internal corridors were picked out as particularly objectionable and described as more like an institution than a home,' she reported.[51] Coleman suggested that short balconies and landings, where only a handful of flats shared the space, were better than the 'anthill effect' of long corridors. Repeating the metaphor, interconnecting walkways or streets-in-the-sky only created 'a great communal anthill riddled with passages'.[52] Thirty years on, in January 2016, then prime minister David Cameron again blamed estate architecture for social ills, 'brutal high-rise towers and dark alleyways [are] a gift to criminals and drug-dealers.'[53]

Where the corridor was once a device for the possibility of social and personal transformation, it has now become an anxious and dystopian site, principally through the rejection of the collectivist politics that inhered in large-scale housing projects. The turning of the utopian corridors of Fourier, the Soviets and the post-war planners into dark passages of menace and threat is one of the principal means by which our imagination about the corridor has changed.

But before we turn to the fully dystopian world of corridor dread, we still need to traverse several other corridor types. The political utopias of Fourier and the Associationists were not the only place where the corridor emerged in the late eighteenth and early nineteenth centuries. There were commercial spaces where corridors became immersive worlds of capitalist delight, and there was also a whole raft of new public institutions that, if not utopian, still believed that corridor structures might reform and regulate the erring human spirit. Let us now turn to these.

4

Corridors of Commerce: The Arcade, the Exhibition Hall, the Mall

The first section of Walter Benjamin's famous essay 'Paris – The Capital of the Nineteenth Century', written in 1935, is titled 'Fourier or the Arcades'.[1] Fourier's utopian dream of the phalanstery had been inspired, in part, by the stone arcades and the central wooden aisle of shops in the Palais Royal, the epicentre of frenzied political intrigue and economic and sexual exchanges in the 1780s. Yet Fourier's aim was to take the structural *form* of these covered walkways and turn it against the violence and inequality of market capitalism. Fourier prompted a whole line of utopian thought about the potential for communal transformation by corridor, as we have seen, but he never quite succeeded in turning the arcades against themselves. Indeed, Paris was the capital of the nineteenth century to Benjamin because it was the apotheosis of the triumph of the mercantile bourgeoisie. The city was Europe's glitzy bauble of vast accumulation of wealth and its ostentatious consumption.

Paris turned into a 'city of arcades' and these architectural forms became for Benjamin the best representatives of the immersive dream worlds of this new stage of capitalism. This was the thesis of his *Passagen-Werk* (Arcades Project), which he left unfinished when he committed suicide while trying to escape from occupied France in 1940. Using Benjamin's account, this kind of corridor was not intended to liberate but rather seduce by hemming you into a narrow promenade where there was no outside, no possible imaginative alternative to the entrancing world of beautiful, alluring, shiny things. Cosseted in luxurious, exotic interiors, separated from any other order of reality, you would be enticed into a light state of trance, tugged this way and that by the pulses of consumer desire. Fascinated by the faded glamour of the Paris arcades in the 1930s, at what he assumed was the end of their life, Benjamin's dialectical ambition was to use these outmoded dream worlds as places where he might wake his reader up from their complacent slumber, to find their fugitive utopian potential again.

This chapter looks at how the commercial corridor has been the vehicle of a different kind of utopia. The arcades that first appeared in the 1790s became laboratories of commodity fetishism. They steadily increased in size as engineers designed new means to extend their length and height, becoming vast iron and glass enclosures, emblems of progress and modernity. Joseph Paxton's innovative 'Crystal Palace' for the Great Exhibition in London in 1851, with its narrow transepts and iron-balconied wings, was the model for the vast display halls that were associated for the rest of the century with World's Fairs. Both the arcade and the exhibitionary universe of the fair would feed directly into the post-war emergence of the shopping centre and its immersive corridors. These corridors of commerce emerge in a clear line of development.

Arcades: Passage Works

The *passage* that first appeared in Paris in the 1790s is 'a glass-covered passageway which connects two busy streets and is lined on both sides with shops'.[2] *Le passage* derived from the Latin *passus* for 'step' and suggests the constant movement through or promenading along of the *passant*, or passer-by. They particularly emerged in Paris because they became a way of commercially exploiting otherwise unused terrain behind street facades, threading through gaps between buildings or inward-facing courtyards. Many are short and straight corridors between parallel streets, but others also bend, turn sharp corners or branch out in elaborate ways along the edges of property lines, splitting into multiple entries and exits. Since the passages were lined with shops on both sides, any natural light had to come from above. This forced innovation in glass and iron roof designs throughout the nineteenth century.

The first Paris arcade – the Passage des Panoramas – was built in the Montmartre district in 1799 by an American entrepreneur on the site of the grand town residence of the Duke of Luxembourg. It was followed quickly by the Passage du Caire, built through an old convent garden in the textile district of Le Sentier (and originally paved by tombstones from the convent graveyard). Both survive: the Passage du Caire is still a working textile market and has branched into an elaborate network of passageways.

Both names provide useful clues. The first *passage* was clearly associated with the new entertainment space, the panorama, which had appeared in London in 1787 and spread rapidly across Europe. The panorama was a rotunda-style building where, after being funnelled through a narrow transitional space, visitors were vertiginously immersed inside a giant 360-degree painted simulation. These images, designed to surround and dwarf the viewer placed in a central viewing platform, were sometimes a total representation of the city outside (as in the celebrated depiction of the entirety of London from the top of St Paul's that debuted in London in 1829), but often depicted far-flung exotic spaces well beyond the experience of those who paid the small fee to enter. Early visitors talked of being completely confounded by the illusion of being transposed into a wholly other exotic world. This, of course, was a technique later explored in many other kinds of commercial environment. That two rotunda flanked the entrance to the first-ever *passage* produced this association with shopping from the very beginning.[3]

The Passage du Caire, meanwhile, invoked the patriotic triumph of Napoleon's invasion of Egypt in 1798, and included Egyptian elements in its decorative designs to hint at this exoticism. Yet the name also revealed that one of the origins of the *passage* lay in the Oriental bazaar, the famous narrow warrens of market stalls and shops that were much visited by Europeans taking the Grand Tour to Cairo or Constantinople. The first direct transposition of the Oriental bazaar to London came with the opening of the Soho Bazaar in 1815, and the Pantheon on Oxford Street was a famous multi-purpose bazaar, described in 1838 as having a 'great hall, a room of noble proportions, from whence a corridor conducts to a beautiful conservatory'.[4] The overwhelming cornucopia of stimulants available there (both the goods, and the women who sold the goods) was described in detail by the leading journalist George Augustus Sala in his *Twice round the Clock; or, The Hours of the Day and Night in London* in 1859. This association of consumption with Oriental luxury, with decadence and fantasies of the harem, was common throughout the nineteenth century.

In England, the first *passage* in London was the Royal Opera Arcade, built by John Nash and George Repton and opened in 1818. It ran parallel to the Haymarket, connecting Pall Mall with Charles II Street, and was designed to provide what was termed a 'covered walkway' to the entrance of the opera house. It was continuous with the portico around the exterior of the theatre and was 3.6 metres (12 ft) wide, with shops on one side that were fitted into the eighteen groin-vaulted bays of the passage and lit from skylights above. It was a place for the ostentatious display of wealth, to promenade before and after the opera, and it soon became known as the 'Fops Walk'. The date was significant: after the British victory over the French at Waterloo in 1815, access to the European continent returned and exotic influences flourished in architectural design. The arcade was undoubtedly associated with a hint of naughty foreign excess. The Royal Opera Arcade survived the opera house itself burning down in 1867, but is

The typical French arcade Passage du Saumon, opened in Paris in 1828. It was renamed Passage Ben-Aïad in 1905.

HÔTEL
LION D'ARGENT
RESTAURANT
BAINS
16 LOTS DE TERRAINS

now marooned behind Her Majesty's Theatre after the audience entrance was moved to the front through the portico on Haymarket in the 1890s.

John Nash was the architect of London's grand attempt at building a processional boulevard through the city. Nash was responsible for the layout and design of Regent Street in the 1820s. The street started at the Prince Regent's palace, Carlton House, then cut north through Piccadilly to the new Regent's Park, although it had to curve at points around property lines to get there, somewhat compromising its spectacle. In Nash's vision, it was to be a street lined with porticos on both sides, like the royal arcaded cities of the continent such as Turin, which still has miles of arcaded avenues and grand squares that start out from the main piazza by the royal palaces. Nash could only partially achieve this 'Corinthian Path' colonnade in Regent Street, defeated by the patchwork of private ownership along the route. The axial route of Regent Street at least succeeded in dividing wealthy Mayfair westwards from the slums and suspicious foreign low-life of Soho eastwards. The Quadrant, the grandest arcade on Regent Street, was built of monumental Doric columns in a 'vast sweeping colonnade' that curved around the lower end of the street as it entered Piccadilly Circus.[5] However, it soon became a shadowy den of prostitution and crime. When it was demolished in 1848 in the name of moral improvement, one newspaper did not lament the loss of this rendezvous 'for beggars, frail fair ones, and cigar-smoking, all-bewhiskered foreigners'.[6] Even demolition did not quite work: Regent Street remained linked with prostitution for another century, a notorious rendezvous during the blackouts of the Second World War.

The association of the arcade with sex and shopping was also very strong with the second arcade built in London in 1818, the Royal Burlington Arcade. This was a construction built along the edge of Burlington House on Piccadilly (now the Royal Academy of Arts) as a way of raising rent for the new owner, Lord George Cavendish. It was consciously designed as an unbroken divider separating the house from the riff-raff of Old Bond Street beyond, who threw their rubbish over the wall into the garden. The architect, Samuel Ware, called the arcade a 'piazza' (the term sometimes used for a covered walkway) in his first plans in 1815. The structure that eventually opened in 1818 was a more sumptuous space with grand columned entrances at both ends. It was around 180 metres (600 ft) long, double-loaded with seventy shops and with enough height for many of the units to have rooms for rent above. Ware built in variety in the vaulted ceiling height and width of the shopfronts so that it avoided a tunnel-like monotony. Entry to the arcade was policed by beadles who were former soldiers dressed in uniforms bearing Lord Cavendish's livery. This emphasized that, although the arcade was continuous with the streets beyond, the arcade was private land and thus subject to its own rules and regulations (and it was locked behind gates at 8 p.m.). It was the kind of pseudo-public space that continues to expand across London in shopping centres and atrium spaces. Cavendish's financial success with this speculative build made the Royal Burlington Arcade the model for the proliferation of this building type across Britain and beyond.

The Royal Burlington was at the heart of gentlemanly London. On the other side of Burlington House was the Albany, the exclusive enclave of a double row of private apartments rented by wealthy bachelors to provide them with 'cloistered quietude' in the heart of the city, a stone's throw from their clubs around St James's, the gentleman outfitters of Jermyn Street, the hunting suppliers and taxidermists on Piccadilly, and the decidedly lower-class entertainments of Leicester Square.[7] The Burlington Arcade had been announced as a place for 'the sale of jewellery and other fancy articles', and to provide 'employment to industrious females', and was initially pitched in the press as a 'very novel' place where 'a Lady, in all kinds of weather, may purchase the various embellishments of art'.[8] Yet it was soon widely known that the rooms above the shops were used for sexual transactions between gentleman promenaders and shop-girls. This is certainly how the London explorer Henry Mayhew understood the purpose of the upper levels in his description in the 1860s. As Jane Rendell observes, 'the connection of arcades with the sexual availability of women, ornamentation, and deceit was reinforced through their origin as a foreign building type.' This was the alluring promise and danger of the Palais Royal transposed to London.[9]

In 1825 the fashionable spa town of Bath opened an arcade called The Corridor that was 84 metres (275 ft) long. It was the only one built with this name, which clearly had less alluring associations. Margaret MacKeith, who wrote a gazetteer of the 118 surviving arcades built in Britain up to 1939, offers highly technical architectural descriptions of each one, but when there is little left to describe of their original features, she refers to them as 'mundane corridors', as if they have fallen out of architecture entirely and become mere infrastructure.[10] The Corridor in Bath had a grand, three-storey entrance with a Doric porch and initially had coloured glass in the roof. The opening day was said to have attracted more than 5,000 people to promenade and it not only had its own police but an orchestra that played in the afternoons.

Back in London, the third major arcade from this early phase was the Lowther Arcade, which was built together with the famous Adelaide Gallery and opened in 1832. The arcade was 74 metres (245 ft) long, with grand turreted entrances into a generous 6-metre-wide (20-ft) passage with very high vaulted ceilings and domed skylights. It was well situated to provide a shortcut between the Strand and Trafalgar Square. Like the Passage des Panoramas, the corridor for shopping was paired with an entertainment. The long, narrow, galleried hall of the Adelaide Gallery was more grandly titled the National Gallery for Practical Science, Blending Instruction and Amusement, and displayed machines, new-fangled technologies like the daguerreotype, and put on spectacular scientific demonstrations of electricity and magnetism. When this lofty pedagogic ideal failed, the Adelaide Gallery became an amusement hall and later the Marionette Theatre.

The arcade had a lower class clientele than the aristocratic Burlington, and was later famous for its cheap toyshops, particularly its Christmas displays. A decade before it was demolished in 1902, it provided a cunning diversion for Dr Watson to shake off Professor Moriarty's spies in what was billed in 1893 as the last Sherlock Holmes story by Arthur Conan Doyle, 'The Final Problem'.

Although the fashion for the building type faded, arcades continued to be built in London into the 1920s (when the functional Market Row and the Reliance Arcade in Brixton were built to cover the markets there). The most extensive project was the arcading of Leadenhall Market on the eastern edge of the old City in 1881, an effective roofing over of a whole network of streets, turning them into corridors with a polychromatic iron and glass superstructure. Other cities that wanted to attract the new phenomenon of this conspicuous consumption also built ostentatious arcades in their town centres: several survive in Glasgow, Cardiff, Manchester and Leeds.

None of these British arcades quite match the grandeur of the continental versions, however. The Galeries Royales Saint-Hubert, constructed in Brussels in 1847 with royal approval, was over 180 metres (600 ft) long (in several sections) with two upper storeys above the shop fronts designed in a uniform Italian Renaissance style that recedes imposingly down its long vanishing perspective. This vast construction capitalized on innovations that could extend iron and glass roofing and was probably the first arcade to be explicitly conceived as an exercise in replacing disorderly streets with a monitored environment for bourgeois strollers. The gallery now linked two markets with a safe, well-lit and ordered space where a warren of dubious slum streets had previously existed. The straight boulevards designed by Baron Haussmann for the centre of Paris in the 1850s after anxious years of revolutionary instability worked on the same principle of the explicit management and control of city space. 'In a very real sense,' Anthony Vidler has argued of Haussmann's Paris, 'the street had become an interior' – an arcade policed by beadles.[11]

Meanwhile, The Passage in St Petersburg opened in 1848 off Nevsky Prospect, the first arcade to use gas lighting to increase the experience of immersion in an entirely artificial world of glittering consumption. The Passage was so vast that it contained coffee-houses, a panorama, an anatomical museum, a concert hall and even a small zoo. Here is perhaps another source for the Soviet 'social condenser', as The Passage survived the October Revolution and eventually reopened as a 'model department store' to showcase the manufactures of the new Soviet Union in 1922.

Also influential was the 1877 Galleria Vittorio Emanuele II in Milan, in which two four-storey arcades met under a vast octagonal atrium domed with an innovative glass and iron roof that cleverly disguised its iron supports so that it seemed to float in air. The arcade connected the Duomo with the famous Teatro alla Scala, but was important in itself as the direct inspiration for the designer of the

Galleria Vittorio Emanuele II, which opened in Milan in 1877.
It later directly inspired the boom in American shopping malls.

first covered American shopping mall, and the reason why malls still sometimes use the Italian term 'galleria'. Mark Twain adored it in his travelogue *A Tramp Abroad*: 'We spent most of our time in the vast Arcade or Gallery . . . I should like to live in it all the time.' In Turin, Twain also admired the sidewalks 'covered over with a double arcade supported on great stone pillars' where at night 'the place is brilliant with gas and populous with a sauntering and chatting and laughing multitude of pleasure-seekers.'[12] Using the arcade as the vehicle for the pompous assertion of the wealth and power of a city or state probably reached its zenith with Berlin's 152-metre-long (500-ft) Kaisergalerie, opened by Kaiser Wilhelm I himself in 1873 along a corridor wide enough to allow his horse and carriage to pass through. In the wake of the Prussian victory over France, this was unashamed triumphalist architecture.

If there is a decided tendency towards gigantism and expressions of nationalism in these arcades, then that is because the Great Exhibition of 1851 radically extended the possibilities of these iron and glass constructions. Famously, the competition to design a temporary structure in Hyde Park big enough to house Prince Albert's vision of a universal display of global trade with the British Empire at its centre produced no feasible building. The solution came from the engineer Joseph Paxton (1803–1865), who had built huge greenhouses for the gardens at Chatsworth House. He proposed extending the modular system of plate glass panels on an iron grid for a temporary building that was soon christened the Crystal Palace. It was built in four months and stood in Hyde Park only for the six-month duration of the exhibition. Close to being a symbolic 1,851 feet (564 m) in length, the two wings stepped down from the central transept with continuous iron balconies along their whole two-storey length, producing long vanishing perspectives. One guide waxed lyrical about 'the long aisles of that unique and beautiful structure', 'its thousands of light and towering columns, its interminable network of girders', and 'the unequalled aerial perspective of its lengthened nave, the noble proportions of its vaulted crystal transept and the wonderful combination of lightness of appearance with strength and stability'.[13]

The six million visitors to the Great Exhibition were notionally directed along pathways that either traced the production process from raw material, through machinery and manufacture to the display and sale of the commodity, or else on a historical trajectory from Greece and Rome to the modern world in a quiet reinforcement of narratives of the virtues of global trade and industrial progress. In practice, these narrow pedagogical pathways were often not easy to discern and the crowds were continually distracted by the sublime spectacle of boundless commodities – more than 100,000 objects were crammed into the Palace.[14]

Joseph Paxton's dreams for monster arcades did not end with the Crystal Palace he built in South London in 1854. Paxton raised shares for his Crystal Palace Company, a private venture rather than a public work this time. The building was slightly shorter (merely 488 metres/ 1,600 ft), but narrower and considerably taller, at six storeys, producing an even stronger sense of a vastly extended arcade. While the French historian Hippolyte Taine called it 'a monstrous great pile devoid of style and bearing witness not to [English] taste, but to their power', Le Corbusier mourned its destruction by fire in 1936, remembering that on his last visit 'I could not tear my eyes from the spectacle of its triumphant harmony. The lesson was so tremendous that it made me feel how puny our own attempts still are.'[15] Actually, the huge temporary halls built in Paris for the international Expositions of 1867, 1889 and 1900, all built as immersive spaces of sublime futurity plonked down in the chaotic nineteenth-century city, outstripped even the gigantism of the Crystal Palace. The Expos in Paris became the vehicle for those utopian rivals of Fourier: the followers of the Comte de Saint-Simon, passionate advocates of international free-trade capitalism.

A year later, he offered a plan to London's Metropolitan Board of Works for the Great Victorian Way, a response to a Metropolitan

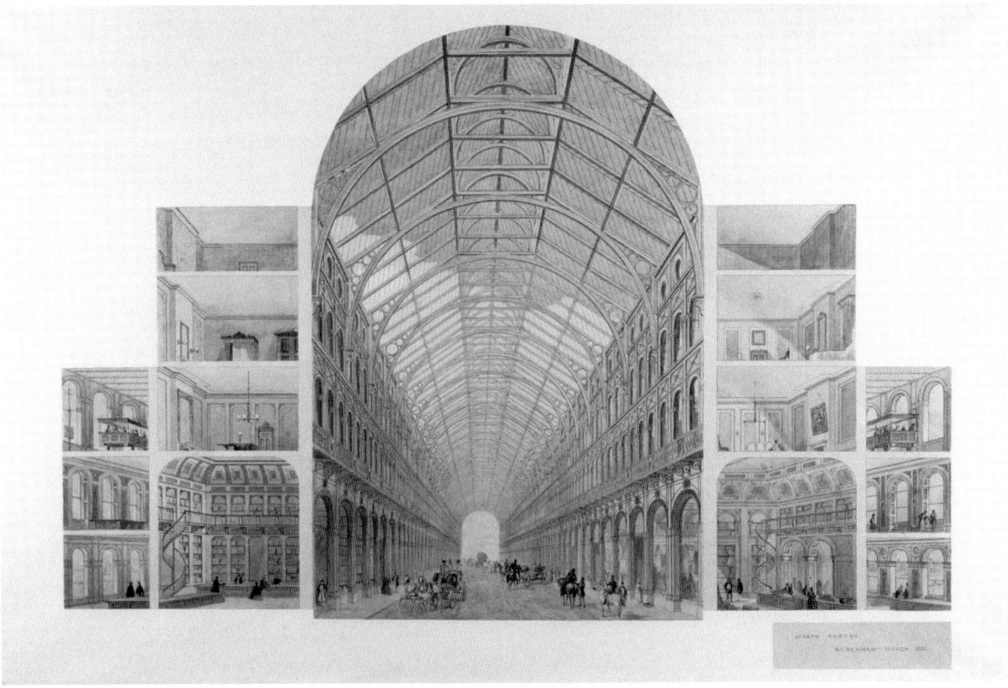

Sir Joseph Paxton's design for the Great Victorian Way (1855), a plan to build an arcade linking all the main railway stations in central London.

Communications commission to address major works needed to transform a London that was under pressure from massive population growth. Paxton's idea was for a circular arcade, over 16 kilometres (10 mi.) long and 22 metres (72 ft) wide with a vaulted glass roof reaching over 30 metres (100 ft) high, that would form a 'girdle' around London to link up all of the capital's major railway stations in one continuous iron and glass structure. This multi-level construction included a wide covered walkway lined with shops, hotels and some housing, beneath which ran railway tunnels with express and local services. The three bridges over the Thames would continue the arcade, recalling the old London Bridge, which had buildings on both sides. The Great Victorian Way would be 'a magnificent promenade – a new source of comfort and enjoyment'.[16]

Other London improvements using arcades included Frederick Guy's 1845 plan for an arcade that ran between the Bank of England and Trafalgar Square (Guy had commissioned the iron and glass extension at the Royal Italian Opera House, the Floral Hall, in Covent Garden, and so was not just an implausible dreamer). Alongside Paxton's 1855 plan, William Mosley offered his own Crystal Way, a promenade and railway that would run between St Paul's and Regent Street. Paxton carefully costed his project at £34 million, calculating an eventual profit from the rail fares. All of these remained London's sadly lost chances to become a European city of arcades. The first cut-and-cover section of the London Underground opened less than ten years later in 1863 between Farringdon and Paddington stations, but this was a very different structure.

In *The Architecture of Failure*, Douglas Murphy identifies Victorian iron and glass buildings as quintessentially modern 'fragments of the drive towards a better world that did not come to pass'.[17] The gigantic Expo halls were fugitive and temporary; the arcades they derived from lost a little of their glamour as the immersive worlds of department stores became the shopping norm in the 1860s. By then the emblematic role of the arcade as the building type of the nineteenth-century bourgeoisie gave it a fascination for writers who wanted to critique the new consumer society.

The young Émile Zola, a relentless provocateur, scandalized his readers with his 1867 novel *Thérèse Raquin*, set almost entirely in the Passage du Pont-Neuf, 'a sort of dark, narrow corridor linking the Rue Mazarine to the Rue de Seine', only thirty paces long and two wide.[18] This is the nightmare underside of the light, leisured world of *flâneurie* or promenading in the grand arcades.

> This Passage du Pont-Neuf is not a place for strolling. People use it to avoid making a detour, to gain a few minutes. Down it walk busy folk whose only thought is to march briskly straight ahead. You see apprentices in their aprons, seamstresses delivering their

> finished work, and men and women with parcels under their arms. You also see old men lurking in the dreary light of the glass roof, and gangs of little children who come running here after school to kick up a row . . . No one speaks, no one stops . . .
>
> In the evening, the arcade is lit by three gaslights enclosed in heavy, square lanterns. These hang down from the glass roof on which they cast patches of yellowish light, spreading pale circles of luminescence around them that shimmer and appear to vanish from time to time. The passageway looks as though it might really be a hiding-place for cutthroats; great shadows spread across the paving and damp draughts blow in from the street; it has the appearance of an underground gallery dimly lit by three funerary lanterns.[19]

Zola forces a confrontation with the hidden financial and sexual transactions that the glittering surfaces of the commodity world otherwise strive to erase. His 1883 novel *Au Bonheur des dames* (The Ladies' Paradise) explored the immersive world of the department store as the arcade's successor, focusing on its seductive, corrupting environments and the lives of the store girls that service this illusion, the quintessential consumer dream world.

In the twentieth century the tarnish on the arcade seemed to accelerate. The brilliant German essayist Siegfried Kracauer, writing in the 1920s about the personal associations produced by the Linden Arcade in Berlin, recalled that as a child the very word *Passage* induced a shudder, as 'in the books that I raced through, the darkened passageway was usually the place of deathly attacks . . . and gloomy plans.' This was the echo of Zola's exposé. Kracauer captures expertly how the slightly tawdry decline of the arcade, the blackened skylights and tarnished mirrors, also takes the glint off all those shiny commodities, now revealed as merely 'transient objects', banal in their grubby everydayness: nail scissors, powder boxes, cigarette lighters, semi-pornographic books implanting perverse desires. What the 'twilight of the thoroughfare' exposes is the collapse of that magical power of the commodity fetish, as theorized by Marx. Instead, this is a world of *kitsch*, a sort of afterlife where things have 'passed, still warm, into death' and their consumers are little more than stumbling zombies.[20]

The crepuscular world of the arcade in its dying days was entirely embraced by Louis Aragon in his 1924 masterpiece of Parisian Surrealism, *Paris Peasant*. Aragon offered a detailed description of the last months of the Passage de l'Opéra, one of these 'sunless corridors' that had been scheduled for demolition in another drive to extend Haussmannization and sanitize the city. The book was intended as a tribute to the place where the avant-garde Dadaists met in cheap cafés and restaurants, and where the Surrealist group began to coalesce in 1919. Aragon works his way through the interlinked passageways of the Galerie du Baromètre and the Galerie du Thermomètre shop by shop, transcribing hoardings, menus, bills of fare and protests about the eviction and demolition. There is no polite evasion of the predominant transaction in the arcade: this is a world of hotel rooms rented by the hour (along a corridor with stairs at each end, to allow for quick exits), prostitutes negotiating their rates, bathhouses with booths for anonymous sexual encounters; a cheap theatre where a 'whole shifting population of women' moves between shady roles of actors, barflies, sexual partners. As Aragon glides between pedantic social realism and oneiric flights of fancy in his text – the ideal combination of sur/realism – the arcade becomes to him an 'iridescent universe' because it houses every low-life, avant-garde shock to the sensibility of the respectable bourgeoisie.[21]

Walter Benjamin approved of the Surrealists because they were 'the first to perceive the revolutionary energies that appear in the "outmoded", in the first iron constructions, the first factory buildings, the earliest photos, the objects that have begun to be extinct . . . They bring the immense forces of "atmosphere" concealed in these things to the point of explosion.'[22] However, the avant-garde never quite found the dialectical levers to overthrow the dream world of capitalism from inside the bourgeois arcade. Not only did arcades live on in a strange afterlife (and have in some cases been glitteringly restored), they mutated after the Second World War into one of the key corridic structures of our time: the shopping mall.

'Elongated Mousetraps': Victor Gruen and the Invention of the Shopping Mall

In *The Malling of America,* William Kowinski calls the shopping mall one of 'the signature structures of the age', 'the strange achievement of the American Way: a utopia fashioned by the not-quite-invisible hand of merchandising'. Margaret Crawford, lost inside the 492,000 square metres (5.3 million sq. ft) of the West Edmonton Mall in Canada, with eight hundred shops, eleven department stores, hotels, cinemas, nightclubs and skating rinks, all 'situated along corridors of repeated storefronts', concludes that 'the world of the shopping mall – respecting no boundaries, no longer limited even by the imperative of consumption – has become the world.'[23] The modern mega-mall is a direct descendant of the European arcade and the gigantism of the iron and glass exhibition space.

The usage of 'mall' derives from the narrow promenade bordered by trees in St James's Park in London, a place associated in the seventeenth century with the game pall-mall (hence the famous street Pall Mall, on which may be found St James's Palace and numerous gentlemen's clubs). The mall, defined as 'a sheltered walk serving as a promenade' in the *Oxford English Dictionary*, became associated with shopping centres only in the 1960s.

The American 'regional shopping center' (later mall or galleria) was largely the creation of one man: the shop designer and architect Victor Gruen. Gruen is another half-forgotten yet major figure in the transformation of the corridic spaces of our everyday life, rarely remembered as an architect because he worked on these purely commercial and 'infrastructural' spaces that roof over and box in artificial public spaces. Gruen was born into the vibrant Jewish community in Vienna (his surname was Grünbaum) and had been active in socialist politics and the subversive cabaret world as well as shop design, and so was in immediate danger when the Nazis annexed Austria in 1938. He travelled to New York and through the émigré network almost immediately began to bring striking Modernist shop designs to a new American market with noted success in the streets of Manhattan. Gruen was always explicit about wanting to reproduce the European world of strolling, relaxation and sumptuous consumption in arcades, and expressly aimed to recreate the atmosphere of Milan's Galleria Vittorio Emanuele II in many of his projects. Even his first small shopfront designs tried to break down the standard two-dimensional 'poster' shop window and build three-dimensional mini-arcades into narrow street frontages by setting shop doors back from the street. This created corridors of dramatically lit plate-glass vitrines, where shoppers could pause away from the sidewalk rush, window-shop, and begin to be seduced across the threshold.[24]

Gruen transferred his practice to Los Angeles in 1940, where he built a succession of stores for the Grayson department store chain, learning how to make bold signature designs to be seen from a passing car. His first free-standing department store, Milliron's, opened in 1943, and used a striking set of scissor ramps to put the parking spaces on the roof and fully separate pedestrians from vehicle traffic. Once they abandoned their cars, shoppers descended into an entirely immersive wonderland below, although this shop floor was on a completely open plan. This was Gruen's constant theme, a European who disdained the American dominance of the automobile and strongly advocated the pedestrian separation promised by the arcade. The next evolutionary stage was to extend beyond the single shop into a designed uniform cluster.

The category of the 'regional shopping centre' was the result of a combination of governmental and commercial factors after 1945:

an active support of suburbanization and highway construction to disperse populations from cities (partly a tactic of civil defence against nuclear war), zoning laws, and a schematic administrative system for trying to distribute services evenly for the new housing tracts. In 1949 Gruen's reputation led to proposals for the owners of the Hudson store to build a suburban shopping centre outside Detroit. Recognizing that downtown was collapsing with flight to the suburbs, the Hudson store wanted suburban branches, but Gruen persuaded them to make the store an anchor for a cluster of other shops and services.

The first to be completed was the Northland Shopping Center, in the suburbs of Detroit in Michigan, which opened in 1954. This was immediately noted internationally as a new building type. It had the large Hudson branch store at the centre, but five other lower buildings clustered around it containing eighty rented shops in a pinwheel plan that created a variety of pedestrianized spaces between them. Gruen later categorized these spaces very precisely in his book *Shopping Towns USA*: 'there will evolve large square-shaped areas (plazas and squares); wide rectangular ones (courts); wide and long ones (malls); long, narrow spaces (walks and lanes); covered or partly covered walkways (arcades); wide spaces enclosed on two or three sides (terraces).'[25] At Northland, the buildings were tied together by long colonnades, the shopfronts under uniform parapets, and the public spaces were landscaped, full of fountains and commissioned artworks, with all traffic kept to the peripheries. Gruen hoped to recall the European market square, and even the critic Jane Jacobs, later the author of the most famous attack on suburbanization and the destruction of the urban fabric, praised Northland's recuperation of the market town plan.[26] Hundreds of imitations were soon spreading across the American landscape with major real estate developers feeding the boom.

Gruen's design for the Southdale shopping centre at Edina, south of downtown Minneapolis, was another leap forward. Designed for the Dayton chain store, it opened in 1956. Here, inspired directly by Milan's galleria, Gruen built the first fully enclosed, air-conditioned shopping mall in America, keeping an even temperature through the Midwest's harsh winters and fierce summers. This time, quite late in the planning process, two rival department stores were thrown into the same scheme, generating a push and pull effect through the cluster. The other architect, John Graham, wanted a narrowed and functional corridor of shops between the stores. This design, which he had used in his own shopping centres, funnelled shoppers from one store to the other through a tunnel. Gruen, though, disdained what he called 'elongated mousetraps' for shopping centres. Instead he built a high-roofed central court over two levels, using the swoops of elevators and more fountains and expensive public sculptures to create a theatrical space, where fashion shows, public events, even theatre shows and public lectures could take place. He wanted to create a seductive shopping environment for his commercial clients, but Gruen also seemed genuinely to believe that he could create a cultured agora in these new social spaces.

Southdale was again regarded as a breakthrough design, even if Modernist architect Frank Lloyd Wright judged the place 'repulsive'.[27] Again, Gruen's model experienced uninterrupted decades of growth with thousands of imitators (many built by Gruen's own firm) before the model stuttered a little with saturation in the late 1970s. The mega-malls, those worlds within worlds, followed in the 1980s and Gruen's successors in design, like John Portman or John Jerde, have continued to innovate while retaining a clear vestige of the original roofed arcade. Jerde's Freemont Street Experience in Las Vegas, for instance, which opened in 1995, has covered over five blocks of the downtown area with a barrel-vault roof 27 metres (90 ft) high and 455 metres (1,500 ft) in length to create a classic narrow street arcade. The innovation is that the underside of the roof is the largest video screen in the world, animated with over twelve million LED lights. A shelter from the desert sun by day, the roof explodes into neon life at night, a rival to the gaudy old downtown casinos next door. The animated roof of the street corridor seems a logical extension of the spectacle sought by the first Victorian iron and glass engineers.

Gruen soon innovated with restoring hollowed-out downtown city centres through experiments in pedestrianization (the pedestrianized street in Kalamazoo, Michigan, was again the first ever tried in America, in 1959). But Gruen famously grew to loathe the legacy of his shopping centres and malls. He designed the automobile out, yet fostered the very suburban freeway sprawl he despised. He longed for a revival of the civilized agora and European stroll but killed most public spaces with commerce, since his replacements for civil society became rigidly policed, privately owned commercial spaces that actively suppress political demonstration or expressions of the public sphere that interfere with business transactions.[28] Gruen returned to Vienna in 1968 despite the silence over the destruction of the city's Jewish population. In 1978, two years before he died, he gave a speech in London in which he said: 'I am often called the father of the shopping mall. I would like to take this opportunity to disclaim paternity once and for all. I refuse to pay alimony to those bastard developments. They destroyed our cities.'[29]

Gruen also gave his name to a particular psychological effect produced by immersion in total consumer environments: the Gruen Transfer. This is the soporific effect of being seduced by an environment into a general state of suggestible openness to any floating consumer desire that can then be shaped and directed by shop windows, escalators, mall avenues or corridors of shopfronts. As Sanford Kwinter describes it:

> The unconsciously bewildered shopper, rendered docile, cannot help but drift into the prepared pathways and patterns of externally induced consumer activity, unfocused but exquisitely suggestible to gentle but firm environmental cues. It is estimated that as much

> as 90 per cent of shopping mall transactions concern goods the shopper had not planned to buy, yet did so after the Gruen Transfer took hold.[30]

In the 1950s, Vance Packard wrote a best-selling exposé called *The Hidden Persuaders*, which talked about the deliberate creation of supermarkets and shopping centres that were designed to lull visitors into a semi-trance state, measurable by slower heart and eye-blink rates and a marked loss of memory or sense of time passing. Packard implied that this automatism particularly affected women and children (moral panics about hypnotic threats always suggest this), but warned that advertisers and designers of shops had probed the neuroses of men too, intent on undermining their rational autonomy. The feeling of being 'carried away' in the shopping environment has been explored both by advocates and those who decry the spaces of consumerist culture.[31] William Kowinski calls this a *mal de mall,* an 'agoraphasic' *mallaise*, 'a sudden inability to concentrate, often accompanied by a loss of coherent speech or thought'.[32] The sense of 'bewildering immersion' in the lobby and shopping space of John Portman's Bonaventure Hotel in downtown Los Angeles even prompted the disoriented critic Fredric Jameson to declare melodramatically that this 'mutation in built space itself' constituted the arrival of a whole new postmodern era. Gone was the Modernist utopian project of Le Corbusier's l'Unité; instead, Jameson proclaimed, the death of the postmodern subject was this subsumption into a capitalist hyperspace now impossible to map.[33]

This state of distraction in the mall is sometimes called the Zombie Effect, no doubt in the wake of George A. Romero's horror film satire *Dawn of the Dead* (1978). The film was largely set inside the 102,000 square metres of the Monroeville Mall, which opened in 1969 east of the industrial city of Pittsburgh, which had experienced the catastrophic collapse of its coal and steel industries in a brutally short period and was trying to rebalance its economy through a consumer revolution. The small band of human survivors of the zombie apocalypse spy the mall from a helicopter and see it as a defensible space, even though the surrounding car park and the corridors below are littered with the drifting, purposeless undead. In a celebrated exchange on the flat roof of the mall, one survivor looks down on these forlorn creatures and asks: 'What are they doing? Why do they come here?' The answer is a mordant reflection on hollowed-out consumer subjectivity, the ultimate Gruen Transfer: 'Some kind of instinct – a memory of what they used to do. This was an important place in their lives.' There are queasily comic scenes of zombies shuffling through the central courts, bouncing down escalators, falling in the fountain features, and pawing at shopfronts. In a bewildering mirror effect, this critique of consumerist malls gained a cult audience of mall-rat teens who would watch it specifically in mall cinema complexes. Monroeville Mall itself contained a zombie museum for some years, full of *Dawn of the Dead* memorabilia, as if content to capitalize on the deadening power of immersive recuperation.

In the zombie genre that followed *Dawn of the Dead*, the relentless power of the zombie mass to overrun and absorb the last remnants of humanity is often represented in corridors, as the narrow space gives their sheer number strength to simply press through any barrier or barrage of gunfire. Corridors feature heavily in Romero's follow-up film *Day of the Dead* (1985), set in an underground military complex, and are obligatory spaces of tension and dread in the abandoned malls, office blocks and prisons that are searched through by the ragged band of survivors over and over again in the TV series *The Walking Dead* (2010–). Hospital corridors are also standard zombie hang-outs, as in the climactic battle in the medical complex of *World War Z* (2013). In computer games like the *Resident Evil* series, the corridor plan is used because it limits player choices and so releases more memory to realize the immersive gaming world. Corridors also amplify the dread of anticipation that comes with every door the player passes.

In the immediate wake of the 2008 financial crash, combined with the shift to Internet shopping and the newfound love of concentrated urban living, the rise of the 'dead mall' has become a noted North American phenomenon. 'Dead malls' are spaces emptied by commercial renters or abandoned by real estate owners, left to fall into various states of ruin. Shopping centre and mall development had offered entirely secure returns for vast conglomerates and property development for decades, but 2008 was the first year since Gruen's Northland cluster had opened that not a single new mall was built in America.[34] Of the estimated 1,200 malls still around in America in 2015, about a third have been considered dead or dying.[35] They are the new ruins of modernity, and have become obsessively catalogued on websites like deadmalls.com in much the same way that Aragon or Benjamin detailed the Parisian arcades one hundred years earlier. Just like the arcade, too, the mall finds ways of living on, not least in the modern imagination of claustrophobic horrors and corridor confinement. Most of the TV horror series *The Mist* (2017) was filmed in an abandoned mall in Nova Scotia. The dead mall is another instance where a corridor once associated with the utopian capitalist dream world for turning citizens into active consumers has developed a darker, dystopian flavour.

5

The Ecstasy of Communication: The Hotel Corridor

I think the corridor most forcefully enters our consciousness in that moment when we leave a large modern chain hotel bedroom, pull the heavy fire door shut, and look down a vast vanishing perspective of identical doors receding into the distance. Perhaps there is an instant of hesitation, as turning left or right seems to offer identical prospects and it is not obvious where the elevators or exits are. Both directions are measured out by identical wall lamp fittings and inoffensively abstract corporate art.

The emotional tone of this experience mixes disorientation with a kind of existential angst, a feeling of what I will later define as *corridor dread*. After all, the corridor presents a view of many individual lives standardized by the identical spatial distribution of cellular private lives along a semi-public passageway. Innumerable doorways foreground a sense of transience, of easy substitution, and the service cart is likely already at work, parked somewhere along the corridor while the cleaners slave away to erase every trace of the last guest passing through. This need not be an entirely angsty experience, though: many find the anonymity of hotels liberating, the hallways awash with all kinds of possibilities, erotic and otherwise, that promise the fantasy of escape from routine selves. The ecstasy of communicating corridors and rooms.

This corridor moment has its specific history, of course. The modern hotel emerged from centuries of communal rooms, dining tables and even shared beds in inns or roadside taverns. In the early nineteenth century, American culture adapted the French term *hôtel* to imbue a sense of aristocratic grandeur to a new type of building. These were on a larger scale than anything in Europe: the building of the City Hotel on Broadway in New York City in 1794 was five storeys high and had nearly 150 rooms, for instance, almost the size of a small phalanstery. Most influential was the building of Tremont House in Boston in 1829, a huge purpose-built hotel among the mansions of the wealthiest quarter of town erected by a consortium of Boston Brahmins and designed in its luxury to announce Boston as an international trading city that welcomed visitors. Its Greek-style portico (of 37 Doric columns) led into a lobby topped by a rotunda, the first ever used in hotel architecture. This in turn was the hub for a long corridor, over 60 metres (200 ft) in length, that ran parallel to the hotel's front elevation and distributed a range of carefully differentiated public rooms along it on the ground floor, with bars for men and parlours for women.[1]

It is significant that within a couple of years of opening the hotel produced a two-volume collection of stories, sketches and skits called *Sayings and Doings at the Tremont House*. 'But every *American* knows the TREMONT HOUSE', its preface states, 'and every *foreigner*, who had visited it, must, in candor, admit, that for comfort, good cheer, and the extent of its accommodations, it is not surpassed, if equalled, by any similar establishment in the world.'[2] The second conversation begins in 'the passage in Tremont House leading to the Gentleman's Dining Room'; the last story in the second volume, meanwhile, is called 'A Ghost Story' and features the comical spectral snorer of room 225. The hotel and episodic fiction, separate stories loosely linked along a single narrative spine, were intertwined from the start.

The scale and the horizontality of the spatial distribution in American hotels led many commentators to argue that it was a building that intrinsically expressed the form of American democracy, whether for good or ill. Towards the end of Anthony Trollope's exhaustive travelogue *North America* (1862), the English author felt it necessary to have a separate chapter on them since 'in the States the hotels are so large an institution, having so much closer and wider a bearing on social life than they do so in any other country.'[3] The Englishman found the spaces of the lobby and bars, which seemed to serve as local exchanges for their towns, bewildering in their size compared to the rooms, which offended his sensibility with their lack of separate dressing rooms or sitting rooms for women. The *publicness* of arriving at the hotel desk, your name signed in the ledger only to be discussed at length in a lobby full of gossipy loungers, Trollope found intolerable. At about the same time another writer, William Chambers, called these wide public lounging spaces and the corridors between them 'flirtation-galleries' because of their relaxed 'qualities as places of general resort and conversation' between the sexes.[4]

American hotels did not have the sense of clear social differentiation and class hierarchy found in the European luxury hotel. The confusing social mix of lobbies and the indeterminate boundaries of the public and private in the corridors are abiding themes of the European literature on hotels. Yet for the American republic, the social levelling of the hotel was a utopian expression of the new mercantile capitalism, with fortunes to be made from a young, mobile population mixing together in a new kind of public realm.

E. M. Statler and the Monster Hotel Corridor

The experience of opening a door onto a seemingly infinite hotel corridor is largely down to the extraordinary career of one man: Ellsworth Milton Statler, the inventor of the 'monster hotel' and now mostly remembered for the phrase 'the customer is always right.' Statler's life story perfectly fits the nineteenth-century self-help, rags-to-riches narrative. He was the son of a German immigrant priest, born in extremely poor circumstances in West Virginia in 1863, became a hotel bellboy at twelve years old and rose rapidly through the ranks to become first night then day clerk. He built up capital by leasing the hotel billiard room and turning it into the town's major social club. He then invested his savings in building a 500-seater restaurant in Buffalo in the 1890s, using innovative advertising techniques and economies of scale to generate profit. His move to the hotel business was for the Pan-American Exposition in Buffalo in 1901. This World's Fair was planned to boost the profile of the city of Buffalo and, since tens of millions travelled to these temporary exhibition spaces from around the world, accommodation was needed. Statler built a temporary hotel out of wood that stood only three storeys high but covered nine acres, with a restaurant that seated 1,200, providing more than 2,000 bedrooms off 8 kilometres (5 mi.) of corridors. As explored in Chapter Four, World's Fairs were typically immersive spaces, funnelling large crowds through corridic iron and glass structures. Statler simply adopted the same spatial solution for the accommodation.

The Buffalo Exposition was famously a disaster: a sluggish start due to poor weather was only worsened after President McKinley was assassinated when visiting the site. Statler, who had invested his life savings in his temporary hotel plan, still managed to make a profit. He did the same thing again at the St Louis Louisiana Purchase Exposition of 1904, building an even larger temporary hotel inside the grounds of the Expo itself, hence calling it 'The Inside Inn'. This had 2,250 rooms and 'acres of public rooms, some corridors that were almost half a mile long, [and] a lobby over a hundred yards long'.[5] The corridors were so long that Statler developed a semaphore signalling system for each door, so that a flag was raised requesting service, with hall-boys posted at each significant corridor intersection to ensure that they responded as quickly as possible.

Everything about the St Louis Expo was meant to be vast: it was twice the acreage of the 1893 Chicago World Expo or Paris in 1900. It had ten gigantic palaces in rather free and fanciful adaptations of Italian Renaissance style to display commercial goods and

Statler's hotel, The Inside Inn, built for the 1904 St Louis World's Fair. It had 9.7 kilometres (6 mi.) of corridors.

technological advances, centred around a mile-long central area called The Pike, which contained the largest artificial waterfall ever created. The Inside Inn matched the scale of the exhibition space. Because it was the only hotel within the grounds, it also became an attraction in itself (you could buy memorial postcards of it). As *Collier's Weekly* reported: 'The Inside Inn is a constant joy. It is not entered on the list of exhibits, but of all the shows at the Fair, it is the most entertaining and extraordinary.' Later the American historian Daniel J. Boorstin called such hotels the 'common man's palace', emblematic of the American 'national experience'.[6]

In the first week of opening of the St Louis Expo, Statler was seriously injured by an exploding kettle in the hotel kitchen, nearly losing his life. However, afterwards he could soon console himself with the $300,000 profit he made in the six months of the Expo: the fair had nearly twenty million visitors. This money Statler then ploughed into his first permanent hotel construction, in Buffalo in 1907. It was here that Statler introduced a host of innovations that are still used today: rate cards that guaranteed a fixed price; a private bathroom in every room; a full-length mirror and closet; the keyhole moved above the door-knob for ease of access; the shaving off of the bottom of the door so that messages, bills and newspapers could be slid under early in the morning without disturbing guests. The staff was organized in rigid hierarchies of responsibility, and was imbued with the principles of exaggerated service: the customer is *always* right, even when they are wrong. They were expected to carry the Statler principles of service with them on a printed card at all times.

He also began to develop what became known as the 'Statler plan', a hotel floor plan that is still basically in use. From a central service core, the corridors distribute rooms in as clear and visible a manner as possible. The rooms open onto a short vestibule with the bathroom on one side, the closet on the other, to create a buffer zone to protect the bedroom from the light and noise of the public corridor. The rooms were paired and mirror images of each other so that the bathrooms backed onto the same service core, sharing the same plumbing, so making repairs easier. In 1919 his New York hotel had a telephone in every room and in the 1920s Statler was the first to introduce a wireless in guest rooms.

Statler refined this in the series of monster hotels he built (in Buffalo, Cleveland, Detroit, St Louis and New York). In 1917 the *Architectural Forum* carried a series of admiring essays on 'The Statler Idea in Hotel Planning and Equipment', including a study of the floor plans: 'In contrast with the usual hotel plans, where one is bewildered by a maze of jumbled units, floors at various levels, and a chaos of spaces, here each of the . . . essential parts is contained complete' floor by floor.[7] This was also recognized as the beginning of the standardized hotel chain, the good psychology of the 'intentional similarity' of Statler's buildings across the country, regardless of local context: 'a studied similarity in the forms and arrangements of the public rooms, corridors, and guest rooms, has given to these hotels a striking family resemblance.'[8]

The Statler hotels grew in size, although largely upwards rather than extending along corridors. As engineers solved the construction issues that limited building height and found ways of powering elevators with electricity rather than cumbersome hydraulics, America entered the age of the skyscraper – of verticality rather than horizontality. The fourth Statler Hotel in St Louis (1917) was on a 70-metre-square block of the city, but was sixteen floors high, with a ballroom on the top floor that opened onto a roof garden. In 1919 Statler was tempted to work with the Pennsylvania Railroad Company to design and manage the then largest hotel in the world, the Pennsylvania Hotel in New York City. This 27-storey building, with 2,200 rooms arranged over four connected towers, stood directly opposite Penn Station. (A rival hotel, The New Yorker, opened in 1930 nearby and was connected to the station by an Art Deco corridor under the road, which was then extended and branched out to other buildings. It is still there, but lies in ruins.)[9]

Statler added just a few touches to his perfected model of service: the hotel had the largest private telephone exchange ever constructed, and the 'servidor' was a service hatch for each room that bellboys could access from the corridors without disturbing the guests. In the first year, the vast hotel reached an unprecedented 99.4 per cent occupancy rate, raking in large profits on a major turnover, and began to transform the area around 32nd Street into a commercial district.[10] Soon enough, the Pennsylvania Hotel was overtaken in size. This era culminated in the Stevens Hotel in Chicago in 1927, which had 3,000 rooms (130 or so on each floor), distributed along a twisting, complex corridor floor plan across four towers. It was billed as a 'City within a City', having its own bowling alley, cinema, drugstore and a miniature golf course on the roof. The Crash of 1929 and the depression that followed put an end to this kind of building. The Stevens hotel bankrupted the family and it was eventually bought by Conrad Hilton in

1945. But even after this era of the monster hotel had ended, Statler was remembered as a major innovator: he died in 1928, but was still named 'Hotel Man of the Half Century' by the industry body in 1950.

These massive structures that anonymized and socially levelled their populations by sheer horizontal and vertical extension have had a huge impact on the cultural resonances of the corridor. This was principally a class levelling, of course: the question of the policy on race only occasionally became visible in Statler hotels.[11] But they are only one end of the social spectrum, and we also need to think about a different function of corridors in the luxury hotel.

The Waldorf-Astoria's Peacock Alley, and 'Puttin' on the Ritz'

In the early 1890s, in a fit of pique and as an act of revenge against his rich New York relatives and neighbours, the fabulously wealthy William Astor decided to bulldoze his father's mansion on Fifth Avenue and build a hotel on the site. The thirteen-storey Waldorf Hotel (named after the German village from which the Astors emigrated) opened in 1893, while William Astor himself resettled in London. The hotel was meant to ruin the exclusivity of the neighbourhood, but in fact the hotel manager George Boldt, from its opening night gala in the Ballroom and Gallery, turned it into a feature of the New York elite's social calendar, and it became a byword in luxury and indulgence, particularly once the famous gambler John W. Gates made the bars and corridors of the hotel the centre of his social scene when he was in town. 'To those without the space at their apartments, the Waldorf-Astoria offers modern accommodation for entertainment and social functions; and to those encumbered with mansions, the sophisticated services that liberate their energies from the logistics of running a small private palace.'[12]

Although this collective salon of the elite was hugely successful, the enigmatic William Astor only once visited the hotel, and the legendary maître d'hôtel of the Waldorf in its golden age, Oscar Tschirky, recalled 'escorting Viscount Astor through the corridors of the hotel. He walked along, a tall man, a little bent, his hands behind his back, his head down, looking, I thought, neither to the right nor to the left.'[13]

In 1897 the neighbouring townhouse, owned by William Astor's aunt, was also bulldozed and the seventeen-storey Astoria Hotel built in its place by J. J. Astor IV. The two hotels, owned by rival factions of the Astor family, were connected together by an opulent 90-metre (300-ft) corridor that ran parallel to 34th Street – although with steel doors built in to shut off the link should the family dispute become irreconcilable and the hotels needed to return to existing as separate entities.

This lavishly appointed connecting corridor itself became one of the major social spaces of New York up to the Crash. It was known as 'the Hyphen': 'Where shall I meet you?' 'At the Hyphen.' 'What do

Peacock Alley, formerly 'the Hyphen', the legendary corridor that connected the Waldorf and Astoria Hotels between 1897 and 1929.

you mean?' 'Aw, between the Waldorf and the Astoria, of course.'[14] But as the hotel became a beacon for the spectacular display of wealth, the corridor was also known as 'The Lane of Strut' or 'Peacock Alley', 'where women of fashion were supposed to play the peacock and strut in their fine frocks for the delectation of the other sex and the envy of their own'.[15] Augustus Thomas's Broadway play *The Earl of Pawtucket* (1903) was partly set in the corridor, and there was a silent film called *Peacock Alley* (1922), remade as an early talkie (1930), both starring Mae Murray, 'the girl with the bee-stung lips'. In what was already an abiding theme of these ambiguous semi-public hotel spaces, the uncertain sexual status of the woman in the lobby and the corridor was the focus of these films.

The Waldorf-Astoria made two key innovations: it allowed both men and women to smoke in the dining rooms (ending a quintessential nineteenth-century spatial and gender divide) and it used glass walls for its famous two-storey Palm Room restaurant. It meant that dining there became a performative act that could be watched from the corridor. As a result, Peacock Alley became a space not just for the wealthy *flâneur* – the 'missionaries of strut' – but also for the crowds to watch a social scene they aspired to join, feeding a new kind of mass cultural celebrity spectacle.[16] As a result, it was also nicknamed 'Rubber Neck Lane'. It was estimated that at its peak before the First World War as many as 25,000 people a day walked through Peacock Alley. This would increase by another 10,000 if a president or prince was known to be staying at the hotel. The crowds drifted from the Palm Room at one end to the Empire Room at the other; it was an obligatory passage for any tourist in town. In 1903 a St Louis literary journal commented: 'The place is like Port Said as Kipling described it in the phrase that if you stopped long enough there everybody in the world that is worth knowing would eventually happen along.'[17] 'For more than a decade', Albert Crockett recalled in 1931,

> that corridor and its floating as well as its more or less fixed population represented a phase of American life; continually changing, it is true . . . All around, in the vast, outstretching corridors, there swarmed and swirled in a bewildering maze an endless, drifting crowd of men and women.[18]

The original site of the Waldorf-Astoria closed in 1929 (the land was sold to build the Empire State Building), and with it Peacock Alley passed into New York legend. The particular melancholia that always afflicts writers on the city who are left beleaguered by constant change, and the sense that for them the golden age has always just passed, set in early for this corridor. 'Peacock Alley, even before Boldt's death in 1916, had become hardly more than a tradition,' Crockett lamented. At the end of its first decade, the Golden Peacocks were replaced by 'mashers who ogle women', said McCarthy: 'You look in the faces of these men and there's no joy therein. The eyes and lips are sad.'

This is partly what horrified Henry James about the 'endless labyrinth of the Waldorf-Astoria' when he returned to New York in 1904 after twenty years away in Europe. As with Trollope, the hotel embodied for James 'the American spirit', summed up by the disdainful novelist as an 'immense promiscuity', a distressing loss of the 'old discrimination in favour of the private life'. He watched with disgust the parade 'through halls and saloons in which art and history, in masquerading dress, muffled almost to suffocation . . . in the gold brocade of their pretended majesties.' The promiscuous crowd here, as elsewhere in America, had been reduced to 'social sameness'.[19]

This is a telling comment, given that unlike Statler's horizontal, democratic model of the hotel, the Waldorf-Astoria was meant to offer a series of careful discriminations – if not by class, then certainly by wealth. In his absorbing cultural history of the elevator, Andreas Bernard notes that the hierarchies of social space were in the process of being inverted as a result of the growing ubiquity of the electric lift around 1900. Before, wealth meant you lived in apartments or chose hotel rooms on low floors; it was the poor who had to climb the stairs. Corridors on low floors in hotels were wide, lavishly carpeted and well-lit with attentive service; the higher you climbed, the narrower and more sparsely decorated the corridors, service thinned out and the rooms were cheaper. These were the floors for long-term residents, travelling salesmen and the hotel staff; above them, you reached the summit of poverty in the garret. However, the elevator equalized the effort of reaching any floor, and by the late nineteenth century wealth and exclusivity was marked by the remoteness of floor height and the expansiveness of view above the streets, while the service functions were increasingly located in windowless basements. Soon exclusive New York hotels had floors with protected access and extra services for the wealthy and powerful, even if this occasionally caused problems. In the second iteration of the Waldorf-Astoria hotel in New York, on Madison Avenue at 46th Street, there was nearly a major diplomatic incident at the height of the Cold War in the 1950s when the Soviet leader Nikita Khrushchev, descending from the exclusive suites of the tower, got stuck in a lift for nearly half an hour. When he was rescued, his panicked guards had their guns drawn.[20]

The functions of exclusivity and differentiation in hotels were more European in origin, and strongly associated with another key figure of this late nineteenth- and early twentieth-century period, César Ritz. Rather like Statler, Ritz had a long career managing hotels for others before finally setting up his own ideal hotel, the Ritz in Paris in 1898. From a Swiss peasant background, Ritz began at the bottom as an apprentice waiter before moving rapidly through the ranks by seeking to provide unashamedly fawning and lavish service to Europe's aristocrats and celebrities as maître d'hôtel at the new breed of luxury hotels in Paris, Nice, Menton, Monte Carlo, Lucerne and Baden-Baden. Every year the Prince of Wales sought out Ritz's service in Baden-Baden, leading to a lifelong dedication to his hotels and his famous declaration: 'Where Ritz goes I go.' Ritz became a celebrity himself when he was brought to London to manage the new luxury hotel on the Strand, the Savoy, in 1889. He introduced a French chef, actually edible food, an orchestra in the restaurant to cover up the fact that the English had no conversation, and wined and dined leading politicians of the day to the extent that they went back to Parliament to change the law to allow the restaurant to open on the sabbath. Ritz then founded a Hotel Syndicate with investors in 1896, and finally opened his own hotel in Paris on the Place Vendôme in June 1898. The Prince of Wales followed him to Paris and other leading figures of the European aristocracy soon made it their obligatory home. It was the favoured venue for 'Little Proust of the Ritz' to eat, and where the novelist wrote some of the sections of *In Search of Lost Time*. Proust died waiting for his servant to return from the Ritz with his favourite tipple. It became the hang-out for the Lost Generation in the 1920s, featuring in the fiction of Ernest Hemingway and F. Scott Fitzgerald.[21] The London Ritz, which opened in 1906, was never quite as storied as this. The Ritz-Carlton opened on Madison Avenue in New York in 1911.

The Paris Ritz contained another famous corridor. This was because the Ritz was effectively three separate town houses that had to be linked together. When the extension in rue Cambon opened in 1914, a 73-metre (240-ft) corridor connected it to the Place Vendôme. Very much like a Paris arcade, the corridor was lined with one hundred gleaming glass vitrines that luxury shops from the city hired to display their wares. The Ritz turned an infrastructural necessity into another immersive consumer dreamworld. In the Jazz Age, the song 'Puttin' on the Ritz', about the American Carlton-Ritz Hotel, communicated an urban performance of wealth and luxury, just like the old days of strutting along Peacock Alley. The original lyrics of Irving Berlin's 1929 song, made famous by Fred Astaire, mocked poor blacks parading in fine clothes on Harlem's Lenox Avenue. The lyrics were quietly adjusted in more familiar recordings to refer to the white Park Avenue crowd.

Unlike the clear lines and horizontal class levelling of a Statler hotel, the smaller luxury hotels wanted to capitalize on the quirks of their labyrinthine layout. The Ritz deliberately had no lobby, no vulgar undifferentiated public space, and the route through the hotel to its bars had no signs or directions and was designed to catch out interlopers. As Stephen Watts explained in his insufferably clubbable history of the Paris Ritz: 'To reach the largest and most celebrated of the three Ritz Bars . . . you walk through the lobby and the *salon du thé* and then, on the threshold of the dining-room, make a sharp right-hand turn, then a left, into the long *galerie,* or corridor, lined with glittering showcases . . .' (and so the description goes, on and on).[22] The Ritz twisted and turned, went up and down levels, tucked offices and bedrooms into unlikely places, and essentially worked like a trap to test the rightful belonging of those who ventured along its corridors.

This is the architectural and cultural history that underlies the high- and low-end versions of the modern hotel. The social impact of this new space seemed to come to a head in the interwar years, in the 1920s and '30s, when the hotel was most intensively explored in cultural commentary, fiction and film.

The Blonde in the Corridor: Hotel Detective Fiction

In the 1920s the 'comedy of manners' genre navigates social mix-ups in the new social space of the hotel. Elizabeth Bowen's first novel, *The Hotel* (1927), for example, is set on the Italian Riviera in a hotel with corridors 'dark, thickly carpeted, panelled with bedroom doors' and begins with a lengthy set-piece about a misunderstanding over the use of a private bathroom that opens onto a communal corridor. There was also a more self-conscious use of the hotel to present a schematic typology of society, as in Vicki Baum's *Grand Hotel* (1929), set in Berlin and almost immediately transposed to American cinema with a star turn from Greta Garbo. The Weimar text was further domesticated to America when this film was remade with Ginger Rogers and Lana Turner as *Week-end at the Waldorf* in 1945.[23] These are almost textbook examples of how sociologist Jürgen Habermas talks about fiction functioning in the bourgeois public sphere, as narratives that offer negotiations of social behaviour for the emergent middle classes. Since the public rooms and corridors of the hotel mean both proximity and confusing social intercourse, gestures of differentiation are rich sources for comedy, all the way up to *Fawlty Towers* or even *Pretty Woman*.

But in a more anxious register, this is also why there is an association of the hotel with crime and detection from early on: the hotel contains both low life and the high life as close neighbours. Guidebooks warn continually about the risks to property in hotels, outlining some of the tricks of the trade: 'Most thieves . . . walk the halls and try doors as they come to them, starting not long before dawn.' They try to slip in when occupants are in the bathroom, and guests are advised to 'spread a burglar cry' as soon as they find valuables missing, as 'the prowler, who may have just left the rooms, may be caught in the corridors.'[24] One strand of *Grand Hotel* features a master cat burglar clambering along ledges in an attempt to steal jewels without using the corridors. In Thomas Mann's unfinished novel *Confessions of Felix Krull, Confidence Man* (1954), the protagonist starts life as a confidence trickster working in a hotel. It takes an acute Miss Marple to see through the sham performance of gentility that hides the criminal conspiracy behind the sedate tea rooms and attentive lobby service in Agatha Christie's *At Bertram's Hotel* (1965). These are the cluttered interiors of overstuffed sofas, Persian carpets and hanging lamps where the bourgeoisie, as Walter Benjamin once observed, sit 'tremulously awaiting the nameless murderer'.[25] Luxury positively invites crime and demands the policing of difference.

Hotels themselves, of course, employed 'hotel detectives' to watch for those hoping to skip out on paying their bills, keep an eye on pilfering among the staff, or look for nefarious infiltrators of the public spaces below or the more private bedroom corridors above. Hotel detectives were lowly themselves, often fired or retired policemen. Raymond Chandler wrote two stories about hotel detectives in the early 1930s, who dream one day of aspiring to the heights of the status of the Private Investigator like Philip Marlowe. At the start of 'The King in Yellow', Steve Grayce, the house dick of the Carlton Hotel, is lambasted for lazing around the lobby and told to go back upstairs and clear an impromptu party out of the corridor 'on a medium-priced transient floor'. Up there, he encounters some addled jazz players, 'a metallic blonde' and her female friend. The women are 'a couple of obvious hustlers' not detected by the night auditor on the lobby desk and who therefore 'managed to get themselves registered'.[26] That they are in the wrong place, at the wrong price bracket, rings alarm bells in this precisely ordered financial and moral universe. The anomaly soon leads to a trail of bodies around the low hotels and dives of Bunker Hill in Los Angeles, and back to the story of a suicide in room 815.

Chandler's classic articulation of the chivalric, private code of honour of the detective means Grayce in 'The King in Yellow' rises above the expectations of his enemies: 'I always thought house dicks were just a bunch of cheap grafters. I guess I missed out on you.'[27] Tony Reseck in 'I'll Be Waiting' is another hotel dick who is sentimental enough to rescue the red-headed girl waiting in the lobby of the Windermere Hotel for her sweetheart just released from prison. The reaction of the ex-con upstairs waiting for her makes it obvious the primary job of the hotel detective is to stop illicit sexual encounters: '"It slays me," he said. "I'm in the dump an hour and the house copper gives me the buzz. Okey, sweetheart, look in the closet and bathroom. But she just left."' The job is later described as 'palming doorknobs': he acts just like the criminals he is asked to track through the corridors.[28]

In his essay 'The Hotel Room', Dutch psychologist D. J. van Lennep talks about the freedom anonymous hotel dwelling brings, the chances for adventures and temporary suspension of the weight of

The ominous corridor of the Hotel Earle in the Coen brothers' *Barton Fink* (1991). *Below*: shoes of the other, unseen guests.

the responsibilities of 'home'.[29] Sexual fantasy, violence and hotels are certainly intertwined in detective fiction, from the hard-boiled 1920s, via the queasy scenes of Scottie's sexual obsession in Hitchcock's *Vertigo* (1958) that are lit by a sickly green neon HOTEL sign, up to the sentimental naivety of the minder George in Neil Jordan's film *Mona Lisa* (1986). George (played by Bob Hoskins) drives the high-class call girl Simone around London's hotels and waits in the lobbies below to fend off hassle from clients and the house detectives. George has no idea where these labyrinths of streets and hotels will lead him. Another brief moment of sexual freedom in *Barton Fink* (1991), the Coen brothers' film set in the cavernous lobby and the terrifying corridors and rooms of Hotel Earle in 1940s Hollywood, leads to appalling consequences. Hotel Earle's faded Art Deco grandeur deliberately evokes the decor of the public spaces of the hotel in John Huston's film noir *Key Largo* (1948), or the seediness of the San Francisco lobbies and corridors haunted by private dick Sam Spade in Dashiell Hammett's hard-boiled fiction. Crucial scenes of John Huston's 1941 version of Hammett's *Maltese Falcon* take place in the downtown Pickwick Hotel, for instance.

Perhaps the most famous blonde in the corridor is the murderous femme fatale Phyllis Dietrichson in an iconic moment from Billy Wilder's noir *Double Indemnity* (1944), when she is almost discovered in her plot to kill her husband after she decides to visit her hapless patsy, the insurance agent Walter Neff, at his cheap rental apartment block. She has to hide behind the door in the corridor (which conveniently opens outwards) just as the investigator, now suspicious of the life insurance policy taken out on her husband, is taking his leave. The scene is not in James M. Cain's source novel: it is a purely cinematic flourish. In the shadows, in the corridor that speaks of amoral anonymity, illicit plots and sexual corruption, Barbara Stanwyck's bottle-blonde hair glares like a warning signal.

Neff's apartment rooms are bleak and anonymous, carefully described in Raymond Chandler's script as furnished with cheap catalogue fixtures and fittings. Some speculate that the absence of any personal touch in Neff's pad was modelled on Billy Wilder's own rooms from his days of early exile from Germany in the famous Hollywood hotel on Sunset Boulevard, the Chateau Marmont.[30] The alienation and despair of film noir is typically discussed in the fatalistic snares of the city streets and in titles like *The Cry of the City* (1944), *Naked City* (1948), *Night and the City* (1950) or *Nightmare Alley* (1947),

Phyllis hides in the corridor outside Walter Neff's apartment, as claims adjustor Barton Keyes voices his suspicions in Billy Wilder's *Double Indemnity* (1944).

but these kinds of interiors, empty lobbies and anonymous hallways also powerfully illustrate the 'homogenized and homogenizing abstract space' that was typical of the genre.[31] Think of the bullets that come through the crack of the door from the corridor of Joe Brody's apartment block, or the darkened corridor where Marlowe is forced to listen to the murder of the grafter Harry Jones, both scenes from Howard Hawks's adaptation of Chandler's *The Big Sleep* (1946). As Andrew Spicer observes, 'The noir city is symbolically homeless, its denizens act out their lives in public spaces: in diners, bars, nightclubs, automobiles, streets, alleyways, impersonal luxurious hotel suites or cheerless, uncomfortable apartments.'[32] It was these new spaces of modernity that film noir set out to interpret for its audiences.

Alfred Hitchcock's sunnier Technicolor *North by Northwest* (1959) also features pivotal scenes in hotels. The moment advertising executive Roger O. Thornhill, listed under the fictitious 'George Kaplan', walks down the hotel corridor in New York and opens the door of room 796 he effectively becomes Kaplan. There is already an absence at the heart of Thornhill ('What does the "O" stand for?' 'Nothing'), which makes him a perfect husk for this kind of coming into being in hotels and corridor trains. The blonde he finds there (and pursues to another hotel) is an equally empty performance of a shell of an identity. Significantly, the proof of Kaplan's existence is merely a list of hotel reservations: one is the Statler Hotel in Boston.

The Weimar critic Siegfried Kracauer, like his contemporary Walter Benjamin, was obsessed with the spectacle of urban crime and devoured detective novels as a child. He started a study of detective fiction in the 1920s, but only got as far as sketching out a fascinating essay titled 'The Hotel Lobby'. This begins with the mass cultural form of detective fiction, but soon turns into a penetrating philosophical account of the alienated self. For Kracauer, the hotel lobby features heavily in crime fiction because it is an exemplary space of the modern world, a place where lots of people mill but never form a meaningful collective. The lobby is 'the space of unrelatedness', individuals together but alone, atomized and alienated from each other. This atomization undoes selfhood itself, reducing people to 'pseudo-individuals': 'faces disappear behind newspapers, and the artificial continuous light illuminates nothing but mannequins.' In Kracauer's evocative phrase people are reduced to 'ungraspable flat ghosts'. Sounding a little bit more pretentious than anything a low-rent detective like Marlowe might spit out, these lonely figures are for Kracauer standing '*vis-à-vis de rien*' (face-to-face with nothing).[33]

An American social study published in 1936, called *Hotel Life*, seems to agree with this conclusion in less grandiose terms. Norman Hayner considered the transience of hotel living increasingly adopted as a permanent way of life by young professionals and transient workers in America to be one that corrupted the moral self and contributed to the decline of civic society. 'The average guest is individualistic, self-concerned and not interested in social welfare. Any attempt at personal contact by strangers or even by members of the hotel staff

. . . is not tolerated.' Staying in a hotel constituted a 'moral holiday' from social obligations, Hayner argued, and this was beginning to develop 'a pathological aspect' with alarming social consequences as it was adopted by more and more people. Hayner's conclusion made the hotel an exemplary space of modern alienation:

> Exaggerated statements about urban life become realities in the hotel environment. Metropolitan problems exhibit themselves in accentuated form . . . The detachment, freedom, loneliness and release from restraints that mark the hotel population are only to a lesser degree characteristic of modern life as a whole. The hotel is, in fact, a symbol of changes that are taking place not only in the manners of American society, but wherever the influence of machine industry is felt.[34]

Here is a nexus that brings the hotel together with the numbing alienation of machinic modernity. It explains why that vista of identical doors receding infinitely down long corridors has become a key representation of the anonymity of modern urban life: 'In the metropolitan hotel the guest is only a number. His mark of identification is a key.'[35] It is in the corridor of the monster hotel where the utopian promise of social levelling turns in the 1920s and '30s into a space that dramatizes the annihilation of any chance of an authentic self and becomes a dystopian space of existential dread.

Hotel Existence

Curiously, the hotel does seem to hover on the edge of the existential philosophy that was being written in this period. Martin Heidegger's foundational existential text *Being and Time* (1927) spoke about the self in situational terms as *Dasein*, Being-there, but one that had become un-housed from its authentic existence. The modern technological world was one that 'enframed' man in artificial environments that closed him off from the rooted truths of being. And in his post-war essay 'Building Dwelling Thinking' (1951), Heidegger intrinsically linked being and dwelling together conceptually, only to suggest that modern buildings like power stations, railway stations, dams or market halls, or the social housing being constructed in Germany amid the rubble, merely provided basic functions like shelter rather than approaching anything like proper, authentic dwellings. Instead, he pointed to the rootedness of old Black Forest farmhouses or the sanctity of the Greek temple whose enclosure brought into presence the divine. In this contrast, Heidegger equates the functional and infrastructural with the inauthentic and soulless. The transient, generic, featureless space of the hotel is therefore an exemplary instance of 'the real plight of dwelling' in the modern world, the problem 'that mortals ever search anew for the essence of dwelling, that they *must ever learn to dwell*'. The hotel is only ever a temporary shelter that reveals the fundamental human condition of *homelessness*.[36]

Perhaps it is significant that it was at a three-week residential conference at the Hotel Belvedere in Davos in 1929 that Heidegger so challenged the received wisdom on the metaphysics of space and time that a young student there, the philosopher Emmanuel Levinas, felt he had been 'witness to the creation and the end of the world'.[37] This is the same hotel, constructed in 1875 and still one of the largest structures ever built in the Alps, that is now used for the annual exclusive gatherings of the World Economic Forum.

Another key existentialist text, Jean-Paul Sartre's *Being and Nothingness* (1943), uses the hotel corridor in one of its most famous examples. In a section called 'The Look', Sartre offers this scenario: 'Let us imagine that moved by jealousy, curiosity, or vice I have just glued my ear to the door and looked through the keyhole' where 'behind that door a spectacle is presented as "to be seen"'. This models the Other as an object reduced to the mastery of the unchallenged gaze. 'But all of a sudden,' Sartre continues, 'I hear footsteps in the hall. Someone is looking at me.' In the shame of this discovery 'I now exist as myself . . . I see *myself* because somebody sees me . . . The Other's look makes me be beyond my being in this world and puts me in the midst of the world.'[38] This primal scene suggests that it is in the transitional corridor space that we come into our 'being-in-the-midst-of-the-world-for-others', and Sartre then points to the inexplicable labyrinths of Kafka's fiction for further examples of this anxious, compromised and yet foundational state. That his primal scene is one of triangulated sexual jealousy (peeping through a key-hole, but getting caught by an Other) inevitably recalls the involved love triangles that structured Sartre's long relationship with Simone de Beauvoir, a woman he fell for at first sight in a shattering *coup de foudre* when he saw her in a corridor of the Sorbonne in 1929.[39] The poet Thom Gunn turned to Sartre's scenario in his poem 'The Corridor' ('The empty hotel corridor was dark./But here the keyhole shone, a meaning spark').[40]

A little later there was a famous denunciation by the Hungarian Marxist critic György Lukács of 'a considerable part of the leading German intelligentsia' for 'taking up residence in the "Grand Hotel Abyss" . . . a beautiful hotel, equipped with every comfort, on the edge of an abyss, of nothingness, of absurdity'.[41] This powerful image evokes the catastrophe swirling under the Enlightenment-influenced philosophies of Europe in the 1930s and in the wake of the Second World War (he was critiquing what he saw as the wilful pessimism of Frankfurt School thinkers like Theodor Adorno). But this metaphor only reinforces once more why the hotel corridor recurs again and again in the film noirs of the immediate post-war period, a genre defined in 1946 as generating 'a specific sense of malaise', 'the state of tension created in the spectators by the disappearance of their psychological bearings'.[42]

What I have described so far is a sense of deracination or unease evoked by the hotel corridor. We have not yet reached full-scale dread or horror, the ocean of blood that spills out of the elevator of the Overlook Hotel in *The Shining* (1980) and comes rushing down the corridor to engulf the spectator. This more histrionic corridor dread in Gothic fiction and horror film will need a whole chapter of its own.

Here, I want to conclude with three texts that use the hotel corridor in quieter tones to underline this subtle existential malaise that creeps into the once utopian structure of the corridor in the post-war era.

Alain Resnais' film *Last Year at Marienbad* (1961) is marked by a restless, roving camera that glides at a glacial pace through the Baroque corridors, grand public rooms and geometric formal gardens of a hotel somewhere in Europe. It is a highly stylized symmetrical design, the figures stiff like mannequins and dwarfed by the baroque splendour of their surroundings. In the first fifteen minutes, a hypnotic voice-over mutters in a rising and falling, soporific tone about the pathways through these 'endless corridors' and 'empty corridors as far as the eye can see'. The narrative, such as it is, was written by avant-garde novelist Alain Robbe-Grillet, who returned obsessively in his own fiction and films to the image of the unfathomable labyrinth. The opening monologue unrolls in an already exhausting, unfinished, unfinishable sentence:

> Once again – I walk on, once again, down these corridors, through these halls, these galleries, in this structure – from another century, this enormous, luxurious, baroque – lugubrious hotel, where endless corridors succeed silent – deserted corridors, over-loaded with a dim, cold ornamentation of woodwork, stucco, mouldings, marbles, dark mirrors, dim paintings, columns, heavy hangings – sculptured door frames, series of doorways, galleries – transverse corridors that open in turn on empty salons . . .[43]

In *Last Year at Marienbad* it seems that the unnamed male protagonist X is trying to persuade the frozen, near catatonic woman A that they met last year, in a hotel in Marienbad, and that he wants to continue their abandoned affair, even though she claims to have no memory of their shared past. It may be that memories of that last year's liaison begin to bleed through onto the screen (traumatic memories, perhaps, of X's violent sexual assault on A), or else these are fantasies, but soon enough the viewer is unanchored from any secure sense of time or space, status of the image or fixed point of view. The film is an unsolvable riddle, an unending corridor shot with no clear exits marked.

Last Year at Marienbad, a post-war Modernist film, coldly formalist yet saturated with anomie, was shot by Resnais not in the Czech spa town of Marienbad (Mariánské Lázně) but mainly in a series of Baroque palaces around Munich, including Schloss Schleissheim and the vast Schloss Nymphenburg, built for Ludwig I, with its elongated

Camera drifting through the hotel corridors and (below) corridors of cold formalism in Alain Resnais' *Last Year at Marienbad* (1961).

galleries connecting to symmetrical wings that were added to the main structure in 1701. The film also used the famous Hall of Mirrors of the Rococo Amalienburg hunting lodge in the grounds, as well as entirely artificial sets constructed on sound stages. The steady glide through these corridic spaces does not reveal volumes in which viewers can ever properly orient themselves. Instead, it stitches together a maddening dreamlike space that utterly confounds – turning an Enlightenment architectural order into its demonic other. Resnais had earlier made another film in the suburbs of Munich, *Night and Fog*, about Munich's main concentration camp at Dachau, and his cinematographer Sasha Vierny used exactly the same camera glides in both films, the echo hinting at the abyss that lies beneath the hotel. Although I love *Last Year at Marienbad*, I confess I can never watch it without being lulled to sleep by its hypnotic glide through the corridors, its insidious voice-over, the camera moving at the pace of a disorienting anxiety dream.

The Coen brothers' *Barton Fink* might seem initially like an empty stylistic pastiche of 1940s film noir, but is ultimately just as confounding as the modernist *Marienbad*. The central character, the self-deluded writer of earnest proletarian plays, Barton Fink, is modelled on Clifford Odets, who was lured from the New York stage to Hollywood in 1935 only to suffer writer's block, the indignity of having his scripts rewritten and later terrible guilt after testifying in 1952 before the House Committee on Un-American Activities investigating communism in the movie industry. The film is set in 1941, in the weeks around the Pearl Harbor attack. As soon as Fink enters the lobby he is lost in what one critic calls the 'existential hell' of the Hotel Earle, an overheated, infernal fever dream of a building.[44] It is a languid, suffocating space where Fink is given a room on the sixth floor as a 'res[ident]' not a 'trans[ient]' – the ominous tagline of the Earle is 'A day or a lifetime'. Along his corridor, with its monstrous swirling carpet, shoes are put out to shine by the residents every night, but none of the other guests are seen or heard except for Fink's neighbour, Charlie Meadows (a gigantic John Goodman playing against the tiny frame of John Turturro).

Before the frenzied finale, the tone of the film is one of creeping unease and suffocation. Fink's door whumps shut as if sealing him in, mosquitoes drone yet can't be caught, the wallpaper wilts and oozes, the camera drifts off and crawls through the piping, as the pressure of his writing block builds. This is a weird subjective realm of mental disintegration, one key influence on the Coens being Roman Polanski's *The Tenant* (1976).

The neighbour Charlie is another of the Coens' embodiments of unconscious murderous rage, a figure who sweats and oozes – exactly like the hotel itself – and eventually erupts into psychotic violence. In the last scenes, Charlie sets fire to the hotel and strides down corridors laced with flames, bringing down an awful punishment. His true identity, Karl 'Madman' Mundt, a serial killer with a penchant for beheading his victims, shares the same name as a Republican Representative (later Senator) who sat on the House Committee on Un-American Activities from 1943 to 1948. It is as if Fink's hubris about 'the life of the mind' has called up a very precise nemesis. Even so, the puzzling resistance of the film to final determination has prompted one critic to suggest that *Barton Fink* is an illustration of Heidegger's discussion of the problem of hermeneutic interpretation (although I'm guessing that's not how the Coens pitched it to prospective backers).[45] As we can now see, the Hotel Earle is not an incidental setting for *Barton Fink* but intrinsic to evoking a certain kind of mid-century unease.

Finally, Will Wiles's *The Way Inn* (2014) is a novel that updates this theme of existential hotel crisis to the rise of those contemporary monster chain hotels that now carefully reproduce the same cocooned environment around the world. This global expansion of familiar spaces goes far beyond the dreams of anything E. M. Statler could have planned. The plot concerns a professional conference-goer, Neil Double, who travels the globe moving from one anonymous hotel to another, becoming an expert in precise semiotic descriptions of the 'latte-coloured carpet' and 'insipid abstract painting' and offering sharp analyses of transnational hotel decor: 'A small sofa sat in the corridor near the lift, one of those baffling gestures towards domesticity made by hotels. It was not there to be sat in – it was there to make the corridor appear furnished, an insurance policy against bleakness and emptiness.'[46]

The book starts as a comedy of scrupulously observed realism about hotels and their transient corporate populations, but slowly slides into fantasy as the protagonist is progressively stripped of his corporate accreditations and is forced to roam the hotel corridors, vaguely hoping to re-encounter the red-headed femme fatale who has talked enigmatically about the 'modern geomancy' she is conducting in these spaces (what if all the abstract paintings on the wall were cut-up sections of one giant work, she speculates).[47] In a key section, Double leaves the security of his room and decides to turn down corridors against the usual shortest route to the lifts. 'I kept moving, left, right, right again, trying to randomise my route . . . to defy any logical path and experience the building naturally, like a forest, without desire, without rational choices.'[48] To his bewilderment, the corridors seem to extend infinitely, and when he encounters the same room numbers he is sure that he has not looped back because this is a subtly different corridor. It takes another hundred pages for Double to come to the revelation that this is 'not a single corridor, a corridor with branches', but a space that seems infinite:

> Behind her, the corridor continued impossibly, until perspective shrank it to an unseeable singularity. But before that point, there was the faintest hint of a curve, a horizon . . .
> Behind her, the hotel went on.
> It goes on.
> The hotel went on forever.[49]

Double has found his way into the secret space of the *inner hotel*, the key to a corridor that secretly connects every hotel corridor together in a hyperspace that can seemingly take you anywhere in the world, a passage that is 'always the same, everywhere the same, forever'.[50] This discovery comes at immense metaphysical cost, however, and begins to unravel Double's wafer-thin corporate identity and any final attachment to the world outside.

Wiles's expert commentary on the transnational space of the chain is a culmination of the sense of unease that always hovered around the communal corridors of hotels, even as they were celebrated for their utopian possibilities in the nineteenth and twentieth centuries. In parallel with the promise of social housing, then, this mode of communal living seems to curdle in the space of the hotel corridor.

'The Corridor' at Pentonville Model Prison, sketched for Henry Mayhew's *The Criminal Prisons of London* (1862).

6

Corridors of Reform: Prison, Workhouse, Asylum, Hospital, School and University

Henry Mayhew, one of the Victorian era's greatest journalists of the people and streets of London, undertook a survey of the capital's prisons in 1862. Just to the north of King's Cross lay Pentonville, the 'Model' prison widely copied around the world as an ideal penitentiary after it had opened twenty years earlier. Rather than delivering dry debates and statistics, Mayhew discovers the prison from the dynamic point of view of someone entering it for the first time. Through the portcullis gate (ostentatiously added by Charles Barry, architect of the Houses of Parliament), you enter the arrival hall and traverse a 'long and broad passage like the lengthy hall to some Government office'. This is mere preparation, though, for arriving at the central atrium, from which four giant wings, three storeys high, radiate out like the prongs of a fan. These 'light and lofty tunnels', 12 metres (40 ft) high, lined with metalwork galleries to access the cells, are 'officially styled' as corridors, Mayhew explains, as if the word is awkward or unusual. They are flooded with natural light during the day and lit with gas at night. 'The first thing that strikes the mind on entering the prison passage', Mayhew says, 'is the wondrous and perfectly Dutch-like cleanliness pervading the place.' Reaching for more analogies to ground all this newness, Mayhew writes that 'the lengthy and high corridors, with their sky-light roofs, seemed to us like a bunch of Burlington Arcades, that had been fitted up in the style of the opera-box lobbies, with an infinity of little doors.' Again, just a page later, Mayhew thinks Pentonville is like 'a bit of the Crystal Palace, stripped of all its contents'. These reference points are the established iron-and-glass immersive spaces of nineteenth-century modernity. The accompanying sketch, titled 'The Corridor', reveals a space of rational order and light, the last speck of dirt being swept away in the foreground.[1]

Pentonville Model Prison was the culmination of an era of reform that had transformed the typical felon's gaol from the dank and diseased dungeons or holding pens of a century earlier. Newgate Gaol still brooded over the old boundary of the City of London as it had for centuries, and was the traditional departure point for the condemned to process along the Tyburn Road to the gallows. In 1767 Newgate had been rebuilt yet again by George Dance (father and son) as a squat tower with a chaotic labyrinth of 42 rooms arranged in no discernible order. Horrendous conditions brewed a corrupting air inside, so it was then believed. Foul miasma sometimes became a fatal 'gaol fever' (outbreaks of typhus) that could break the bounds of the walls and infect the streets beyond. In 1750 a gaol fever from Newgate infected everyone in the courts of the nearby Old Bailey, killing the then Lord Mayor. The medieval Newgate, first built on the site in 1188, was finally demolished in 1904. This was why Mayhew said of the shiny new corridors of Pentonville that 'the prison is utterly unlike all our imaginary pictures of prisons.'[2]

The era of English reform began on the Nonconformist margins of the Enlightenment but finally found purchase in national policy in the 1830s. It was embodied in the building of large-scale institutions. For the criminals, a network of new prisons. For the miscreants, the reformatories. For the sickly poor, the pauper hospitals. For the deserving poor, the factory; for the undeserving poor, the workhouse; for the mad, the asylum. Institutional reform and rebuilding later extended to schools, universities and the administrative structures of government itself. This state architecture had distinctive waves of signature styling: Neoclassical or Gothic, while the later Board

Schools favoured more secular Queen Anne facades. But whatever the style of ornament, each of these institutions distributed space in ways that were foundationally *corridic*.

Charles Fourier had organized his utopia around the internal 'street-gallery' of the phalanx. His corridor was meant to joyously transport and transform people out of their alienated existence. No one would fund his eccentric vision, yet at exactly the same time other groups had far greater success with the idea that architectural space might effect more modest yet significant reform of character. The architect Ernö Goldfinger once proposed that 'A person within a defined space is subject to psychological effect; the *sensation of space*. It is a subconscious phenomenon, and the impression on the person subjected to it . . . varies with the degree of enclosure, the size of the enclosed space and the shape of the enclosed space.'[3] Reformers between 1750 and 1850 understood this explicitly: they thought of their new structures as reshaping human character, and in doing so invented the typology of the modern institutional public building. The ambition was, to use Robin Evans's phrase, the *fabrication of virtue*, a population 'raised towards perfection by administration channelled through a carefully distributed architecture'.[4] Space inhabited people and (re)made them, not vice versa.

Marginal dissenters first pressed for reform: it was Quakers who recast the gaol as a penitentiary not to condemn but to redeem prisoners from the 1770s. The first modern asylum, the York Retreat, was also built to serve the Quaker community and opened in 1795, before becoming a worldwide model. Early factory schools were either Quaker experiments (Thomas Firmin ran a combined school, factory and shop in London in the late seventeenth century) or were the eccentric projects of reformers like Robert Owen, who founded his Institute for the Formation of Character in New Lanark in 1816. Evangelical Christians of more acceptable hue also sought reform of cruel and punitive regimes. The Seventh Earl of Shaftesbury fought for labour laws to protect children in factories and mines, and helped establish the lunacy commission to improve conditions in madhouses.

Reformist projects like this found greater purchase through the more secular proposals of the Utilitarians, who steadily moved into positions of influence or direct government power by the 1830s. The leading Utilitarian philosopher, Jeremy Bentham, having worked out his calculus of the 'greatest good for the greatest number', campaigned relentlessly for his House of Inspection, or Panopticon, after publishing his plans in 1791. Bentham eventually had personally to underwrite the first ever National Penitentiary at Millbank, London (1816), as an experiment. He was intent on extending his method of reform through constant surveillance to every other building, ranging from schools and factories all the way to chicken coops.

Bentham was too far outside government machinations to have much direct influence on policy. Instead, his philosophical allies James Mill and John Stuart Mill effected major changes in the Civil Service, education and government from the 1820s. Bentham's last personal secretary, Edwin Chadwick, went on to be appointed as secretary to commissions that redesigned the new Factory Acts of 1833 and the New Poor Law of 1834, as well as collecting the data for the Report on the Sanitary Conditions of the Labouring Population of Great Britain in 1842, the basis for the major public works associated with the Public Health Act of 1848. These established a network of national institutions, an army of inspectors that developed uniform standards, collected data, conducted the Census, and performed statistical analysis that calculated the norms and standard deviations of birth, life and death in the population. This was the machinery by which the Victorians 'were forcibly subsumed into a single social body', the arrival of the modern bureaucratic state.[5]

The most influential historian and theorist of this era of reform has been Michel Foucault. Foucault upended Whiggish histories of progress and enlightenment (the mad unchained, the poor enfranchised) to suggest that the birth of the clinic, the asylum, the prison and reformatory were the concrete forms of a new kind of power that moved from the blunt threat of external violence to an internalized regimen of pervasive and constant self-discipline and self-reformation. This power was never simply repressive or coercive; it disciplined and punished but also pleasured subjects into new kinds of social being, rewarding conformity to biopolitical norms. The institutions of this new formation were distinct disciplinary structures that exercised 'a new microphysics of power' that ensured power flowed into the finest capillaries of society, entirely suffusing it. Rather than hurling criminals into undifferentiated incarceration or the mad into the chaos of Bedlam, the institutions of reform separated, categorized, discriminated and hierarchized, relying on a partitioning of space, an obsessive set of spatial divisions and subdivisions that encompassed large populations but sifted them down to the individual level. Foucault spoke of this 'great form of distribution of individuals' as reaching down into 'class[rooms], corridors, courtyards'. This is the architecture 'that would operate to transform individuals' beyond simple enclosure, instead presenting a 'calculation of openings, of filled and empty spaces, passages and transparencies'.[6]

Foucault takes Bentham's Panopticon as the ideal form of this 'subtle, calculated technology of subjection', even though in concrete architectural terms very few buildings were constructed on this plan, since it proved impractical.[7] While the broad trajectory of Foucault's account remains compelling, it loses specificity in its level of abstraction, particularly when it comes to the architectural forms pursued in allied yet distinct reform institutions. Many of these institutions might indeed look the same: imposing, large-scale facades housing cellular subdivisions of rooms distributed along lengthy corridors. Yet the internal divisions of their spaces could serve very different purposes. My interest in this chapter is in pursuing how the corridor plan of the large-scale public building promised to reform the recalcitrant self by building very different pathways through the architecture of the modern state.

The Hub-and-Corridor Prison

The modern prison reform movement began in the 1770s, driven in England by dissenting Quakers who objected to the unforgiving condemnation of the courts, the continuing use of capital punishment, the use of fetters, the arbitrary cruelty of the regimes of local gaol keepers, and the general physical and moral contagion represented by the system. There was a loose categorization of different prisons (bridewells for the indigent, houses of correction for the idle and immoral, debtors' gaols, and gaols for felons), but as local prisons were often improvised spaces in gatehouses, above taverns or in walled-off cul-de-sacs, separation of the convicted was difficult.

In 1773 John Howard was elected High Sheriff of Bedfordshire with responsibility for gaols in the county, which were paid for on local rates and run locally. Howard was appalled at the conditions of his gaols and set about organizing an investigative survey. He published a plain list of the terrible conditions of incarceration: some gaols no more than a room with inmates crammed inside, some chained together so closely that they could not lie down. This led to parliamentary scrutiny and soon a study of the entire country, *The State of the Prisons in England and Wales* (1777), a journey that Howard undertook personally. This evidence base coincided with American independence and thus the end of transportation of serious criminals there. With overcrowding causing more fatal outbreaks of gaol fever, the conditions for reform were ripe.

The very naming of the Penitentiary Act of 1779 showed that a quiet moral revolution had taken place. Rather than regard prisoners as always condemned, what if they were considered as penitents, the subjects of possible redemption? Could the architecture itself foster this reformation? The French monk Jean Mabillon had proposed the model of the Carthusian monastery for a penitentiary in an essay published posthumously in 1724: each prisoner confined in a solitary cell, with no contaminating contact with others, and left to the silent contemplation of their sin, their reflection leading to redemption and rehabilitation. This cloister and cell system had been adapted for the Hospice of San Michele in Rome in 1703, a reformatory for boys with sixty cells along tiered galleries, and this was a model also explored in the Maison de Force in Ghent in 1773. In England, Jonas Hanway, co-founder of the Magdalen Hospital for the Reception of Penitent Prostitutes, extended this reformatory impulse to prisons, expounding the idea of solitary confinement in *Solitude in Imprisonment* (1776). 'The walls of his prison will preach peace to his soul,' Hanway confidently predicted.[8]

Another prison reformer, Sir George Onesiphorus Paul, also concluded that this system would prevent physical as well as moral contagion, writing in 1784 that 'Separation both day and night is the principle of all improvement . . . there is no possible degree of separation that will not bring with it additional perfection: – it favours every species of reform.'[9] The cells were distributed along gallcrics and insulated as much as possible from any communication. Walls were sometimes built down the middle of galleries to prevent any cross-corridor signalling, and there were sometimes systems of narrow corridors along the outside of the ribbon of cells to allow warders to observe inmates through one-way observation points, all to amplify the sense of what Bentham called the 'inspective force' of the architecture, the internalization of the feeling of being permanently watched and judged.[10]

In practice, the idea of complete solitary confinement was rarely adopted because it was found that it tended to drive people mad rather than into religious or social rectitude. Instead, most prisons adopted the 'separate system', individual cells for incarceration at night, with various forms of communal exercise and purposive work during the day for strictly segregated categories of prisoner.

The provisions of the Penitentiary Act were constructed in stone by William Blackburn, a working-class Quaker architect who provided plans for seventeen prisons and advised on many more in a short career that ended with his sudden death in 1790. Blackburn won the design competition run by the Commission for Penitentiary Houses in 1782, and soon became a close associate of the reformer John Howard. Blackburn was responsible for the first radial prison designs in England, clearly influencing Bentham's later Panopticon. At the Northleach House of Correction, for example, completed by Sir George Onesiphorus Paul in Gloucester in 1792, Blackburn arranged five separate blocks in a semicircular D-plan, all facing the governor's residence and the chapel. The two-storey blocks had stairwells at each end, with the individual cells approached on iron walkways inside. There were further exterior walkways on the second floor to increase surveillance of the outside spaces and exercise yards. In later plans these blocks would be turned round into a hub-and-spoke shape, the governor's all-seeing eye able to penetrate the entire length of each of the block's tiered corridors from a single central point. This increased the efficiency of the surveillance of all interior and exterior spaces outside the penitent's cell at a stroke. The isolated blocks separated categories of prisoner and the clarity of clean sightlines along well-lit vistas was central to limiting the moral contagion of association between prisoners. Blackburn also experimented with new kinds of ventilation to prevent physical contagion.

The fundamental contradiction between the need for isolated enclosure for moral containment and open, circulating air for physical health was a problem that vexed every prison architect in the era of reform, of every ideological hue. Whatever design was adopted, the ingenuity of prisoners, overcrowding, underfunding and change of philosophy or function usually subverted best intentions and prompted ceaseless waves of reconfiguration and design.

The theological hopes of redemption that underpinned the penitentiary never went away in the nineteenth century, and indeed Quaker influence on penal policy has remained important into the present day. But there was always a rival language of privation and punishment – that the wide communication of awful conditions would usefully serve as the principal deterrent against crime. In part this was why prison gates and walls kept to the associations of sublime Gothic terror in their crenellated forms late into the century, even as the internal distribution of space altered. Tory governments, foreign wars and recession led to an increasing pessimism about the virtues of reform in the 1810s. Instead, semi-military regimes were favoured, such as the one run at Cold Bath Fields gaol in Clerkenwell, where experiments in solitary confinement were ended in 1816.

A second wave of reform, however, came from Quakers in Philadelphia, a community founded by William Penn with a reformed penal code at its core in 1682, following Penn's own awful experience of imprisonment for dissent in England. A century later, after independence, Philadelphia was a rapidly expanding hub of the new republic. Quakers were at the heart of the Philadelphia Society for Alleviating the Miseries of Public Prisons, which included the founding father, philanthropist and reformer Benjamin Rush. They campaigned against the system of hard labour then employed as the sole instrument of punishment in Philadelphia. Rush closely followed the work of prison reformer John Howard in England. In 1790 this group built a small, experimental Penitentiary House to trial solitary confinement at the Walnut Street Gaol. This was a two-storey block with only eight cells on each floor, each with a mattress, a tap and a high window. The central corridor had a dividing wall to prevent communication. Prisoners were not permitted to leave their cells at any time. This was only ever intended to isolate the most disruptive prisoners inside the main gaol, but like the larger experiment at Auburn in New York (which placed inmates in tiny cells less than 1.2 × 2.4 metres, or 4 × 8 ft), pure solitary confinement was found too harsh a regime to produce the desired reformation of character.

What emerged a few years later was the most influential 'separate system' reform prison of the nineteenth century, Philadelphia's Eastern State Penitentiary at Cherry Hill. It was designed by the young architect John Haviland, a recent emigrant who had trained in London under an architect with experience of building prisons to Howard's reformist ideals. The Eastern State Penitentiary was commissioned in 1821 and the first sections opened in 1829. The design was copied around the world for decades following many inspections by international visitors. It was the basis for Pentonville's Model Prison, but was also borrowed in Germany and France, in St Petersburg in Russia, and then in Buenos Aires, before becoming the blueprint in more than thirty territories across the Far East, China and Japan: 'Details of cells and corridors, exterior style and several basic layouts of cell buildings, are all repeated endlessly in nineteenth-century prisons throughout the world.'[11]

The prison wall at Cherry Hill was a looming 9-metre (30-ft) facade on slightly raised ground, with castellated towers at the corners, embattled parapets and an entrance gate that had an octagonal tower above and an ostentatious portcullis below, 8 metres (27 ft) high, that was closed at night behind a heavy wooden door with iron rivets. The style was borrowed from the English Gothic vernacular and intended to evoke tyranny and dread so as to 'convey to the mind', the Commissioners said, 'a cheerless blank indicative of the misery which awaits the unhappy being who enters within its walls'.[12] This perimeter wall alone cost $200,000 to construct. Once beyond the deterrent effect of the walls and towers, however, the principles of reform took over. A long entrance corridor ran to a central octagonal rotunda, from which came (once they were all completed in 1836) seven separate blocks radiating out like spokes. From the cupola of this central octagonal room a guardsman could see down the corridors and across the grounds. When more buildings were added, a system of mirrors and reflectors was installed 'so that one guard standing in the centre of the rotunda may see throughout all the corridors'.[13] The plan featured here shows the classic shape of the hub-and-corridor radial prison.

Yet even in the process of completing the first plan of the prison to Haviland's design, the architecture was being forced to adapt to

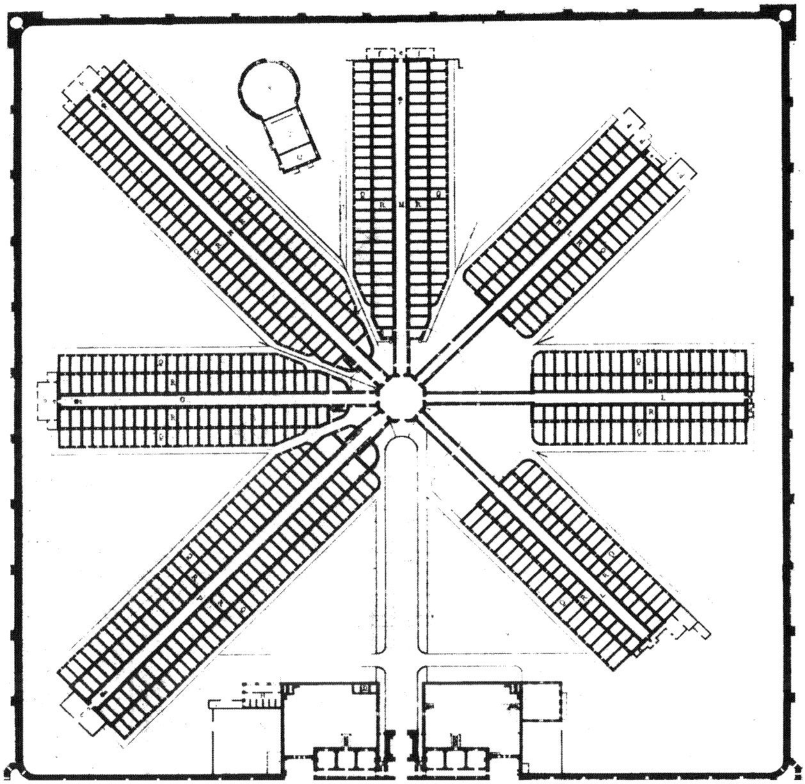

The 1836 plan of the wings of the Eastern State Penitentiary, Philadelphia, Pennsylvania. The number of wings doubled by the time it closed in 1970.

changing philosophies of incarceration. The first three blocks built were single-storey only, with very spacious cells (3.7 × 2.5 metres / 12 × 8 ft) and each provided with its own enclosed exercise yard, exactly as a solitary Carthusian monk might have expected in his pious solitude. There was a food-hatch, a one-way peephole, separate plumbing, and each was lit from above by what Haviland called a 'deadeye' in the ceiling, a ventilator and light reflector that was also meant, presumably, to figure as an emblem of the all-seeing Quaker 'Father of light'. All of these elements focused on reformation through solitary confinement.

Yet by 1829 the state had legislated a move away from this approach and mandated elements of communal labour in prisons: the separate system. As prisoners were now expected to move around outside the cell, the corridors became central spaces. Cell doors were moved from the rear of the cell to open onto the internal corridor, and a system developed with prisoners wearing masks and hoods to restrict their communication and destroy any sense of criminal community while in these communal spaces, or at work. The architecture had already been required to change: the prison was now turned inward and focused on its internal galleries, walkways and corridors. The authorities also had to respond urgently to a city population that was rapidly expanding and sending ever more people to gaol.

Consequently, the next blocks constructed were two storeys high – the size of the upper-level cells initially larger to compensate for loss of outside exercise space. This forced the need to supervise external exercise yards, and communication between cells now became much easier from the windows above, fundamentally compromising the core principles of penitence through silent reflection. The later blocks were also extended in length, further skewing the rational symmetry of design. Indeed, further additions transformed the ideal plan of the Eastern State Penitentiary into a chaotic, improvised labyrinth: three extra blocks were added in 1877, an eleventh in 1894, and a twelfth, of three storeys, in 1911. A thirteenth block of windowless cells for solitary confinement added a couple of years later saw the ironic return of a reformist method, but now used purely for punishment and containment of the most unruly inmates. The fourteenth block was built in the 1920s, with underground punishment cells, and a fifteenth in the 1950s. A model prison for 250 prisoners had turned into an overcrowded maze for nine hundred. It operated until 1969, before being shut down and sold to the city for one dollar. It has had a lively afterlife as a cult ruin, preserved as a National Historic Landmark, but principally now visited for ghost tours and events at Halloween. The decorative Gothic facade has infected the whole site,

A guard in one of the 1836 radial wings of the Eastern State Penitentiary.

which is now suffused with the shivery horrors it was initially built to banish with the sweetness and light of reformation.

At the height of its influence, it was an obligatory destination for important visitors. In 1831 the French diplomat and ardent political reformer Alexis de Tocqueville spent a whole week at the Eastern State Penitentiary on the invitation of Roberts Vaux, the Quaker chair of the board of governors. Tocqueville's researches at the penitentiary informed his famous study *Democracy in America* (1835). Only two years after its opening, Tocqueville visited a small gaol with large cells where prisoners were kept mostly in solitary confinement. He elected to visit every prisoner alone, without prison officials, and was impressed to find them all voluntarily in favour of this separate system (many had transferred from the overcrowded 'congregate system' in operation at the Walnut Street Gaol). 'It is incontestable', Tocqueville concluded, 'that this perfect isolation shelters the prisoner from all harmful contagion.' He noted, however, that solitude came with 'days full of phantoms' unless it was relieved by some form of communal labour. Ironically, all found Sunday, the religious day of rest spent entirely alone in spiritual reflection, almost intolerable.[14] Tocqueville publicly praised the system, but considered the cost of the gaol madness and unworkable in France.

Ten years later Charles Dickens also visited the Eastern State Penitentiary, virtually the only institution he crammed into a short stay in Philadelphia in 1842. He was polite to the earnest Commissioners and also spent time visiting those in the famous solitary cells, but his lengthy and savage denunciation of the system in his *American Notes* caused much offence. Of course, Dickens had traumatic experience of debtors' gaol as a child when his father was imprisoned. In debtors' gaol, the boundaries of the prison were much more permeable. Prisoners lived with their family, who were able to come and go for set hours during the day. In the penitentiary, it was the solitude Dickens found 'cruel and wrong'. Led to the central rotunda, 'from which seven long passages radiate', he thought 'the dull repose and quiet that prevails' in these 'dreary passages' was awful to contemplate. The black hoods worn by prisoners as they moved about were a 'dark shroud, an emblem of the curtain dropped between him and the living world'. It was a place of people 'buried alive' and in his interviews he read countenances that held 'a kind of horror, as though they had all been secretly terrified'. He thought short-term experience of solitary confinement might have some effect, but was certain the long-term effect was to destroy souls rather than reform them. After his visit he wrote privately to a friend: 'The prison is beautifully – exquisitely – kept, and thoroughly well managed: but I never in my life was more affected by anything which was not strictly my own grief.'[15] Dickens had a strikingly different response to the more communal use of corridor spaces in St Luke's pauper lunatic asylum in London, as we shall see.

Despite these reservations, the separate or 'Philadelphia System' and its radial design was the one imported to England at Pentonville Model Prison, which opened in 1842. The first National Penitentiary in England on Millbank in London was acknowledged as an expensive failure. It opened in 1816 to Bentham's over-elaborate design of six interlocking hexagons in a petal shape around a central inspection house, a plan that cost several million pounds and required 5 kilometres (more than 3 mi.) of labyrinthine corridors. Mayhew called it a 'gigantic puzzle' and 'ungainly', and it was demolished in 1893.[16] In contrast, Pentonville borrowed the radial simplicity of Philadelphia. Designed by the engineer Joshua Jebb, the Surveyor General of the new prison commission, Pentonville had four radial corridor wings, with three tiers on iron walkways under a barrel-vaulted ceiling, creating space for 520 separate cells. The corridors were flooded with light from cathedral-like windows, leaving no hiding place from the central observation point, which had sightlines down each corridor. Over the next few years, Jebb would follow this design in more than sixty new prisons across Britain, and his design spread across Europe.

The regime for prisoners at Pentonville started with eighteen months of strict solitary confinement; silent communal work came later as a reward. 'In the cell of the criminal', one of the chaplains of Pentonville wrote, 'his privations are aggravated by REFLECTION, by bitter recollections and anticipations.'[17] Prisoners lost their names, being referred to only by number (warders would be docked pay by their superiors if they were heard using names). In the corridor, prisoners wore sackcloth hoods with eyeholes and a restrictive peaked cap to hide their faces. At night, guards wore sack wrappings on their shoes to maintain strict silence and shuffled along the corridors, dimly lit with gas lamps. 'By the time the hour of nine sounds through the galleries,' Mayhew reported, 'all is as still as a catacomb.'[18]

Prisoners were compelled to attend the prison chapel on Sundays, where they were locked into a series of partitions within an ingenious structure of tiered wooden pews that isolated each prisoner in a blinkered box that only allowed them to see the priest. For the prisoner truly resistant to reformation, there were also the notorious 'refactory' or 'dark cells' in the basement, windowless spaces of confinement, a 'terrible place', Mayhew reported, with 'something intensely horrible in absolute darkness'.[19]

The commissioners of Pentonville were committed ideologues of the separate system. Their annual reports were staunch defences of a system that targeted the 'divine law of love' on the individual prisoner, the architecture finally in harmony with the principle of the reformation of character. From afar, the Philadelphian reformers declared London's Model Prison 'a triumphant refutation of anti-separation arguments'.[20]

The evidence on rehabilitation was skewed, however, because Pentonville at first only took prisoners awaiting transportation. The degree of their willingness to reform determined whether they would be reimprisoned when sent to the colony, or allowed into the community. There was little data to determine the rehabilitative success of the separate system, only lots of invested opinions. In 1847 William Crawford and Whitworth Russell, the main ideological advocates who secured the separate system in English penal policy, both died. This, combined with the inevitable constantly rising pressure on prison numbers, meant that the strict principles of Pentonville were loosened less than five years after opening. The assistant chaplain at Pentonville, John Burt, was forced into print to decry the reduction of the length of solitary confinement to nine months and the increasing kinds of destructive association being allowed. It meant for him that Pentonville was now, a decade from its triumphant opening, a lapsed system unable to undertake a 'general renovation of the moral character'. Instead, it was a technology that could only produce 'unchanged or imperfectly reclaimed' people.[21]

The mix of theological and utilitarian ideas underpinning the hub-and-corridor reform prison came undone fairly rapidly, then, as harsher conceptions of punishment prevailed. The 1865 Prisons Act finally transferred all British prisons to the central administration of the Home Office and also regularized a new regime of punishments. To supplement a short initial period of solitary confinement (now only one to three months), this separate system opened out to include deliberately pointless, crushing physical labour, including several hours a day either on the treadmill or the hand crank while being deliberately underfed under a careful system of 'scientific starvation'. 'Hard Labour! Hard Fare! Hard Bed!' was the cry of those who preferred the logic of deterrence.[22] In the later nineteenth century the biological determinism of new theories of 'criminal anthropology' (influential after the publication of Cesare Lombroso's utterly spurious *Criminal Man* in 1876) considered criminality a matter of biological inheritance. In this framework, reform was impossible: crime was in the very convolutions of the brain, the sinews of the body.

Yet the shape of prisons did not change even as the architecture slid out of sync with this pessimistic philosophy. Corridor structures built to distribute and separate prisoners soon became the principal locus for unregulated association – precisely what they had been built to avoid. It was the terror and humiliation of proximity that meant Oscar Wilde was sent first to Pentonville in 1895 before his transfer (on a public train) to the Gothic pile of Reading Gaol, built by George Gilbert Scott in 1844 on the same radial plan. The treadmill at Reading, as it was meant to do, destroyed Wilde's physical health and he died less than three years after his release. After Newgate was pulled down in 1903, Pentonville was also where executions took place. This was where Sir Roger Casement was executed for treason after the Easter Rising in 1916.

In 2015 nearly 1,300 prisoners were crammed into Pentonville Prison in terrible conditions, a place almost annually condemned in the reports of the Chief Inspector of Prisons. The Howard League for

408

WORKHOUSE FOR 300 PAUPERS,—GROUND PLAN, No. 1. (E.)

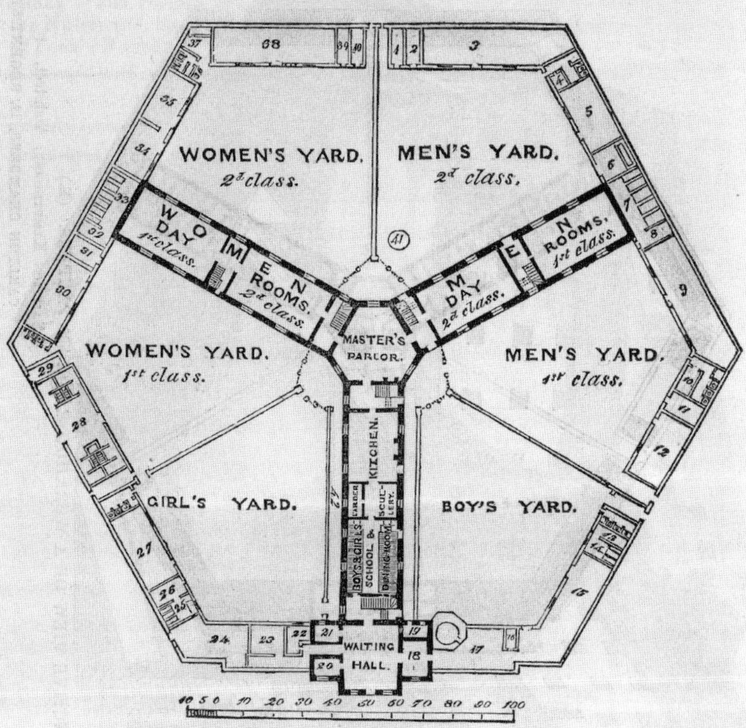

SCALE OF FEET.

1 Dead House.
2 Refractory Ward.
3 Work Room.
4 Dust.
5 Work Room.
6 Washing Room.
7 Receiving Ward, 6 beds.
8 Bath.
9 Work Room.
10 Dust.
11 Washing Room.
12 Flour and Mill Room.
13 Washing Room.
14 Receiving Ward, 3 beds.
15 Work Room.
16 Coals.
17 Bakehouse.
18 Bread Room.
19 Delivery Room.
20 Porter's Room.
21 Searching Room.
22 Store.
23 Potatoes.
24 Coals.
25 Receiving Ward, 4 beds.
26 Washing Room.
27 Work Room.
28 Piggery.
29 Slaughter House.
30 Work Room.
31 Washing Room.
32 Bath.
33 Receiving Ward, 6 beds.
34 Wash-house.
35 Laundry.
36 Dust.
37 Washing Room.
38 Work Room.
39 Refractory Ward.
40 Dead House.
41 Well.
42 Passage.

Hexagonal workhouse plan prepared by Sampson Kempthorne in the 1835 *Report of the Poor Law Commissioners.*

Prison Reform continues to campaign for reformatory principles from its Quaker roots, while politicians still appease populist tabloid demands for deterrence over reform. Once the ideal Model penitentiary, Pentonville was declared in 2015 by the Minister for Justice 'the most dramatic example of failure within the prison estate', no longer a corridic world saturated in divine light, but full of 'dark corners' where drugs and violence are dished out.[23] This is the trajectory of many Victorian reformist institutions that live on long after their ideological moment of design. Yet while the corridor plans of many Victorian prisons have survived in ill-adapted forms because the building of new institutions was no longer funded by a sense of civic duty, those of the workhouse had such a dreaded place in the collective imagination that very few have lasted in recognizable form today.

The Workhouse: Corridor and Anti-corridor Plans

The British state's commitment to the reformation of character in the early nineteenth century was best exemplified in the arrangements for the New Poor Law of 1834, after a report orchestrated by Bentham's former secretary Edwin Chadwick. Relief of the poor was to be administered by a network of boards of local worthies, distributed evenly across the country to encompass the entire population. Within ten years there were nearly six hundred Poor Law Unions, and each one was required to build a central workhouse. The system demanded that charity must be administered only through entry to the workhouse, where the living and sleeping conditions and the quality of the food had to be demonstrably worse than outside, making it the 'less eligible' option in order to maintain a strong deterrent. The Royal Commission under Chadwick expressed the view that 'work, confinement and discipline will deter the indigent and vicious', and the hated Poor Law tests became the device to separate the poor from the paupers, the deserving from the undeserving.

This reform was always about framing the new concentrations of the urban poor inside the strictures of productive labour, and to manage criminal vagrancy. Even someone as ostensibly enlightened as the socialist Robert Owen considered the environment of his factories and communal quarters as fine-tuning what he called the 'machinery' of his workforce. Working-class agitators, though, like William Cobbett nicknamed this new architecture of coercion *bastilles,* after the Paris prison whose liberation had signalled the start of the French Revolution. When scandalous details emerged of reduced rations that forced labourers at a union in Abingdon, England, to gnaw on the rancid animal bones they were meant to be crushing for bonemeal in 1845, the fear and loathing of the system grew.[24]

Large-scale workhouse buildings had been established after the Gilbert Act of 1782, when parishes were allowed by law to form unions to share the infrastructural burden of housing the poor. The first wave of Unions built after 1834 (more than three hundred went up before 1840) were designed like prisons with the intent to intimidate, terrify and deter. Some had Gothic facades that towered over the slums, asserting their implacable rule over the populace, although there was a strong resistance to frivolities of ornament in these ideologically Utilitarian buildings, making most of them functional and plain in the early years. Their internal spaces were divided by gender and age, separating man and wife and children from parents. Like prisons, this separation favoured designs with wings, often in cruciform or radial shapes. The barrack-like living and working quarters forced a collective association, but not out of any real reformatory principle and certainly not out of the socialist ideals that had shaped the internal structure of the phalanx. Rather, living communally – in public – was simply the worst punishment the middle-class framers of the law could imagine. Living in halls and dormitories and along corridors was meant to *shame.*

The Royal Commission suggested four model designs for Union workhouses in 1835.[25] Sir Francis Head offered the courtyard form, very much like a closed medieval cloister, to house up to five hundred of the rural poor, dividing the sleeping space into rooms of 3 by under 5 metres (10 × 15 ft), each dormitory to sleep eight. These dimensions were determined to be no larger than the space of a workman's cottage, 'well built, substantial rooms being a luxury'.[26] This design was only adopted in Head's local Kent Union. The three other plans were the conception of Sampson Kempthorne, a young and inexperienced architect who got the job purely through family connections to the new Poor Law Commission. The first was a Y-shaped radial form, dividing a hexagonal ground-plan into six partitions, allowing neat division into the separate categories designated by the Poor Law (three for aged and infirm women, able-bodied women and girls, another three for infirm men, working men and boys). The first of these was built by Kempthorne at Abingdon in 1836. His second plan was of four wings in a cruciform shape, easily the most regularly used as it was the most adaptable in terms of scaling up or down, or adding extensions as the pauper population expanded. His third design for a smaller workhouse for only two hundred was barely used, given that the economic recession that started in 1837 deepened in the 'Hungry Forties' and numbers seeking workhouse relief grew. Kempthorne was criticized for loosely adapting radial prison designs (possibly by Chadwick himself in an anonymous denunciation in the *Illustrated London News* in 1846), and his influence was limited when he decided to emigrate to New Zealand in 1841.

The next twenty years of large-scale, single workhouse structures were dominated by two architects. George Wilkinson designed several around Oxford before moving to Ireland with a commission to build the entire network of nearly 130 workhouses, completed between 1838 and 1843. Kempthorne's assistant was a young George Gilbert Scott, who established his own practice with William Bonython Moffatt. Scott and Moffatt built more than fifty workhouses in the 1840s, the later ones escaping the harsh utilitarian strictures of local commissioners to explore 'Elizabethan' styles in more rural areas (as at the Dunmow or Amersham Unions). In the cities, the pressure of the parish poor, and the growing problem of 'casuals' or vagrants, pushed the creation of larger buildings. Marx's ally Friedrich Engels denounced the terrible conditions in England of Manchester's 'Poor Law Bastille', which housed 1,200 in 1845. A vast edifice was built for the Greenwich Union in 1844, with a long central corridor that had to be barred by gates periodically to keep different classes of inmates separate. The old City of London, known to be a jurisdiction rich with charitable institutions, was the area most beset by 'casuals' seeking food and lodging for the night in the capital, particularly in the harsh winters. The city solved this problem by using a workhouse located over 6 kilometres (4 mi.) across London in the poorer district of Peckham, intended to displace a population that was considered worryingly disorderly and riotous. Later, the commissioners built the City of London Union in the East End on Bow Road, 'externally, at least, resembling an Italian palazzo', says one historian sardonically.[27] This housed eight hundred, but was strictly for the aged and infirm and refused to take the able-bodied.

This specialization of function was a key shift in the 1860s. The 1834 plans were all single buildings, complexly divided. The problem, as with prisons, was that the rigidity of architecture could not keep up with the changing ways of categorizing the poor. On top of the initial divisions, the young were soon divided between infants and children (ages seven to thirteen), and then were added the categories of 'harmless lunatics and imbeciles', the sick, aged married couples who should be allowed to lodge together, probationers, and casuals or vagrants. Separate solitary cells were required to punish the refactory: these were for Reform's ungracious resistors.

The historical survey of fifty years of building included in *Knight's Guide to the Arrangement and Construction of Workhouse Buildings*, published in 1889, was most critical of this middle period of simply expanding buildings into monster workhouses. Between 1850 and 1870 the design had moved from dormitories with window ventilation on both sides to a larger scale where 'wards and dormitories were arranged along both sides of a central corridor'. Ventilation and thus health was badly affected:

> The corridors in the lower storeys were but poorly lighted, and gratings provided in the floors of the upper corridors for the purpose of lighting the lower ones serve to diffuse the impurities of the atmosphere throughout the entire building . . . It is difficult to conceive of any arrangement of a building . . . better calculated to act prejudicially on the health of the inmates.[28]

In consequence, after changes to the Poor Law in the 1860s, workhouse buildings separated out many of their functions. The infirm and pauper lunatics were housed in separate hospitals and asylums; children were placed in separate schools (although many still suffered from ophthalmia as a result of the unhealthy conditions). There were even branch schools set up in seaside towns like Herne Bay and Broadstairs for what were called 'delicate and scrofulous children'. Vagrants were addressed by other laws and institutions. When, as in cities with dense populations, different workhouse buildings were situated on the same site, *Knight's Guide* had useful tips about how to link the buildings together while maintaining their separation. This was to be done strictly by 'covered walkways', open to the air if possible, like colonnades. 'Enclosed corridors between several blocks or pavilions should be avoided.'[29]

In an influential report on workhouse infirmaries written by Edward Smith in 1866, the guidance was that any corridors must be 'light and airy' and always 'leading to the outer air at the end of each set of wards'.[30] These were separate 'pavilion' designs that aimed to maintain healthy circulation of air in wards, and emerged from Florence Nightingale's relentless campaign of hospital reform.

It is worth pausing briefly to acknowledge the immense influence on health institutions of Florence Nightingale's *Notes on Hospitals*, two papers issued as a short book in 1859. Nightingale, the legendary 'lady with the lamp', became an English heroine of the Crimean War for her defiance of the conservative Army Medical Corps in Turkey, where she had volunteered to organize a team of nurses to treat the troops. The battlefield losses were massive in the Crimea, but the hospitals set up by the army managed to kill off a further 19,000 British troops from the avoidable transmission of communicable diseases. Nightingale noted, through rigorous statistical analysis of mortality rates, that it was safer to be treated in temporary medical tents than to enter the death trap of the Scutari Hospital. As a result, Nightingale issued imperative orders about the building of healthy hospitals.

Her pavilion plan isolated the ward, which came off at right angles from a long corridor that purely serviced controlled access to the wards. This meant each ward was able to have windows on both sides, to secure a healthful crosswind, and to alternate beds with windows. This was entirely driven by Nightingale's adherence to the incorrect 'miasmatic' theory of disease (that illness was generated from foul air), but it inadvertently assisted the isolation of disease pathogens anyway. Nightingale's plan was profoundly anti-corridic, regarding any functional use of corridors other than as pathways as extremely dangerous and an enemy to health. 'Without the most perfect ventilation, there is always more danger of effluvia being driven by a draught till it accumulate in one part of a very large ward, as was the case in the long corridors of Scutari,' she said.[31] Nightingale's ceaseless badgering of the authorities meant that domestic hospital architecture began using her designs in the 1860s. The most prominent multiple pavilion hospital was St Thomas's, rebuilt opposite the Houses of Parliament on the Thames, which opened in 1871. It had six ward pavilions, each four storeys high, all built on the same cross-ventilated design. The whole complex was serviced by a 274-metre-long (900-ft) corridor. This was the origin of the bewilderingly long hospital 'link' corridor. The pavilion design was dominant for thirty years, after which steel-frame and elevator technology allowed hospital wards to be stacked on top of each other in towers.[32]

Some of the earliest pavilion link hospitals were infirmaries built to service the pauper poor through New Poor Law requirements. For instance, the Chorlton Union Workhouse in Manchester was one of the first to be organized on this separate set of pavilions around a central cruciform building, able to house 1,500 souls for reform. However, the constant local pressure to keep building costs down still often resulted in large, lowering, labyrinthine single structures that now brought further opprobrium from health reformers.

The specialization and separation of functions in Poor Law institutions reveals how the New Poor Law drove the development of a network of large public institutions: infirmaries, geriatric homes, schools, asylums, hospitals and dosshouses. When the post-war Labour government finally abolished the last remains of the Poor Law in 1948 with the National Assistance Act, many of these buildings became council housing or were transferred into the National Health Service. If they were not demolished but remodelled and repurposed by extension and alteration, the physical presence of the workhouse faded from the terrain. What survives is a strong cultural memory of an architecture that was principally designed to shame, intimidate and deter. There is no starker contrast to this intended effect than the reformist aims of the new asylum.

The Reform Asylum: The York Retreat Corridor

The reform of the treatment of the insane in this period followed a similar path to prisons, from undifferentiated confinement in almost completely unregulated private and charity institutions in the eighteenth century towards a network of large-scale public buildings by 1850 that were complexly subdivided. In the new asylum the cure was meant to be effected by 'the architecture itself, the organisation of space, the way individuals are distributed in space, the way they move around it'.[33] Unlike the prison or workhouse, though, corridor spaces were not merely there to distribute people to the cells where the actual work of reform was done in contemplative solitude. In the asylum, the corridor *itself* was often meant to serve as the passage to health, a space that, if properly used, could become a technology that reintegrated the inmate back into the social world beyond the asylum enclosure.

The whole era of institutional reform is often summed up in one iconic event, which is located in the madhouse. This is the moment in 1797 when Dr Philippe Pinel broke the chains that bound the two hundred men incarcerated on the lunatic ward of L'Hôpital Bicêtre in Paris. Pinel was a post-Revolutionary appointment tasked to bring reform to the chaotic world of this gigantic hospital. Although it was a combined effort of many doctors, Pinel was said to have made a revolutionary gesture equivalent in symbolic importance to the storming of the Bastille by freeing the patients from their restraints. He sought to overturn the idea of the mad as filled with a bestial rage that could only be locked away with criminals, and instead spoke 'in favour of the moral qualities of maniacs' and their 'most estimable virtue'.[34]

The year before, in England, a group of Quaker reformers led by Samuel Tuke opened the York Retreat to treat members of the Society of Friends (more widely known as the Quakers) who had lost their wits. This was in response to revelations about the horrifying conditions in the local asylum, where the Quaker Hannah Mills had died six weeks after her committal, all requests to provide her with religious consolation denied. The York Retreat signalled the birth of the 'moral treatment', again emerging from the dissenting, religious margins but which became the adopted public method of treatment over the course of fifty years. In 1838 Lincoln Asylum pioneered the lifting of all 'mechanical restraint' from its patients, a tactic more famously adopted by John Conolly when he became the superintendent of the Middlesex County Asylum at Hanwell, then Britain's largest institution, the following year. By 1845 the ending of restraint and moral treatment in vast asylum structures – one for each county – was established in British law by the Lunacy Act and the County Asylums Act. It remained the dominant mode of treatment until new medical paradigms emerged in the late nineteenth century. Moral treatment also dominated the building of state asylums in America in the nineteenth century, with the corridor plan at the centre of asylums constructed on the model of the pioneer Thomas Kirkbride. Like the radial prison, these vast public asylums long outlived the philosophy that built them. Their therapeutic value was openly questioned, yet they were occupied for decades after, and only began to close in the 1980s, their structures often left to rot, becoming minatory ruins on the edges of towns.

Let us start with the famous York Retreat, which opened in 1796. After the incarceration and death in appalling circumstance of Hannah Mills in the general asylum at York, the Society of Friends raised funds to build an institution that would embody, Samuel Tuke explained, 'a more mild system of treatment' in accord with the principles of the reformation of the soul.[35] The *Description of the Retreat* (1813) offers a detailed account of the building. It was set in grounds with large, unbarred windows to provide aspects onto the gardens, so abolishing all echoes of the prison. The bilateral symmetry of the main block had its administrative core at the centre, and two wings, laid out on a straight corridor (unusually for 1813, the plans use the term 'corridor', although the textual commentary only refers to the 'gallery'). Men occupied the ground floor, women the first floor; there was also a class separation, with patients of the 'higher class' given rooms in the centre of the block, away from the main corridor. Ribbons of cellular rooms for the majority of patients were distributed on both sides of the main corridor, again with unbarred windows and disguised locks and simple bedheads, all designed to dispel any notion of restraint. There were dayrooms at each end of the corridor, gender segregated like the exercise gardens outside. The double-loading of the main corridor Tuke somewhat regretted, 'for, though a large portion of light is admitted, by the windows at each extremity of the building, yet, the galleries on the ground floor, at least, are rather gloomy.'[36]

The 'moral treatment' at the Retreat used no coercion, no corporal punishment, no fear or menaces, and was instead premised on Quaker principles of an appeal to the kernel of the moral and rational soul that survived the onset of madness. 'Insane persons generally possess a degree of control over their wayward propensities. Their intellectual, active, and moral powers, are usually rather perverted than obliterated.'[37] The tactic of persuasion, of an appeal to the 'desire for esteem' in patients, was about the limit of treatment. And it was the space of the building, its focus on social conformity in the communal spaces of the dayroom or the reward of dining with the director in the main block, that was meant to push inmates back towards the norm. There was already a quiet recognition that there were sometimes recalcitrant cases that refused to respond after the managers of

The Retreat in York, the Quaker asylum that opened in 1796. This view of the north front is from Samuel Tuke's *Description of the Retreat* (1813).

the Retreat raised more money to add a separate annex, called 'The Appendage', on the site. Tempting the redeemable back into sanity required their absolute segregation from the incurably or resistantly insane, the catastrophic indifferent mixing that was criticized in old madhouses by John Conolly at the start of his career. Already this early asylum embodied the reformatory path to sanity in its spatial design: on the far edges, the recalcitrant or incurable; along the corridor, moving ever closer towards the rational administrative centre, were stages marking the degrees towards the return to sanity. In the Retreat, the corridor was a suasive device, an orderly, rational design, its social pressures almost more important than the cellular rooms where patients slept: 'Architecture itself was moralised.'[38]

The Retreat was very influential, despite its capacity to treat only about thirty residents, and only those from its own Quaker community. Samuel Tuke's principles were used for the much larger Wakefield Asylum, built in 1819 with three storeys and eight long gallery wards. Wakefield's published plans and elevations then became an early model for scaling up the reformist lunatic asylum.

Attempts to extend this model and to abolish the cruelty and indifference of the for-profit private asylum system were consistently blocked by vested interests through the early nineteenth century. The Madhouse Act of 1828 allowed for the first system of inspection, but only in London and its environs by doctors who were easily corruptible. A national Lunacy Commission and the requirement to build large county asylums arrived in 1845 with the pressure of the evangelical reformer, the seventh Earl of Shaftesbury. He dominated the Commission for forty years and was wedded to moral treatment and often resistant to new medical ideas about insanity.

Before the rise of the county-funded asylum in the era of reform, there was also a network of large charity hospitals dedicated to the care of lunatics. The most famous of these, the Hospital of St Mary of Bethlem, in London, had been relocated from its medieval monastic building in Bishopsgate to a vast building beyond the city limits

Fourth gallery of the Retreat, York (shown in 1887).

in Moorfields, first erected in 1676 and then extended with wings in the 1720s. It had a classical Greek frontage that was nearly 207 metres (680 ft) long, with echoes of the Tuileries Palace in Paris, and traversed by a long single gallery said to allow 'for a gentle breeze'.[39] But behind the orderly architecture the chaos of indifferent incarceration ruled. For a fee, this spectacle of madness could be visited, much like a visit to the zoo, 'with cells opening on wide galleries where visitors still amused themselves by mocking the patients through the hatches in their doors'.[40] As a site of depravity, Bedlam featured as the final, terrible destination in William Hogarth's 1733 series of paintings 'A Rake's Progress' (and the engravings that followed two years later), where the spaces depicted are nightmares of disorder. This version of Bedlam, built on inadequate foundations, soon began to crack and sink into the London clay.

To establish a different kind of charitable treatment, a group of reformers began to raise funds in 1750 for what was to become a new model charity institution, St Luke's Hospital for Pauper Lunatics. It was initially located very pointedly next to Bedlam, but moved in 1786 to a grand purpose-built institution at Old Street on land owned by Bart's Hospital. Here there was less use of physical restraints, no public visits allowed, and cases were treated at much lower fees

Engraving of the second Bedlam Hospital, built at Moorfields outside the city walls of London in 1676.

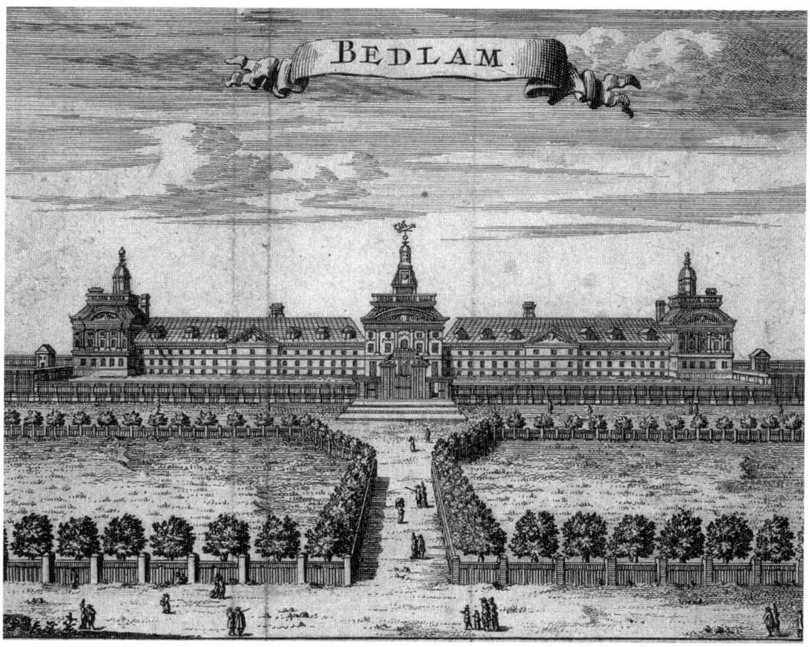

Mid-19th-century illustration of St Luke's Hospital for Lunatics, established in 1751.

than its Bedlam rival. The Old Street building had a high enclosing wall, but beyond it George Dance, aided by John Soane, built an elegant classical building in brick with a Greek portico and symmetrical wings, separating men and women, that produced an imposing frontage along Old Street that was 152 metres (500 ft) long. It was designed to house three hundred patients.

The distinguishing feature of the internal space was the very wide galleries for the wards. The individual cells had small high windows covered with wire and so were very dark. In contrast, the galleries – at least as they were illustrated in the aquatint published by Rudolph Ackermann in the third volume of *The Microcosm of London* (1808–10) – were flooded with light from long windows (other reports, however, tended to stick with the adjective 'gloomy'). The prospect from the wards was somewhat blighted by the detail that the male ward overlooked the pauper cemetery attached to the hospital.

Charles Dickens noted the gallery spaces on his Boxing Day visit to the hospital, reported in *Household Words* in January 1852. The outward aspect of high walls and 'dismal little iron-bound windows' prepared him for gloomy incarceration, the individual cells of solitary imprisonment that had appalled him at the Eastern State Penitentiary. He noted that the cells still had grooves in the floor and walls where restraining chairs had been nailed to hold patients down. But these were traces of a regime abolished after the Lunacy Commission began regular inspections from 1845. In the 'long, long gallery' of both the female and male wards, Dickens instead came across social spaces of eccentric communality:

> I passed into one of the galleries on the male side. Three men, engaged at a game of bagatelle; another patient kneeling against the wall, apparently in deep prayer; two, walking rapidly up and down the long gallery arm-in-arm . . . one man, with a newspaper under his arm, walking with great rapidity from one end of the corridor to the other.[41]

He went on to witness a Christmas carol concert with a choir of patients, giving his approval to these signs of intrinsically social rather than solitary therapeutics. St Luke's became the model for many of the charitable lunatic hospitals built before the 1840s and clearly had an influence on the wave of reform institution plans. Samuel Tuke was known to have visited it before building the York Retreat. By 1837 W.A.F. Browne's book *What Asylums Were, Are, and Ought to Be* thought that the 'long and spacious gallery', which could be 'used as a common hall and as a work-room, or as the place where the night keeper or nurse may watch', was central to the 'perfect asylum', an achievable Utopia.[42]

Thomas Kirkbride's Corridor-plan Asylum

At mid-century, asylum architecture obviously shared the transformation in scale and extent of other reformatory institutions, but continued to emphasize the therapeutic importance of the corridor. The single most influential figure in this regard was the American doctor Thomas Kirkbride, responsible for massively extending the asylum on a linear corridor plan. As with the prison reformers, Kirkbride came from the Quaker community. He trained as a medic in Philadelphia, specialized in psychology, and then helped design and build the Pennsylvania Hospital for the Insane, a symmetrical Neoclassical building in spacious landscaped grounds. It was conceived as moral architecture, and was opened to much acclaim in 1841. The plan scaled up the York Retreat, using a rational administrative central hub and grand entrance with symmetrical linear wings built on 3.7-metre-wide (12-ft) transverse corridors double-loaded with rooms, leading to shorter end-wings, placed at right angles, with even wider corridors. As with the Retreat, later additions included separate blocks, placed further out from the main block, for incurable (or unreformable) patients.

Kirkbride was representative of the new professionalization of asylum treatment in medical terms, helping to launch a new Association of Medical Superintendents and the *American Journal of Insanity* in the 1840s. The distribution of patients to separate wards was now done on a differential diagnosis of their *type* of insanity by a new kind of expert, the 'alienist', not just on general categories of gender, class or wealth. Indeed, Kirkbride considered madness 'the great leveller of all the artificial distinctions of society', affecting all classes, with no blame attached other than to a vague sense that the 'high state of civilization' was causing an increase in nervous collapses.[43] The key to asylum treatment was the firm belief that the patient must be removed from their social and family environment, but be given asylum with patients on wards at the same degree of difference from the norm. The stages of cure could be marked by a progressive movement along the corridor, from outlying psychotic wards at the far end, through the general paralysis and dementia wards towards the gentler nervous disorders. More privileges and private space were accrued as you moved through the wards, and the closer you moved to the superintendent's rooms, the closer it was to the social and rational norm – and the exit. Punishment might mean a move back down the wards – a system that was still in operation in the 1940s, as recorded in Mary Jane Ward's autobiographical novel about her committal to an asylum, *The Snake Pit* (1947), which became a celebrated Hollywood campaigning melodrama.

As in Britain with its County Asylums, America developed a State Asylum system, which provided one major asylum per state. These structures became gigantic institutions because they followed the linear corridor principles laid down in Kirkbride's *On the Construction, Organization and General Arrangements of Hospitals for the Insane*, first

New Jersey State Lunatic Asylum at Trenton, which opened in 1848.

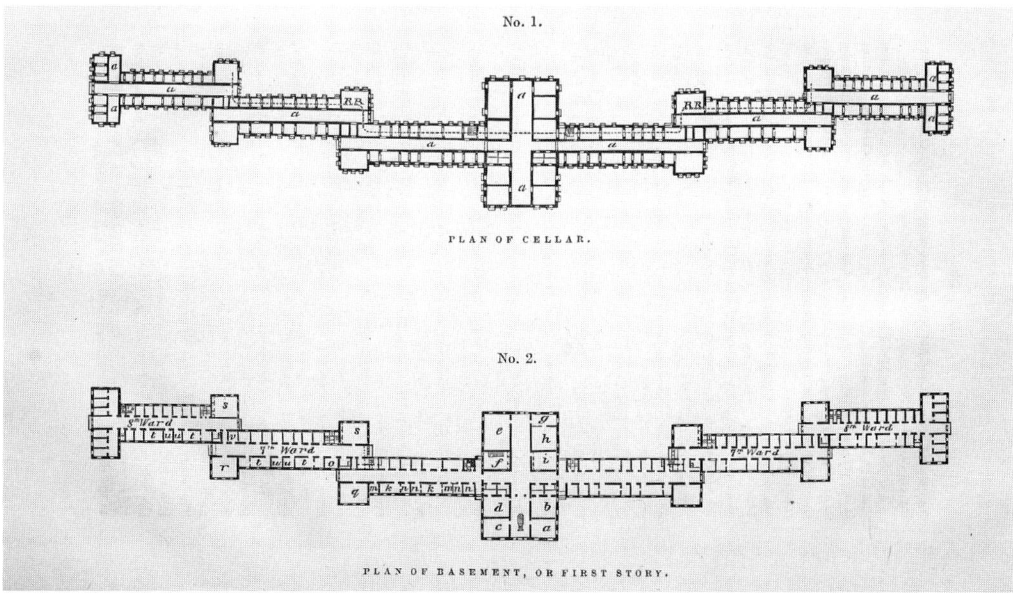

The Kirkbride Building, built in 1883, at Oregon State Hospital, Salem.

published in 1854. He advocated building asylums to be populated by about 250 patients in 40 hectares (100 ac.) of land built to be retreats but accessible by transport, on city limits. By this point, Kirkbride's classification required eight subdivided corridor wards on each gender-divided side of the central administrative building, meaning sixteen corridor wards stretched along a vast facade: 'The rooms are arranged on both sides of the corridors which are twelve feet wide and have their extreme ends mostly filled with glass.'[44] To allow light in at either end, and for ventilation, Kirkbride's designs often used chevron patterns (sometimes called 'broad arrow' plans), setting back each additional ward as it was added, so that the extended linear design was not in a straight line, but staggered. The wings were generally only two storeys high, in a plain unadorned style, but Kirkbride did suggest producing an imposing central block to signal the authority of the medical and administrative hub. These often adopted Gothic styles. This was the archetypal architecture of the asylum as *persuasive institution*, and some of the largest reformist structures ever built. They spread across America and held a dominant role in asylum architecture for the next thirty years, Kirkbride's ideas pushed by Dorothea

Lynde Dix, a passionate campaigner for asylum-building. A gigantic structure like the New Jersey State Hospital at Trenton went up in 1848; upstate New York was served by the Hudson River State Hospital built in Poughkeepsie, which opened in 1873. It was designed in High Gothic style by Frederick Clarke Withers and extended to more than 457 metres (1,500 ft) in length. Many asylums were so large that villages grew up around them to provide staff and services.

Historian Nancy Tomes suggests that Kirkbride's linear designs reflected the classless nature of American society – and perhaps they can indeed be seen in parallel to the aspirations of the Associationists, who were building utopian phalanxes in exactly the same era. Britain, in contrast, had more 'class-specific forms of architecture and management'.[45] This may be too crude a divide, however, for the County Asylums system adopted the same monumental style of the single dominant structure in the 1840s. The most important figure in England was the professional asylum superintendent John Conolly.

Conolly had been an indifferent doctor and inspecting physician for Warwickshire asylums before his appointment as Resident Physician at the Middlesex County Asylum at Hanwell in 1839. Conolly was celebrated as the superintendent who finally brought Pinel's ideas of freedom from mechanical restraint to Britain, although he had observed this earlier under Robert Gardiner Hill at Lincoln Asylum. Conolly's 'mild and humane treatment' and his radical decision to teach a lecture course on insanity *in situ* with patients rather than in the lecture theatre placed him at the centre of professional alienism, running new journals and chairing new bodies.[46] In 1847 he ventured into architectural matters with *The Construction and Government of Lunatic Asylums*, aware that a major period of construction was to commence shortly after the 1845 Acts. He was concerned that there was no master plan for the asylum and wanted to avoid 'unscientific' ad hoc designs by architects with no understanding of the needs for treatment. Conolly noted that Pinel's devoted pupil Jean-Étienne Esquirol had commented on his experience of designing his own asylum at Rouen, and knew of Maximilian Jacobi's work on asylum construction in Prussia, which favoured either Rouen's quadrangles or the Glasgow Asylum's radial forms, but disliked the 'lineal form' of the York Retreat, 'where its inconveniences have long been felt, and yet are only partially remedied'.[47] Even so, Conolly concluded that of the available plans there was 'none so convenient as one in which the main part of the building is in one line'.[48] These were to be even more extended than the Kirkbride plan, because the bedrooms were located on one side only: 'It is evident that a building of this shape, long and narrow, consisting of a succession of galleries or corridors, with bedrooms on one side only, may be moderately perflated by every wind that blows – an advantage extremely salutary.'[49]

Conolly was precise about the ideal proportions of the county asylum corridor, 4 metres (12 ft) wide and 3 metres (11 ft) high. At this size, 'spacious, well-lighted, cheerful galleries' meant that 'what are called dayrooms can scarcely be required' – and were easier to supervise and surveil. Conolly reinforces the asylum corridor as a key therapeutic device and as the principal social space for patients. He was also explicit on distributing 'the noisy, the refractory, and the dirty' to the far ends, and approved of the solution adopted at Derby Asylum to avoid disrupting calmer wards by moving these patients around the building 'by means of a corridor on the outside of the building, running underneath the windows'.[50]

Conolly was the principal adviser to the building of the new county asylum for Middlesex at Colney Hatch, designed by the architect Samuel Daukes on this linear corridor plan. When Colney Hatch opened in 1851, the *London Daily News* recorded that 'It is not only the largest lunatic asylum in the world, but it is hereafter to be regarded as the model for all other asylums in this and other countries.'[51] Built for 1,250 beds, the structure was slightly longer than the Crystal Palace, which had opened just two months before in Hyde Park. The comparisons are sustained: like the Crystal Palace, Colney Hatch was 'flooded with light; there is not a dark corner in the whole

Middlesex County Pauper Lunatic Asylum at Colney Hatch, designed by John Conolly, and opened in 1851.

of it'; like the Crystal Palace, Prince Albert took a close interest in the asylum and praised it as a model of advanced social engineering, an emblem of British modernity.[52] It was then the largest single standing structure in Europe and could claim to have the longest corridors too – more than 9 kilometres (6 mi.).

The complex at Colney Hatch was first extended in 1857 because it could already not meet demand, and it was continuously extended throughout the nineteenth century, reaching a peak of 2,500 in-patients in the 1890s (an improvised wooden extension burnt down in 1903, killing more than fifty patients). The Colney Hatch corridor plan was soon replicated in other monster asylums around the perimeter of London and across the country. By 1914 there were 119 county asylums with over 100,000 patients.[53]

In the 1860s the sensation fiction melodrama craze in Britain frequently involved plots of wrongful committal to both public and private asylums, most famously in Wilkie Collins's *The Woman in White* (1860). Eminent alienists found themselves involved in very public court cases and caricatured in lurid popular fictions. Conolly

The link corridors of the Middlesex Asylum at Colney Hatch, sometimes claimed as the longest in Europe.

was the model for Dr Wycherley in Charles Reade's exposé of the private asylum system, *Hard Cash* (1863). Scandals similarly engulfed the 'suburban palace-prisons' of America, with a famous exposé of the Bloomingdale asylum and Pennsylvania Hospital in *The Trial of Ebenezer Haskell* (1869). The medicalization of the role of the asylum superintendent also increasingly questioned the therapeutic value of moral treatment, the same sort of doubts that had crept into prison reform. As biological determinism, neurological studies of the brain, and theories of inevitable degenerative decline suffused alienism, the reform principles of moral management were eclipsed. Yet the buildings remained and were even further expanded, the new medical taxonomies of mental illness forced to improvise divisions of the old architectural space.

Design modifications did occur through the century that displaced, to a degree, the linear corridor plan. Wards were separated on the 'pavilion' design, with the main 'link corridor' returned to its purely instrumental, connective function. This was a result of the tendency to merge the asylum into the hospital system, and again showed the influence of the reforms of hospital architecture pushed through by Florence Nightingale. There was also a later nineteenth-century shift to the villa or cottage system, moving away from the single monumental structure towards smaller buildings scattered across a rural setting. This was a system pioneered on the Continent by Albrecht Paetz in Gheel outside Leipzig, which aimed to abolish all associations with not only prisons but giant asylums, looking instead for a new ideal of a small community for healing with no obvious boundaries between the sane and the insane, sometimes even bleeding directly into already existing villages with a system of 'fostering' the mad into the wider community.[54]

Yet because the state and county asylums remained so dominant in a perpetually underfunded system in England and America, these corridic structures remained the ones that dominated the imagination of the lunatic asylum. The pulp modernism of Sam Fuller's film *Shock Corridor* (1963), for instance, takes place almost entirely in the corridor of the ward called 'The Street', intended for patients to socialize but frequently a place of chaotic breakdown. In this central corridor the *Daily Globe* reporter, who has feigned madness to get inside the asylum to break a story, slowly descends into a real 'catatonic schizophrenia'. The corridor is evidently now seen as an environment that induces lunacy rather than cures it.

Anti-corridic Anti-psychiatry

This was a suspicion that grew after 1945, marked by the radical experiments of asylum director Franco Basaglia in Italy from 1946, the 'anti-psychiatry' movement that emerged around R. D. Laing's *The Divided Self* (1955) in Britain and its sustained attack on the asylum, and the critiques of Michel Foucault in France with *The History of Madness* (1961) and Erving Goffman in America with *Asylums* (also 1961). Goffman researched his study from the inside of St Elizabeth's Hospital in Washington, which then had 7,000 patients. He declared the asylum to be a 'total institution' that, after the waning of any hope in moral persuasion, had become 'forcing houses for changing persons', places where the 'territories of the self are violated' by erasing the boundary of self and environment.[55] Goffman's long-term immersion in the hospital meant that he was able to track what he termed the 'underlives' that developed in unobserved corners of the regime, 'free spaces' in toilets, porches, disused basements or hallways that became tolerated autonomous zones. Goffman examines a short hallway at right angles to the main administrative corridor, 'large, high-ceilinged, and cool', that became a refuge in summer, or another hallway 'between the dormitory and the maintenance offices'.[56] Rather than the technology of the ward corridor, these are spaces of refusal, where the autonomous underlife is tolerated, even encouraged by an overburdened official regime.

In 1967 Mayer Spivack published his study 'Sensory Distortion in Tunnels and Corridors'. This was an analysis of the strange effects associated with a 905-metre-long (2,970-ft) link corridor, which took twenty minutes to traverse, and the very long ward corridors in the vast complex of an unnamed Veterans Administration Hospital in America. In a building that treated upwards of 1,000 schizophrenic patients, among others, Spivack argued that such corridors were like 'looking down a gun barrel' where, 'because of the extreme length and uniformity of the passageway, one feels no sense of progress'.[57] Because of the slight slope, Spivack continued: 'One feels victimized here. Something inexplicable is happening as one walks along, disoriented in space and time, fighting gravity to climb forever to a far door while growing enormous, or compelled by the slope to race downhill.' He worried that these 'weird echoing spaces' exacerbated illness and were the 'nuclei' for the growing cultural unease about the hospital as a dehumanizing machine.[58] Spivack's study was at the very end of the life of the monster hospital complex stitched together by corridors, tunnels and walkways. The move to abolish hospital corridors and to open up the plan with atria modelled on hotels or malls instead started soon after in the Medical City development in Dallas in 1974.[59]

In 1961 the then British Health Minister, Enoch Powell, condemned the failing asylum system. He was speaking at the vast Cane Hill Asylum in Surrey, which was dominated by a brick service tower:

> There they stand, isolated, majestic, imperious, brooded over by the gigantic water-tower and chimney combined, rising unmistakable and daunting out of the countryside – the asylums which our forefathers built with such immense solidity to express the notions of their day. Do not for a moment underestimate their powers of resistance to our assault.[60]

This last rhetorical flourish, at least, was prescient: Powell undercut an entire system, but offered no real alternatives. Asylum treatment limped on into the 1980s, when Sir Roy Griffiths produced an advisory report for the government, *Community Care: Agenda for Action*, which formed the basis of the Community Care Act in 1990. At its core, this Act called for the wholesale de-institutionalization of the mentally ill and the closing of the asylum system. It took an equivalent length of time to start to close the state asylums in America.

In consequence, we are still surrounded by the ruins of this reformist asylum system. Often the core Victorian buildings have heritage protection, but the sites have proved somewhat resistant to repurposing, and many stand empty until arson or neglect prompts their demolition. Parts of Colney Hatch became luxury flats, renamed as Princess Park Manor to erase their history. Cane Hill in Surrey, where Enoch Powell announced the end of the asylum, only closed down in 1991 and became a wild ruin until the site was almost completely demolished in 2008 (only the chapel, main administration building and the famous water tower remain). Before that Cane Hill was a destination for urban explorers and 'place hackers'. Indeed, asylum ruin photography is a subgenre in its own right, producing many coffee-table books. Mark Davis's *Asylum* typically offers a cover with a shot of a vanishing perspective down a ruined wide corridor from the West Riding Pauper Lunatic Asylum, and the book is replete with such images, the walls peeling, the ceilings cracked or open to the sky, the angles low and menacing down the hallways to emphasize the distance. The genre requires 'corridors leading to unseen destinations' and if possible abandoned psychiatric paraphernalia of rusting bedsteads or ominous signs of surgery or restraint. John Gray's *Abandoned Asylums of New England* does the same for notorious ruins like the vast Gothic pile of the Kirkbride-plan Danvers State Hospital, which was only finally demolished in 2007.[61]

These ruins of modernity stand as a 'cipher for the temporal and spatial doubts that modernity always harboured about itself'.[62] Ruined asylum corridors point down pathways built with tremendous optimism in reformist theology and enlightened scientific progress, projects now left in tatters. The ruin is ambiguous because it is meant to testify to our advance over a naive or primitive past, and yet unnerves with the sentiment it invokes about our own inevitable future. There is a standard Latin tag for the contemplation of ruins: *sic transit gloria mundi* (so pass all the glories of the world), cemented in English literature by Percy Shelley's 'Ozymandias' or the settings of the

Gothic romance. Because asylum architects often favoured Gothic facades, the corridors and rooms of this reform institution have merged with the tradition of ruined castles, haunted houses and mad doctors intent on monstrous experiments. It takes mere seconds for the TV series *American Horror Story: Asylum*, for instance, to invoke every single one of these clichés in its opening episode. The couple trespassing along the ruined corridors of Briarcliff asylum are swooped back in time to the early 1960s, when mad doctors and evil nuns persecuted the inmates in tiresomely conventional ways. This feeds on the Gothic anxiety of horrifying return, only what we fear now is not the feudal tyranny or Catholic priesthood that menaced the writers of the eighteenth-century Gothic but the dismantling of the agency of the self and its coercive reconstruction by the Victorian reform institution. The architecture of the asylum persisted the longest of all these reformatories, long into the late twentieth century. This is why it continues to grip our imagination.

I could end this chapter here, at this bleak assessment of the failures of the project of reform by corridor. The prison, the workhouse and the asylum, although they had different spatial distributions and purposes, were ultimately all incarceral and coercive. The failure of these particular architectural mechanisms of reform is one of the reasons why I think we now associate corridors with menace and dread. Even the monster hospitals, dedicated to managing sickness and cure, became dystopian places. These institutions all crawled out of the belly of utopian religious, scientific and administrative ideas of earnest Victorian reformers, but ran aground.

And yet, just to emphasize that there is nothing intrinsic about this set of affects, let me briefly turn to a couple of other Victorian reform institutions where the architecture of the corridor had somewhat different associations.

School and University Corridors: To Infinity and Beyond!

The education system must also be considered part of the great reformist ambition for the fabrication of virtue in the nineteenth century. In Foucault's view, every aspect of school space was part of the new biopolitical diffusion of power: 'The space for classes, the shape of the tables, the planning of the recreation lessons, the distribution of the dormitories (with or without partitions, with or without curtains), the rules for monitoring bedtime and sleep periods – all this referred in the most prolix manner, to the sexuality of children.'[63] The Marxist theorist Louis Althusser considered education and its architectural forms as the principal Ideological State Apparatus in bourgeois capitalist societies, designed to reproduce the relations of production, '*realized* in institutions, in their rituals and their practices'.[64]

In England, systematic state school reform came later than mainland Europe, with the Elementary Education Act of 1870 and its subsequent extensions in 1881 and 1890. This shift to compulsory state education, with a network of school inspectors to enforce it, prompted the formation of school boards and a massive programme of school building in the early 1870s. The first architect of the London School Board, Edward Robson, undertook a comparative survey across Europe and published his findings in *School Architecture* in 1874. There was a great deal of attention paid by reformists to the Prussian hierarchy of different educational state institutions, now that Germany was emerging as the main rival to English economic dominance. Matthew Arnold had unequivocally praised the Prussian education system as superior to England at every level, from elementary to their polytechnics and universities, and lamented the English suspicion of state education (and its cost) in his report to the Schools Inquiry Commission in 1868.

In Prussia, students were separated out by gender and age and distributed into separate classrooms along the central corridors of the *gymnasium* building. The school-teaching convention in England, in contrast, had been to collect all students into one large hall, with one teacher supervising the whole through a few student assistants. This was cheaper, considered more efficient (one teacher could supervise up to 1,000 children), and had been codified in the 1810s by the Quaker Joseph Lancaster, among others, as 'the monitorial system'.[65] The 'barn' style of school halls was overtly modelled on the new factory, and factory schools disciplined children into a life of industrial labour. This had been the whole point of Robert Owen's New Institution for the Formation of Character at his factory complex in Lanark: to maximize the efficiency of his 'living machines' by moulding his subjects from a very early age.

Sixty years later, Robson tried to find an architecture of reform for the London School Board that took the best from the evidently superior continental system, but retained aspects of the English assembly hall. His designs were intrinsically suspicious of corridors as essentially redundant, a 'luxury and waste' for buildings underpinned by local taxation, the same spirit that rendered workhouse architecture rudimentary and unadorned. Robson insisted that 'the corridor considered only as a passage should be eliminated as far as possible' and if corridors appeared they were either there only for morally dubious displays of 'style and show' or else otherwise showed bad design, 'a want of forethought'.[66] Corridors limited ventilation and multiplied staff costs as it required more staff to maintain full surveillance of school space. The only use for covered galleries was sometimes for outside areas, for physical exercise and military drill – spaces that were sometimes called 'marching corridors', echoing the disciplinary forms of military barracks and parade grounds.

The German *gymnasium* was evidently a suspect model for Robson. In the early years of the London School Board, a model Prussian-style school was built in Stepney, but was judged a failure. After Robson moved on to another post and was replaced by T. J. Bailey in 1884, the London School Board soon found a local vernacular style that marked out these state schools among the slums of Whitechapel or Shoreditch. Passing through Clapham Junction by train, a sentimental Sherlock Holmes exclaims to Watson: 'Look at those big isolated clumps of buildings rising up above the slates . . . Lighthouses, my boy! Beacons of the future!'[67] The London School Board style developed a hybrid Queen Anne design, which was seen as more secular and progressive than the Gothic. The schools rose out of the surrounding streets in three high storeys in London red brick, with large sash windows, pedimented gables and hipped roofs. Inside was a central assembly hall, usually with classrooms leading directly off it (still no corridors!) – a model eventually fixed as a much-reproduced plan by the prolific architect J. J. Stevenson and codified by Felix Clay in *Modern School Buildings* (1902).[68]

By 1914 the longitudinal corridor of the German *gymnasium*, combined with the idea of pavilion classrooms along corridor spines taken from the Nightingale hospital, became the norm in English school designs. My own state school (built in 1939) was typical in having a central assembly hall with a long spine corridor leading to two quadrangle blocks – the sciences slightly elevated above the arts – at either end. I still dream about those corridors, which at least had recessed windows onto the internal courtyards, providing some hiding places from the swishing cane of the roving deputy head if you had been sent to stand in the corridor.

It was around 1914, too, that British universities embraced German educational ideas and their corridor architectures. For centuries, the 'ancient' English universities retained the cloistered medieval quadrangles of their monastic origins. The scholastic tutorial system of education did not require large halls for lectures or demonstrations: the cell remained the basic architectural unit. The first modern reform universities in Britain appeared in the nineteenth century, at first in often makeshift spaces until local philanthropy and civic pride in London (University College in 1828 and King's College in 1831), Birmingham (Queen's College in 1828), Manchester (Owens College in 1851) and other cities began to build their own 'beacon' monuments to higher education. These were designed in what became codified by the 1860s as 'Collegiate Gothic', still based on broadly quadrangular plans, although often scaled up. Another wave of civic university construction in northern industrial towns in the 1870s was retrospectively grouped under the term 'redbricks'. The focal buildings of these establishments, built in the city centres of Leeds, Liverpool or Newcastle, were imposing structures, often on a vast scale. In 1912 W. M. Childs complained of 'buildings of imposing frontage, storey above storey . . . full of echoing corridors and stone stairways'.[69]

As Matthew Arnold had recognized, the economic power and influence of the newly unified Germany was a result of its efficient modern state institutions, including its technical education and the scientific research universities that had been established in Berlin (1809), Bonn (1818) and Munich (1826). Unchanged medieval scholasticism in England, combined with a suspicion of both state funding and the new scientific knowledge's challenge to traditional authorities of classics and theology, saw Britain face serious competition in the latter half of the nineteenth century. In his introduction to Friedrich Paulsen's outline of *The German Universities* of 1906, the English university reformer Michael Sadler warned that 'we are still far behind Germany in real appreciation of the fruitfulness of disinterested but systematic research, and of the value of scientific precision in the administration of public affairs.'[70]

As research institutions, German university buildings distributed their space in different ways, requiring lecture halls for theoretical elaboration and laboratory spaces for practical exercises. Universities were not tiny communities cloistered away from society, but public buildings with flexible spaces distributed along communal corridors. Corridors where staff and students mingled and moved between classes also carried their own pedagogical opportunities for the informal circulation of knowledge, even the sparking of new connections. Rather than a place of punitive differentiation or separation, the university corridor adopted from Germany has become emblematic of a certain utopian conception of interdisciplinarity. Sociologists of corridor conversation in educational institutions (of which there are seemingly very many) still see these as liminal spaces where 'there are multiple interdisciplinary and learning opportunities' precisely because they are informal and dynamic spaces outside the classroom.[71]

One of the most sublime adaptations of this German model was realized in Boston when the Massachusetts Institute of Technology moved across the Charles River from the town centre in 1913. The new MIT building, designed by William Welles Bosworth, had an exterior in a Beaux-Arts style, but the elements of the plan were linked together by a long transversal east–west corridor to allow passage through the campus. This corridor was intersected at right angles with snaking symmetrical corridors on each side of the lateral building, forming open arms onto the river-front, and producing a corridor 251 metres (823 ft) long. This is known as 'the infinite corridor', and it has since been extended seamlessly into other buildings after first opening in 1916. The idea of this corridor was to allow the scientific disciplines to flow into each other seamlessly, encouraging new connections.[72] As you walk the double-loaded corridor, glass walls periodically allow you to see into laboratories or classrooms, ponder mathematical problems left on blackboards, read oblique messages left on the pin-boards, or pause in social spaces built under the cupolas in various lobby-junctions. The corridor is a space of student rituals – the nose of George Eastman (inventor of the roll-film Kodak camera and MIT benefactor) on the bronze frieze in one lobby is shiny because students rub it for luck before examinations. The corridor also becomes the occasion for scientific experiment when, twice a year, the long transversal corridor aligns with the Sun like Stonehenge, flooding the entire length with sunlight. Since 'MIThenge' generates enormous crowds in the corridor on these occasions, there is even a website announcing the next conjuncture and the social etiquette for the

The Infinite Corridor at Massachusetts Institute of Technology,
the utopia of interdisciplinarity.

best viewing experience. Just as the corridor plan was entering into crisis in the asylum or prison, the university was adopting it as a new generative space for scientific-technical advance.

This optimistic corridor plan was carried into the post-1945 era of massive university expansion in England. These new universities were planned on the campus model, an American term derived from the open 'field' settings for universities that were in contrast to the cloistered Oxbridge quadrangle.[73] In the post-war era of grand plans, the campuses of the so-called 'plateglass universities' – Sussex, York, UEA, Essex, Lancaster, Kent and Warwick – were 'conceived of as a continuous whole rather than a set of separate blocks', linked by concrete walkways and plazas like the megastructures of social housing dreamt up by radical town planners.[74] Essex University had the most radical vision of Brutalist high-rises and elevated walkways, although budget cuts inevitably curtailed its full realization. Michael Beloff, the old Etonian and Oxonian who coined the rather sneering term 'plateglass

Two vistas down the 'Red Route' Corridor, University of Leeds, designed by Chamberlin, Powell and Bon, and built between 1963 and 1975.

universities' in 1968, called these campuses 'anti-human', full of neon light and harsh metal and glass surfaces. They seemed to him to be 'sited along or between corridors and always places of transit, never places of rest'.[75] Another malcontent proclaimed of Manchester University in 1965 that

> The architects and planners have pronounced our doom . . . It is to spend the rest of our days in this university . . . in identical cells, forever wandering down long, dark tunnels, lurching against doors that will always open the other way, searching for the numbers alone that will distinguish one cell from another.[76]

All the same, these grand visions could also produce impressive gestures of utopian interdisciplinarity. The expansion plans for Leeds University in the 1960s were overseen by the modernist practice Chamberlin, Powell and Bon (who built the Golden Lane and Barbican 'social condenser' housing projects). The design unified different scientific disciplines along a continuous concrete corridor that was meant to stretch from the halls of residence to lecture rooms (separated into a magnificent single block) to different disciplinary units that were modular and thus could be reconfigured according to unforeseen future changes in knowledge. The initial vision was to extend this corridor beyond the campus and into town. The surviving sections are far longer than MIT's 'infinite corridor': Leeds University thus reached to infinity – and beyond. Now known as the 'Red Route', joining buildings together in corridors on slender concrete podiums, it seems like another lost vision of corridic campus utopianism in the brief moment when university expansion was properly funded. It was typically left incomplete by budget cuts in the late 1960s, leaving the principal architect, Peter Chamberlin, in bitter dispute with the university, the dons privately advising that he needed psychiatric help. Even so, the Leeds project was 'formative for every subsequent proposal' for cohesive university campus design.[77]

Like the hospital, contemporary university spaces now tend towards the model of the shopping mall, with large open atriums and a suspicion of corridors as anything other than fire exits to be hidden in the backroom parts of the service infrastructure. Atriums are the new model of interdisciplinary fluidity. Within a year of opening, however, the scientists of the £700 million Francis Crick Institute in London, the most advanced scientific research complex in the world, designed expressly to encourage cross-disciplinary collaboration, complained that the building was 'too noisy to concentrate'.[78] Researchers wanted offices, corridors, doors that could close. There's no pleasing some people.

This long history of the corridor in the reform institution reveals the continuing conviction that architectural space can make and remake the citizen-subject of the modern state. Just as often, it suggests that utopian conceptions and dystopian results are coiled within each other, but unpredictably, helping to create our sense of profound ambivalence about the public corridor.

Nearly every architectural space I've explored so far in this book has linked the corridor to public buildings and the apparatus of the state. But the nineteenth century was also the era when the private space of the domestic house was transformed by the arrival of the corridor.

7

Passages to Privacy: The English Gentleman's House

So far this history has focused on the meanings of the public corridor and the multiple functions it has served in distributing the space of new kinds of public institution. Yet modernity is marked by the simultaneous transformation of the architecture of the private house too, and it is the pivotal arrival of the corridor in the domestic sphere that I now want to consider.

In terms of domestic architecture, the authors of the monumental *A History of Private Life* track the development of the house from the communal Anglo-Saxon hall to increasingly separate and specialized spaces. These spaces include the division of the *solar* (the lord's family retreat) from the more public hall in the medieval period, and the emergence of specific rooms such as the *camera* (a space to store the most valuable family documents), which originates from the French term *chambre*, the bedroom and its *ruelle* (the boxed-in space between the bed and the wall furthest from the door) and the *studiolo,* cabinet, closet or study for retreat or retirement, based on the model of the monk's cell. The technology of the fluted fireplace allowed for further domestic differentiation in the Renaissance. Rather than a single, central fire, there were now separate rooms with lower ceilings that could contain fireplaces. With more internal room divisions, this allowed for an increasing separation of both master and servant, and the male and female members of the household.

The Palladian villa, transported to England in the seventeenth century by Inigo Jones and others, starts to show the recognizable shape of the modern house plan, 'the true type of the English home', as one architectural history put it in 1904.[1] The rational order of the narrow Georgian house plan has proved remarkably enduring. In England the migration to urban centres in the eighteenth and nineteenth centuries housed that population typically in terrace or row houses that could be scaled up or down depending on wealth. The majority of labouring class two-up, two-downs had no hallway; the lower middle classes with five or six rooms had a half-hall entrance from the front door to the stairwell, imperfectly dividing the front and back of the house; larger houses used halls, landings and passages to distribute functionally differentiated rooms. Semi-public parlours versus private (with-)drawing rooms, the division of space between the sexes and between the family and servants – these become the axes for the domestic dramas of Victorian middle-class domestic life. This is the first lesson of the private corridor: its existence and extent precisely marks out the hierarchies of social class.

Nevertheless, for the majority, as Orest Ranum observes: 'Despite the installation of innumerable hallways, doors, antechambers, and partitions in old buildings, there may have been little increase in privacy before 1860.'[2] This way of organizing domestic space is strikingly modern and really blossoms in the Victorian era, reinforced by a bourgeois ideology of separate private and public spheres. By the Edwardian period, the corridor has been declared 'the chief instrument for achieving privacy' in the English middle-class home: 'it was essential to have passages, or corridors, so as not to have to go through another room, as was so often the case in continental dwellings.'[3] Indeed, the German author Hermann Muthesius observed in his 1904 study *The English House* that 'the most striking difference is the lack in England of communicating doors between the rooms, which means that the only access to a room is from a passageway or hall. Thus the English room is a sort of cage, in which the inmate is entirely cut off from the next room.'[4]

In what follows, I want to look first at the impact of the corridor on the aristocratic stately home, starting with the building of the Grand Corridor at Windsor Castle for George IV in the 1820s. Then I'll turn to the key textbook of High Victorian domestic architecture, Robert Kerr's *The English Gentleman's House* (1864), which makes the corridor the pivot of the house's whole design, whatever its budget and scale, but which obsesses anxiously about its contradictory functions of separation and communication. A sense of how this anxious domestic circulation is played out in nineteenth-century domestic fiction can help consolidate the place of the corridor in the domestic imagination. I'll make a final turn to what is surely the apotheosis of the private corridor: the bizarre network of miles of underground tunnels and corridors built over 25 years at Welbeck Abbey by the eccentric fifth Duke of Portland, who spent millions on his system of passages to avoid the shame of being looked at.

Windsor Castle's Grand Corridor, 1829

I outlined the arrival of the corridor in Vanbrugh's borrowings from palazzo designs at Castle Howard and Blenheim Palace in Chapter One. The proper domestication of this form, however, took place later, alongside the arrival of the long tangential corridors in public reform institutions and the rise of corridic public spaces such as arcades in the early nineteenth century.

For centuries an important royal seat, the Windsor Castle complex had become a messy accumulation of old buildings, falling into a period of neglect under the mad king George III, and was in urgent need of modernization. The scandalously spendthrift Prince Regent spent vast sums on the architectural follies of Brighton Pavilion and the Royal Lodge in the grounds of Windsor as he waited for his father to die. When the Regent became George IV in 1820, he sent John Nash to build Buckingham Palace at great expense and a competition was opened for plans to modernize the Upper Ward at Windsor, the old palace built by Charles I and left largely unchanged. The circulation or movement between rooms was poor and often improvised from a chaotic interior. In 1823 the project was given to the king's favourite architect, the plain-speaking Derbyshire builder Jeffry Wyatt (shortly to change his name by permission of the king and to be knighted as Sir Jeffry Wyatville). Wyatville was set a strict budget of £150,000, overseen by parliamentary committee to keep a tight rein on the expense, although in the end the changes cost over £900,000.

Wyatville transformed the exterior silhouette of the Upper Ward into a picturesque faux-medieval castle with fanciful towers and crenellations, but the interior was very modern. At the heart of the modernization was a new way of connecting the formal State Rooms to the Private Apartments of the Royal Family. This new method of communication got rid of improvised *enfilades*, the cascade of one room into another that had never been as successful as the carefully wrought perspectives of the Sun Palace at Versailles or the grand procession of halls along the Neva River facade of the Winter Palace in St Petersburg. Instead, the elements of the Upper Ward were linked by the new architectural device: the corridor. Wyatville had already experimented with modernizing corridors in his reworking of the ancient aristocratic seats of Longleat and Toddington Manor, working to improve their internal circulation. At Windsor Castle he linked the southern and eastern sides of the Upper Ward's quadrangle of buildings together with a continuous corridor along the first floor. Wyatville pushed the king to think of this corridor as no longer a purely functional channel but the chance to create a grand processional space. Its name, the Grand Corridor, seemed to stabilize by the 1840s, having been called the Long Gallery or Great Gallery in the plans. It was in three sections, the South Corridor, the Angle of the Corridor and the East Corridor, and ran continuously for 158 metres (520 ft), 6.5 metres (22 ft) wide for much of its length, although it tapered in places as it negotiated awkward older elements. The longest single section was the East Corridor, at 90 metres (300 ft). It was framed by deep royal

Joseph Nash, *South Section of the Grand Corridor* (Windsor Castle), 1848, watercolour.

red carpets and draperies, had a flat-panelled cornice ceiling with gilded gold detailing, Gothic window seats designed by A.W.N. Pugin, and was lined with artworks in matching frames (including the royal collection of paintings by Canaletto). The length of the corridor was marked out by 41 identical marble pedestals to display an array of busts that consolidated the genealogy and power of the British throne. Indeed, the redesign of the State Apartments meant the corridor ran towards St George's Hall and the Waterloo Room, new ritual spaces fashioned by Wyatville, the Waterloo Room being a celebration of the 1815 victory over the French and a mark of the renewed imperial power of the British state. Meanwhile, a suite of private rooms was constructed for the Royal Family, all accessed from the corridor. Given all the pomp and circumstance of the State Rooms and the embrace of a rooted nationalist Gothic for the new Upper Ward, George IV ironically preferred to decorate these private rooms in French style. This was a new spatial arrangement that was markedly middle-class even in its grandiosity. The Grand Corridor was therefore an intrinsically hybrid structure.[5]

When it was completed in 1829, Lady Dover proclaimed that 'The first *coup d'oeil* of the long gallery or corridor is the most strikingly beautiful thing you can conceive . . . it is now splendidly furnished and lighted, filled with pictures and admirably arranged.'[6] George IV had already declared Wyatville the official architect at Windsor and even suggested naming one of the new towers after him. The King died in 1830, however, and his successors ended the spending spree and the patronage of Wyatville.[7]

Joseph Nash's 1848 book of lavish prints, *Views of the Interior and Exterior of Windsor Castle*, was a glimpse into the private world of Queen Victoria and her Consort twenty years later. There were three prints of the corridor, grandly termed 'a noble and spacious ambulatory'.[8] The print of the South Corridor used the classic single-point perspective to emphasize its length, the eye led along the framing carpet and panelled ceiling into the vanishing point. The East Corridor, the longest, was noted for its 'beautiful specimens of cabinet-work, consisting of buhl, marquetrie, ebony, and other inlaid objects of use or ornament'. It is the prints of the Queen's White, Green and Crimson Drawing Room and the Private Dining Room and Sitting Room, though, that take the viewer beyond the more public and processional elements of the design. For Nash, the prints of these private spaces offered 'a truly royal picture of the domesticity of a great Monarch', and a later courtier confirmed that the 'great corridor itself' was 'sacred to the private life of Queen Victoria'.[9]

At Osborne House, the Queen's retreat on the Isle of Wight built in 1848 with the enthusiastic close participation of Prince Albert, the main house was organized around galleries that separated family and guests, and a long link corridor completely separated the family from the servants' block and the more public events associated with the ballroom (which was accessed by its own corridor). While regally appointed, these spaces were also in a recognizable distribution that could be imitated in houses up and down the scales of class and privilege. This is how the Grand Corridor led towards a more general adoption of the device in the Victorian period. The key book for disseminating this plan was Robert Kerr's *The English Gentleman's House.*

Robert Kerr's Anxious Corridors, 1864

Robert Kerr was a quintessential establishment figure, a professor of architecture at King's College in London, a board member of the Royal Institute of British Architects in its early years, and from 1862 the District Surveyor for St James's in Westminster. His guide on how to build the ideal house was pristinely orthodox too.

Kerr's sketch of the architectural history of the English house is surely the first to be organized around the epochal arrival of the corridor. The quest for privacy in pre-modern domestic architecture was entirely hampered by being pre-corridic, in Kerr's view. Kerr complained that the thirteenth century might have seen the emergence of parlours and withdrawing rooms, but 'thoroughfares through all rooms alike were too common.' He marked the design of Oxburgh Hall in the fifteenth century as important for its innovative passageways, but 'there are as yet no continuous corridors', with 'a large number of external doors towards the court, and internal doors of intercommunication between the rooms, [which] constitute an awkward substitute'. The Tudors saw the benefit of 'the addition of internal Passages (although not many of these)', but with Hengrave Hall in Suffolk, completed in 1538, we finally arrive at the opening of the epoch of the continuous corridor. Kerr thus dates the first sight of this innovation much earlier than Vanbrugh's Blenheim

Palace, whose spaces of circulation he declares 'deplorable'. Even the central architects of the Enlightenment, like Robert Adam or Colen Campbell, fail to learn this lesson: 'one that is more singular perhaps than all else, as indicative of positive want of skill, is the striking deficiency of ordinary Passages, and the readiness which is universally exhibited to create thoroughfare-rooms – not excepting even the chief apartments of the house'. This suggests it is only Kerr's contemporary Victorians that have truly finally grasped the centrality of the corridor. The historical ground has been cleared of rubble, and Kerr can establish the first principles of how to build the English Gentleman's house along a continuous scale from the smallest parsonage to the grandest palace.[10]

Kerr's overriding architectural aim is to multiply privacy, using rooms and passages to enclose the family. 'It is a first principle with the better classes of English people that the Family Rooms shall be essentially private, and as much as possible the Family Thoroughfares.' Even in the very smallest gentleman's house (he simply ignores what he calls 'dwellings of inferior class'), there should be a clear divide between family and servant quarters, and either separate corridors or routes established so that 'the family have free passage without encountering servants unexpectedly, and let the servants have access to all their duties without coming . . . unexpectedly upon the family or visitors'. In an admirably blunt statement, Kerr declared: 'Whatever may be their mutual regard and confidence as dwellers under the same roof, each class is entitled to shut its door upon the other, and be alone.'[11]

Kerr works through the elements of the ideal house, separating public reception rooms, guest and visiting rooms from private family rooms, women's withdrawing rooms and men's smoking rooms, libraries, studies and billiard rooms, before marking out upstairs bedrooms, boudoirs and dressing-rooms, and the distinct functions of the servants' quarters below stairs, the separate gendered worlds of the domestic offices of the butler's pantry, the kitchen and housekeeping. As Kerr progresses through the plan of the house, it is the thoroughfares and corridors that become the pivotal devices to separate these demarcated zones. The 'whole is greatly dependent on the means of communication – the Thoroughfares communicating them. To confer upon these a proper degree of importance is most essential.' He calls thoroughfares 'the skeleton of its plan' and devotes a chapter to these, followed by a more specific taxonomy, entitled 'Gallery; Corridor; Passage'. For these gradations, Kerr confidently stated, 'a Corridor is a wide and stately Passage: a Gallery is a wider and more stately Corridor.'[12]

In these chapters, Kerr tries to balance the need for compactness – to avoid passages that are 'involved and circuitous' – with a recognition that privacy requires multiple routes or 'lines' through the house: family thoroughfares, public routes between central halls, dining rooms or saloons, the separate routes for servants, and the pathways to bedrooms, nurseries or the gardens. The contradictory forces are evident, since every route requires a clear line through the house, yet also wants to curl around ever more enclosed, private spaces. On the one hand, Kerr commands that the design should 'avoid as far as may be possible for all principal routes of intercommunication twisted and involved lines', yet on the other needs to separate the family's Principal Corridor from any unexpected passage of the domestic staff. Kerr ends up with the almost impossible injunction: 'let the route of a servant to and from the entrance be so contrived as to cross the Corridor in some almost unobservable way.'[13]

These tensions became evident in Kerr's own design for the grand country retreat Bearwood House in Hurst, Berkshire, built for John Walter III, the proprietor of *The Times*. Commissioned as a result of the publication of *The English Gentleman's House* and completed in 1870, the plan multiplies thoroughfares and passageways to illustrate Kerr's philosophy, with separate subdivisions of corridors for different classes of servants, family and guests, and the nursery wing. The house, which was given up as a family home and became a school in

1921, was judged 'impossibly unwieldy' in Jill Franklin's survey of the country houses built in the Victorian era: 'The entire plan is a show-piece of Victorian specialisation and segregation, and a prize example of how cumbersome the final result could be.'[14]

When J. J. Stevenson wrote *House Architecture* in 1880, a book that proved influential on the next generation, the sensibility and economics of house-building for the gentleman had shifted. There was less chance of a large body of servants, and less 'veneration for the upper classes'. Consequently, houses were more compact, with shorter corridors – long corridors being best avoided as 'not beautiful' as they risked ending up looking 'like a railway tunnel'. 'All space occupied in passages is lost,' Stevenson warned, 'increasing the size without adding to the accommodation of the house.' Instead, corridors were to be short stubs, broken up by windows and staircases and flooded with light from light-wells, the design in general avoiding 'passages where one must grope his way in the dark'.[15] Late Victorian and Edwardian houses were built on different principles from Kerr's distinctly mid-century, High Victorian ideals. Even so, the German commentator Hermann Muthesius observed in 1904 that it was 'still a major concern in the English house that the paths of the servants and of the family and visitors shall never cross – a requirement that a designer does not always find it easy to meet'.[16]

Kerr wanted the gentleman's house to be a machine that worked cohesively yet acted at the same time to hold apart a complex array of functions, bodies and classes. The corridor was the hinge, the juncture that ensured both connection and separation. It was, therefore, 'a spatial-social paradox' at the heart of the Victorian house.[17] No wonder it is a place in the domestic economy that is often rushed through or overlooked in house histories, because it is commonly a liminal space of passage that is at once over-determined in its imprecise multiple functions yet under-determined compared to the settled insignias of status and function that mark, say, the drawing room or the parlour. The English middle classes secured their domestic identities in the 'eruption of objects' that stuff the parlour – all that heavy furniture, fire screens, antimacassars, photographs, knick-knacks, ornamental glass, net curtains, draperies, hearthrugs, candlesticks, vases, and clocks.[18] This is the dense semiotic environment where bourgeois selves are secured. Yet the family also sits amidst their precious commodities, as Walter Benjamin once observed, reflecting on the origins of detective fiction in the nineteenth century, 'tremulously awaiting the nameless murderer' to steal into the room from the passage outside.[19]

What is evident on reading Kerr is that his segregation of private space, enclosed rooms placed in ribbons along corridors, has to be grasped dialectically with the reconfiguration of the public sphere and the rise of large-scale institutions in the nineteenth century. The workhouse is humiliating precisely because it removes a middle-class conception of privacy from notions of 'home'; public housing along shared corridors is demonized because it is the exact inversion of the idealized Anglo-Saxon home as retreat, as drawbridged castle. In Kerr, this privacy of the home was a privilege of class and wealth. *The English Gentleman's House* did not consider any house below the cost threshold of £1,250. His one contribution to the fervent mid-Victorian debates about social reform and the structural inequalities of laissez-faire capitalism came with his lecture 'On the Problem of Providing Dwellings for the Poor in Towns' in 1866. In this, he claimed that needless social niceties were prudishly demanding that poor families needed a minimum of three bedrooms, but Kerr was quite content that the poor required only one shared room for the whole family that could be built at £70 per unit and rented for 4 shillings a week, thus solving the housing crisis in an instant. The coarse nerves of the poor obviated any question of 'delicacy' in this plan.[20]

It is seemingly only in aristocratic palaces or houses that a corridor might accumulate sufficient interest to be worthy of architectural comment, whether at Windsor Castle or for instance the semicircular linking Family Corridor of the Curzons at Kedleston Hall, built (perhaps) by Robert Adam in the late eighteenth century and stuffed with *objets* that speak of family and colonial history.[21] As I have observed, though, guidebooks like *How to Read Houses* or anthologies of writings on everyday domestic space routinely overlook passages and corridors, despite their pivotal role in the distribution of space in the house. It's for this reason that Victorian domestic fiction can provide a more telling resource for exploring the fraught social space of the corridor.

Domestic Fictions/Crooked Corridors

Charlotte Brontë's *Jane Eyre: An Autobiography* (1847) works its plot through the spaces of buildings very precisely. *Jane Eyre* is staged as a progression through six houses, each very exactly described. Jane's tumultuous inner life, pulsing between constraint and escape, is exteriorized in her pathways through buildings. As Karen Chase has observed, Jane is 'ceaselessly engaged in the opening and closing of windows and doors, the ascending and descending of staircases, the crossing of thresholds . . . [and] rooms and passages serve as inner and intricate spaces.'[22]

In the Gateshead house, Jane is a class anomaly, the loathed penurious cousin, marginalized in the domestic family space, forbidden the drawing-room or parlour, and pushed to the back stairs or servants' quarters. She retreats to the very edge of the house to hide in window seat nooks. The traumatic punishment of being locked in the red room is amplified with sounds from the 'outer passage', Mrs Reed coming 'along the corridor . . . rustling stormily' – a repeated scenario of threat throughout the novel. Jane is next sent to the 'Orphan Asylum' of Lowood, an evangelical 'charity' school of sorts. This is revealed subjectively in Jane's journey 'from compartment to compartment, from passage to passage, of a large irregular building' when she first arrives. Brontë accurately describes the evangelical 'monitorial' system of teaching, all eighty starving girls kept together in one large hall, divided by task, constantly ranked, surveilled and punished. Compliance through shaming is further enforced by shared dormitories that destroy any last vestiges of the private self, and prove fatal when typhus strikes.[23]

Jane's third home, at Thornfield Hall, shows Brontë's subversive attack on the country-house ethos. There is a tradition of panegyrics to the manorial lord who in the seventeenth and eighteenth century, during periods of immense social instability, came to symbolize a social microcosm of order, hierarchy and continuity.[24] But instead of this, Thornfield is riddled with patriarchal disorder and Gothic secrets. Jane is again a class anomaly in this house, this time as the paid governess. She occupies servant spaces in the house and is aligned with the housekeeper, yet she is also expected to sit in drawing rooms, where she is slighted at evening entertainments by her supposed class equals and again chooses marginal nooks and crannies to avoid attention. She is barely tolerated there and never invited into the more informal class intimacy of the dining-room or the billiards room, unlike Blanche Ingram. Even so, Jane clearly has a bedroom on the 'long gallery' of the family floor, rather than on the servants' floor. This is the agony typical of the Victorian governess.

The space of Thornfield is precisely mapped when Jane is taken over the house by the housekeeper from the grand 'large front chambers' of the reception rooms on the ground floor, the long gallery of the family, guest rooms and nursery above, and finally up the 'narrow garret stairs' to the third floor that leads to 'the long passage . . . narrow, low and dim, with only one little window at the far end, and looking, with its two rows of small black doors all shut, like a corridor in some Bluebeard's castle.' This is the realm into which Jane retreats to find privacy and rail against the narrow constraints of her life: 'Then my sole relief was to walk along the corridor of the third story, backwards and forwards, safe in the silence and solitude of the spot.' The knowledge that this is the domain of Rochester's monstrous first wife Bertha Mason, locked away in a room within a room hidden behind heavy tapestries, redoubles the menace of this labyrinthine interior in the upper part of the building. It is from this location that the microcosm of order will come undone. Bertha's 'savage', colonial exteriority has been folded into the secret heart of the servants' quarters of the house, but proves uncontainable.[25]

Jane's flight into the woods frees her from the Gothic enclosure and social shame of 'the insolent vault' of Thornfield – but her descent into vagrancy nearly kills her. Even so, Jane believes that to die on the heath is a better fate than a 'workhouse coffin', reflecting the iron values of her class. Her refuge at Moor House is an ancient family house, a 'crumbling grange' of modest scale where the kitchen and single small parlour is the focus of the impoverished Rivers family. It represents a return to lower middle-class moral order under the strict religious authority of St John Rivers, where there is 'no superfluous ornament' and only sequestered respectability. When Jane takes up the role as schoolteacher in the village of Morton, even she privately smarts at her rudimentary cottage quarters, her 'little room with white-washed walls' and a single bedroom above. She returns to Moor House, conveniently restored to her proper class by a family inheritance, spending money to turn the house into 'a model of bright modest snugness' (which is done by putting 'canvas on the passage, and carpets on the stairs').[26]

Threats and weird psychical intrusions creep along corridors in *Jane Eyre*, Gothic elements that scratch at the doors of respectable domestic interiors. Bertha seems to have the freedom of the gallery and corridor at night in Thornfield, and later, at the moment of maximum patriarchal pressure on Jane to marry her cousin St John and subsume her life into his missionary work, she receives a kind of telepathic distress call from Rochester. She hears a spectral voice: 'I flew to the door and looked into the passage.' This simple gesture is an architectural realization of her instinct to escape middle-class enclosure, and she leaves Moor House immediately. She first finds Thornfield the ruin that her prophetic dreams had predicted, before heading to Ferndean, the last retreat of the mutilated and blinded Rochester. This house is virtually subsumed by the forest: it is called an old 'manor house' but serves as a largely abandoned hunting lodge with 'no architectural pretensions' and with only three rooms in use, befitting Rochester's fallen state. Here, at the centre of the labyrinth, the minotaur is finally tamed. Jane and Edward marry and seem content to reside in this retreat – the cottage pastoral of the Victorian middle classes.

The spatial obsession of *Jane Eyre* is perhaps unusual in being so intrinsically linked to the psychological journey of its central character – what one critic has called the 'portal desire' of Jane expressed at doorways, thresholds and in passageways.[27] Yet the house of fiction was a generic metaphor of the period, culminating in Henry James's famous statement in the Preface to *The Portrait of a Lady* (1881):

> The house of fiction has in short not one window, but a million – a number of possible windows not to be reckoned, rather; every one of which has been pierced, or is still piercable, in its vast front, by the need of individual vision and by the pressure of individual will.

James's late Victorian impressionism emphasizes the subtly different angles of subjective perception from myriad viewpoints, rather than the omniscient narrative voice associated with mid-Victorian Realism. His novels increasingly delighted in never giving the overview or taking the straight route, but formed crooked corridors. 'You approach the subject too *immediately*,' James once advised another author in 1899, recommending instead 'the ante-chamber or two and the crooked corridor before [the reader] is already in the Presence'.[28]

James saw *The Portrait of a Lady* as 'a square and spacious house', built around the 'corner-stone' of the central character Isabel Archer, the plot constructing 'fine embossed vaults and painted arches', filling out every detail from his pile of bricks, and slowly swinging shut the iron door that will imprison her in the perfect yet deathly interiors of her sham marriage.[29] This novel, like *Jane Eyre*, progresses through a series of precisely described houses. The theme of duplicity and double-dealing begins in the very space of Isabel's childhood home in Albany, which is described as two houses knocked through, a 'double house' with 'two entrances, one of which had long been out of use but had never been removed'. The ominous tinge continues beyond the large and spacious public rooms on the ground floor where the family is on display: 'On the third floor there was a sort of arched passage, connecting the two sides of the house, which Isabel and her sisters used in their childhood to call the tunnel and which, though it was short and well lighted, always seemed to the girl to be strange and lonely.'[30] These are the spaces that will catch Isabel increasingly inside restricting frames, compelling her action just where she had thought she was most free.

I will return to James's use of corridors and passages in his ghost stories in Chapter Nine, but here *Jane Eyre* and *The Portrait of a Lady* serve to demonstrate how often the passageways of domestic fiction are critical spaces of action, even as we overlook them for the more overt meanings of the parlour or boudoir. This can be picked up across very different modes and styles of fiction. In comedies of lower middle-class life, hung up on status anxiety, we find H. G. Wells's Kipps at a loss for all his perusal of 'Manners and Rules for Paying Calls' when a servant fails to answer the front door and he has to squeeze past the daughter of a house 'in a rather narrow passage'. Similarly, the comedy of the Pooter family in the Grossmiths' *Diary of a Nobody* (1892) can hinge on the absence of a proper hallway, which punctures their class pretensions. The presence of a servant marks their ambition to rise up the class hierarchy, yet her lack of servility and embarrassing proximity as they share the same cramped spaces shows how the ideals of privacy and segregation in domestic space recommended by Kerr or Stevenson are impossible for the new majority of the lower middle classes, the world of suburban clerks so damned by Edwardian commentators for their mediocrity.[31]

If these fugitive fictional moments can make the role of the corridor in domestic space become more visible, it is the eccentric tunnelling obsession of the fifth Duke of Portland that can really bring home the significance of the corridor to the operation of the Victorian concern to secure privacy.

The Apotheosis of Corridors: The Fifth Duke of Portland

Between 1854, when he became the fifth Duke of Portland, and his death in 1879, the strange and reclusive William John Cavendish-Scott-Bentinck spent well over £100,000 a year building tunnels and corridors on the private family estate at Welbeck Abbey in Nottinghamshire. The original fourteenth-century abbey building had been replaced after the dissolution of the monasteries by a mansion built in extensive grounds for the Cavendish family in 1604. Even the usually deferential *Country Life* had to confess that the buildings that accumulated over the years were 'a sombre pile, massive and ugly in many styles'.[32] Here the new Duke built miles of stately brick-lined and paved tunnels that allowed him to be driven in his carriage to the nearest railway station unseen (he remained in his carriage behind closed curtains, when the whole contraption was loaded onto the train). He constructed a vast Riding School in iron and glass to stable his beloved horses, a building that stretched nearly 122 metres (400 ft), and which was lit by 4,000 gas jets. The long narrow gallop, at over 305 metres (1,000 ft), he also covered in iron and glass. The original riding house was turned into a vast ballroom. He built a kitchen garden of 9 hectares (22 ac.) – pointedly larger than the one at Windsor Castle – protected by gigantic walls. There was an extended fruit arcade and a plant corridor. 'This arcade is nearly one thousand feet in length, and is formed of a series of ornamental iron arches, and over the whole of this are trained a number of apple trees up one side, and pear trees up the other, and bearing profusely over the whole of this immense length.'[33] When he converted one block to the new kitchen, it was connected to the main house by a long tunnel with a narrow gauge railway, so that the food would stay warm. It was said that the Duke required a hot roast chicken to be available at a moment's notice, any time of day or night.

Most of these massive works were achieved by the simple 'cut and cover' method, digging trenches and then roofing them over to make tunnels, a technique used for the first London Underground lines. Indeed, the Duke employed thousands of workers directly from these construction sites in London, creating whole temporary cities of dwellings for them on his estate (the Irish workmen called their encampment 'Sligo').

Inside Welbeck Abbey – or rather underneath it – the Duke excavated a room that was, for a time, the largest private room in Britain, with an innovative 19-metre-span (63-ft) iron girder roof covering a quarter of an acre. Intended first as a chapel, it became the gallery for the family pictures. Pleased with this, the Duke then burrowed on, creating a lengthy suite of five rooms that became his library, each room opening onto the next in an *enfilade* but 'at the side of these runs, on one side, a charming glass-roofed corridor of considerable width, and, on the other, an arched covered corridor of great length'. These rooms in turn were 'connected with the rest of the mansion by underground corridors and passages'.[34] He also extended the south wing of the house, raising the whole structure by another floor.

The Portland dukedom was fantastically wealthy from the rents raised from their extensive estates in the north of England and Scotland and from owning large swaths of the West End in London, as well as the profits from a number of coal collieries in the northeast. The millions spent on these building works did not really dent the Duke's income. He owned Fullarton House in Troon and Langwell in Caithness – estates he managed carefully by letter without ever actually visiting. He did spend time at the large mansion on London's Cavendish Square, Harcourt House, which had passed into the family in a previous generation when it was won in a game of cards.

At Harcourt, the fifth Duke hid behind a high blind wall at the front, but much to the consternation of his wealthy neighbours he built a 24-metre-high (80-ft) smoked-glass wall along the boundary to stop any chance of the garden being overlooked from the street. He retreated to Harcourt when he became ill in September 1878 and died there a year later.[35]

For all this building of reception rooms, ballrooms, extra wings and communicating tunnels and corridors, the Duke was legendary for living in seclusion. He never received company, refusing to associate with fellow aristocrats, never taking up his seat in the House

The 'New' Riding School at Welbeck Abbey, built in the 1860s, one of the largest iron and glass structures in the world, photograph taken c. 1905.

of Lords, and rebuffing honours offered by Queen Victoria or Prime Minister Disraeli. He accosted trespassers on his land, who frequently came in the 1870s once the Duke had become a 'mass of legend' in the press for his eccentricities, and bad-temperedly dressed them down.[36] He lived at Welbeck only in a small set of three or four modest rooms in the main house, which was known as 'The North Closet'. The Duke was often seen surveying the works on his estate in his peculiar outfits: two overcoats, very high starched collars, a top hat over half a metre tall, and his trousers tied at the knee to avoid mud. He played with children on the estate, but often avoided contact with his staff. One servant from the laundry serenely recalled that, after the Duke had let the servants boat on the lake, 'I remember going once or twice, and His Grace was in the shrubbery at the time.'[37] A compulsive letter writer, he preferred to direct works by written note, handed to his servants through a specially designed letter box in the door to his rooms, which cut down almost completely on face-to-face encounters in his private rooms.

The Duke had no children and so the estate passed to a cousin after his death. The bizarre building was consequently where the notable Modernist eccentric Lady Ottoline Morrell grew up. She recalled arriving at the main hall to find 'a grass-grown morass covered with builders' rubbish . . . The hall inside was without a floor, and temporary boardings had been laid down.' She continued: 'The late Duke was so absorbed with his vast work of building that he was oblivious of everything else. He pursued this hobby without any idea of beauty, a lonely, self-isolated man.'[38]

Welbeck Abbey has been called 'the culmination of a type of corridor segregation', where 'the corridor-cell complex reached its greatest dimensions to date'.[39] The Duke's motivation, of course, remains somewhat opaque. He suffered from psoriasis and neuralgia, but stories of a worse facial disfigurement (perhaps a euphemism for hinting at the visible marks of syphilis) do not seem to be true according to the testimony of servants who saw him regularly in the grounds.

He turned away from polite society after a youthful obsession with the soprano Adelaide Kemble came to nothing in the 1840s (she was in fact already married, but secretly, to continue working on stage), and perhaps this was decisive in making the Duke prefer seclusion. Some accounts suggest he began tunnelling when he realized the law could not intervene to stop the public rights of way that passed through his private land and the building burgeoned from there.[40] Psychologically, the heavy shadow of the public political service of his father and grandfather may have pushed him to the opposite extreme. And if he was insane, it was what a Victorian doctor would have termed a monomania, a reasoning madness that directed energy into a singular path of obsession with engineering and mechanical detail. The Duke was eager to use the latest advances in traction engines and steam ploughs, or try new architectural innovations, then work to surpass each achievement. It may simply have filled empty time.

The particular form his obsession took, though, suggests that his compulsion found its perfect expression in the new Victorian device of the corridor, the innovation that ensured privacy and spatial segregation in the private home. The Duke was a fervent Protestant of English aristocratic stock. His rare forays into the letters pages were to denounce the threat of disestablishing the Church of England. He fought to maintain the influence of the Church over schools after the 1870 Education Act risked creating a secular state curriculum. Did a Puritan twist of shame amplify the Duke's need to secure and segregate the private self? Shame is a social, relational emotion, a fear of losing face. The Duke's fear of being looked at features in all aspects of his personal behaviour, in his plans for tunnels, closed carriages, and even in the alleged design of his boxed-in bed. This was always a class-based aversion to his social equals rather than children, servants or the navvies he directed on his works. Contact with his inferiors, of course, could be managed entirely on his own whimsical terms – even a modest and deferential laundry maid could sense as he went around Welbeck that 'sometimes he was a little amused' at his ability to manipulate everything around him.[41] Ottoline Morrell reported that 'The Duke wished his housemaids to skate, and if he found one of them sweeping the corridor or the stairs, the frightened girl was sent out to skate, whether she wanted to or not.'[42] It is worth noting that the family motto was 'Craignez Honte' or 'Fear Disgrace'. Was it this injunction that led him to concretize the motto in this bizarre apotheosis of the private corridor as a device for containment and control?

8

The Dystopia of Corridors, I: Bureaucracy

The modern corridor, I have argued, has often been imbued with utopian possibility, whether of collective living in Charles Fourier's phalanx, communist 'social condensers' and welfarist public housing, or as immersive capitalist dreamworlds of consumption in arcades, shopping malls and luxury hotels. The aims of reform institutions that began to be built in the late eighteenth century processed people along corridors in different ways, but always in the earnest hope of the transformation of the recalcitrant self into the obedient citizen who would emerge into the light at the end of the passage. If many of these dream buildings began to seem accidentally coercive or deliberately punitive, that is because the public corridor was always shadowed in its development by its diametric opposite, the private corridor, which was designed to preserve and defend the boundaries of the self rather than break them down and reform them.

The sustained critique of the limits of public housing built around corridors and walkways, and the critique of the destructive force of the corridor-plan design of institutions like asylums, accelerated in the 1960s. This is when the term 'institutional neurosis' was formulated, a condition 'characterized by apathy, lack of initiative, loss of interest more marked in things and events not immediately personal, [and] submissiveness'. In the wake of Foucault's *Madness and Civilisation* and Erving Goffman's attack on the 'total institution', many suspected that the 'institutional career' could only be one of dehumanization.[1]

In this chapter I want to argue that this institutional critique was further fomented in the latter half of the twentieth century by attacks on the soulless corporate office and the labyrinthine spaces of bureaucracy. If the utopian corridor is best represented by soaring streets in the sky, then dystopia is often depicted as a windowless and oppressive corporate corridor where receding identical doors mark out the systematic destruction of the individual by the instrumental rationality of corporate number-crunching or state administration.

Dystopia is a distinctly twentieth-century genre, symbiotic with the total institutions of the totalitarian state, both left and right. It is symptomatic that the coinage of dys-topia, the worst of all possible places, is ascribed to John Stuart Mill (the utilitarian Jeremy Bentham preferred 'cacotopia'), although it has only come into common use after 1945. One of the first of these dystopias, E. M. Forster's 'The Machine Stops' (1909), was written as a direct riposte to H. G. Wells's technocratic vision of the future and envisions the complete isolation of individuals into cellular pods, all relations mediated by the machine. On a rare and anxious journey outside, the protagonist looks down from an airship onto 'corridors of shining tiles [where] rooms, tier beyond tier, reaching far into the earth' house the population 'buried deep in the hive'.[2] Yevgeny Zamyatin's premonition of the ossification of the Bolshevik revolution, *We* (1921–2), ends in the sclerotic offices of 'The Bureau of Guardians': 'Inside, in the corridor, stood an endless chain of Numbers, holding small sheets of paper and many notebooks.'[3] In Arthur Koestler's *Darkness at Noon* (1940), his denunciation of the Stalinist purge of the 1930s, Rubashov's inevitable execution comes outside his cell: 'A long corridor received him; its walls were blurred and he could not see the end of it. The man in uniform kept always three steps behind him.'[4] All the way up to Terry Gilliam's steampunk dystopia *Brazil* (1985), with its interminable labyrinths of offices, ducts and tubes and endlessly multiplying paperwork, bureaucratic dystopia has often been figured through the corridor. The office corridor is the architectural shape of inhuman bureaucratic processes where, to quote the last line of Zamyatin's *We*: 'Reason must prevail.' In this very modern condition, instrumental rationality is exercised through the orthogonal grid of the corridors of corporations and state bureaucracies.

First, I am going to sketch out the rise of the office and its ambivalent relation to the corridor, an architectural space that becomes associated with self-generating bureaucratic processes. As the army of clerks grew from the mid-nineteenth century, this generated some enduring fictions of its peculiarly maddening rationality. I then want to track how the emergence of the open-plan or 'Action Office' in the 1960s coincided with a significant cluster of anti-corridic artworks that spoke to the wider context of the emergent critique of total institutions and deadening bureaucracy.

From Counting House to Office

The emergence of a distinctive class of clerks and office workers and state bureaucrats was a product of the mercantile capitalism that built the modern Western state from the late eighteenth century. Before, clerks had been few in number, highly specialized, and often appointed to sinecure posts by patronage. The Prussian state was the first to introduce competitive examinations for entry into its Civil Service in the 1780s. Consequently the earliest uses of the term 'bureau-ocracy' in English tended to refer derogatively to Teutonic systems, a rhetoric continued in the ongoing identification of the European Union with 'red-tape' regulation. In England the Civil Service remained tiny and unreformed until the 1870s, despite the energetic attempts of Benthamite reformers, but private businesses expanded enough by the 1840s to generate a puzzling new petit bourgeois class of black-coated clerks, above artisans but below gentlemen, who required conduct books like *The Young Clerk's Manual* (1848) to know how to behave.

As historians of the blackcoated clerk have noted, the detail of the daily grind of this class has largely vanished between the cracks and is glimpsed most richly in fiction.[5] Mr Dombey's counting house in Dickens's novel *Dombey and Son* (1848) depicts the emerging office hierarchy through older, more exotic courtly metaphors:

> Between Mr Dombey and the common world, as it was accessible through the medium of the outer office . . . there were two degrees of descent. Mr Carker in his own office was the first step; Mr Morfin, in his own office, was the second. Each of these gentlemen occupied a little chamber like a bath-room, opening from the passage outside Mr Dombey's door. Mr Carker, as Grand Vizier, inhabited the room that was nearest to the Sultan. Mr Morfin, as an officer of inferior state, inhabited the room that was nearest to the clerks.[6]

There is a similar structure in Herman Melville's enigmatic tale 'Bartleby, the Scrivener' (1853), where the elderly lawyer creates an inner office away from his lowly copyists with a flimsy folding door, but then places his new appointment Bartleby inside his own room for him to be 'within easy call', behind a folding screen 'which might entirely isolate Bartleby from my sight'.[7] Bartleby's polite refusal of workplace hierarchies creates an escalating disturbance in the order of things.

These moments of spatial description show improvised adaptations of older buildings. Francis Duffy has proposed that the purpose-built Oriel Chambers in Liverpool of 1864 was a breakthrough in creating small suites of rooms specifically for small enterprises, with offices that were 'programmatically modular – a neat congregation of small undifferentiated units' placed along shared corridors. Oriel did not hide this novel layout behind a traditional Gothic or Italianate facade, but announced its unadorned functionalism overtly in ways that anticipated the International Style of universal office space a hundred years later.[8]

In the 1851 Census less than 1 per cent of the British population identified as clerks, but as small-scale mercantilism morphed through joint-stock investment and amalgamation into monopoly capitalism in the latter half of the nineteenth century the numbers of office workers grew. This is the much reviled world of the Pooters in *The Diary of a Nobody* (1892), or the precarious financial existence and constant cultural discomfort of the clerk Leonard Bast in Forster's *Howard's End* (1910).

If the modern office increasingly 'splinters the workforce among departments and through occupational differentiation', it follows that the complex stages of workflow undertaken by increasing numbers of clerks can be broken down into steps best organized spatially in linear pathways – along corridors. Frederick Winslow Taylor's 1911 book *The Principles of Scientific Management* was overtly directed at segmenting the 'brutish' heavy labour of a steel works into a series of mindless repetitive acts, and was the basis of Henry Ford's innovation of the linear factory assembly line. But Taylorism was also enthusiastically transformed into the new science of Office Management as American capitalism boomed. In Schulze's *The American Office* (1913), office space was organized in a logical flow of 'constant forward movement':

> There should be no doubling back in the progress of work through the office. Every order should begin at one point and go steadily forward until the office work on it is completed. One of the most frequent causes of waste is the constant shunting backward and forward of work which should go smoothly ahead in one direction.[9]

Quick and easy communication between offices made clear corridor circulation between departments vital, at least in Schulze's view. His diagrams for the ideal office featured public corridors for clients shadowed by linear private corridors for backroom staff functions, laid out in efficient logical sequence.

Yet corridors could also be seen as the exact enemy of the efficient modern office. This was the basis for the radical design of the

Larkin Administration Building in Buffalo, built by the key Modernist architect Frank Lloyd Wright and opened in 1906. The Larkin Company was a soap manufacturer, but had become an innovative national mail order business that by 1900 needed to process more than 5,000 orders by letter every day. Wright built a brick monolith that pushed service stairwells and elevators into the pylon-like corners, thus freeing up the central floor plan within. A central atrium flooded the four office storeys with light from the vast span of the iron and glass roof. Wright then inverted the usual office plan, placing the central office at the foot of the atrium in a large, undivided space, and used the balconies above as specific zones of office activity. Letters arrived in the basement, and were processed through successive stages of a building that was effectively a giant filing and card-indexing system (filing cabinets were built into the walls; metal desks had fixed cantilevered seats to regularize posture). The office operation was all supervised by the management from the ground floor, turning the usual office structure upside down, in what was effectively one of the first open-plan offices. Fixed structures of differentiation like corridors were entirely abolished.

Innovations in air ventilation in the Larkin also freed Wright from the need to construct a narrow building with offices placed along ribbons of windows. Air could now circulate in the deep space of an artificial environment. This was a further element in erasing corridors from the office. The Larkin heralded (although somewhat ahead of time) the American business view that corridors were inefficient, uneconomic, dead space.

The Larkin Administration Building was much admired around the world. The German architect Eric Mendelsohn wrote back home in 1922:

> I am sitting in the inner court . . . Four floors, lit on all sides give out on to this hall. There are a thousand people at work here. You hear no single sounds. The general noise from the working

The Larkin Administration Building, Buffalo, New York.
This open-plan office was completed in 1906 by the architect
Frank Lloyd Wright, and demolished in 1950.

> of a thousand individually almost silent typewriters, calculating machines and adding machines simply forms the background hum for the ordinary field of activity.

Another European visitor in 1921 said that 'one senses the tempo of our times' in the Larkin.[10] The vast army of clerks were exalted to the virtues of efficient work by slogans sculpted into the balconies overlooking the central atrium: INTELLIGENCE ENTHUSIASM CONTROL. The open-plan office certainly amplified the possibilities of control through ease of supervision and surveillance of the clerks, many of them women, sorting vast volumes of paperwork.

Although the building was demolished in 1950 to much outcry, the architect Ludwig Mies van der Rohe had also visited the Larkin and declared it a major influence on his Seagram Building in New York in 1958. The Seagram was the office block that secured the post-war signature of the business HQ as built on functionalist open-plan floors replicated in stacks into the sky behind uniform glass-plated curtain walls. Mies's office was an embodiment of the De Stijl concept of 'universal space', making for a grid-like delimitation of offices that transcended any local context for an ideal form, translatable into any city space. Externally, office blocks assumed a standardized International Style. Internally, in this model of the office, the corridor was now relegated to shameful service functions and obligatory fire escapes hidden behind glossy atrium and lobby spaces.[11] Survivals of dark double-loaded corridors in office buildings from the 1920s and '30s became design problems to redress in building refits.[12]

In the 1960s there were various attempts to transform the possibilities of the open-plan office. *Bürolandschaft*, or 'office landscaping', was a set of radical proposals that emerged from Germany. The modern office no longer worked along the lines of power or fixed hierarchies examined by Taylorism, but now needed to respond to constantly shifting conditions and flat networks. This was a recipe for abolishing all walls, corridors and private offices for an entirely open plan. 'Office

Bureaucratic doom: the generic corporate corridor.

landscaping is a *total* planning approach in which the cybernetics of information processing are fundamental,' said one guide in 1969, reflecting the investment of management consultants in the scientism of systems theory, viewing the office as a holistic self-regulating ecology.[13] It was meant to be open and democratic, in the spirit of the times, but remains the most universally hated of office layouts because it abolishes all private, personal desk space.

Oddly enough, the parallel proposal for the 'Action Office' in 1968, which was meant to provide fluid and responsive modular furniture for open-plan offices, was actually the beginning of the cubicle system.

Robert Propst, inventor of the Action Office, confidently dismissed 'the egg crate concept, with rows of enclosures connected by corridor' as obsolete because it was 'a form of linear communication based on almost totally vertical organization'.[14] Within a few years, though, his utopian open plans had solidified into cheap mazes of cubicles, labyrinths of what Douglas Coupland calls 'veal-fattening pens', 'small, cramped office workstations built of fabric-covered disassemblable wall partitions and inhabited by junior staff members'.[15] The cubicle office is an indifferent, dystopian world – the kind of place occupied by the cartoon character Dilbert or Keanu Reeves in *The Matrix*, before his life as Mr Anderson ends and he becomes the messianic hacker Neo. Meanwhile, the managers escaped back into private offices along the executive corridor, their status measured by square footage and exterior windows.

The Anglo-American office took an anti-corridic turn in the 1960s, but comparative work has shown that the corridor-and-cell design has been largely retained on the European mainland. Juriaan Van Meel noted in the year 2000 that if you visited the offices of the Dutch bank ABN Amro in Amsterdam 'you find a building with corridors and spacious rooms on either side. Inside these rooms you can see people working behind computer screens, next to a window.' The offices for the same bank in London, however, finds the same work being done 'in relatively small cubicles in large open areas'.[16]

This is partly a result of a different economic relationship to office space. Anglo-American companies rent abstract space in generic office buildings and spend minimally on interior design, whereas European businesses often invest in and design their own headquarters. Mainland European countries also have compulsory worker participation in office design (an anathema to Anglo-American business models), leading to laws about proximity of workers to window space, and thus long, narrow ribbon designs often centred on wide interior streets or corridors. As Francis Duffy notes in *The New Office*, in buildings such as the Scandinavian Airlines (SAS) HQ at Frösundavik,

Sweden (built in 1988), the ING Bank HQ in Amsterdam (1987), or the edding International HQ in Ahrensburg (1990), the offices are built around split-level galleries and interior streets that encourage serendipitous encounters. At the edding HQ, more than a third of the interior space is corridor: 'People are actively encouraged to circulate along the split-level galleries.'[17]

Unlikely as it seems, these model European offices have the ring of Fourier's utopian street-galleries about them, their advocates folding them into a benign vision of enlightened unalienated labour, often in glossy coffee-table brochures of post-Fordist workplace puffery. If these spaces seem unlikely outside of *Silicon Valley* parodies, it is not just because the abstracted deep space of the Anglo-American office is more familiar; they are also countered by much darker visions of the bureaucratic corridor.

Corridors of Power: Bureaucratic Dystopias

Max Weber's chapters on the rise of bureaucracy in his study *Economy and Society* were written just as the discourse of Office Management in America was emerging to join the expanding state bureaucracies of modern mass democracies. The statistical society that developed in the nineteenth century managed populations through biopolitical norms and regulations, targeting the abnormal and dissident for punishment and corrective reform. The state required systems of documentation, paper records, filing systems and informational circulation to bring its citizens into being. For Weber, the distinctive features of bureaucracy include its tendency towards increasing specialization and segmentation of tasks in the name of technical efficiency. This logic leads to an ideal of impersonal abstraction in systemic processes: 'Its specific nature, which is welcomed by capitalism, develops the more perfectly the more bureaucracy is "dehumanized", the more completely it succeeds in eliminating from official business love, hatred, and all purely personal, irrational, and emotional elements which escape calculation.' The apparatus generates and programmes the bureaucrat, not vice versa, producing 'the personally detached and strictly "objective" expert' who can only operate within the parameters of the machine.[18] Another of Weber's key insights is the self-replicating nature of bureaucracies, their intensive enlargement, since autonomous systems generate ever more protocols, measuring only the internal processes of the system itself until the signal is drowned by noise and efficiency gains undergo entropic collapse. Yet once they are set up, Weber warned, bureaucracies are 'among those social structures which are the hardest to destroy'.[19]

In 1941, in the depths of global war, James Burnham's *The Managerial Revolution* polemically argued that across the political spectrum the fascist state, Stalinist communism and the managed state interventions of the New Deal in America all manifested the same rise of a particular class of manager – 'operating executives, superintendents, administrative engineers, supervisory technicians, or, in government . . . administrators, commissioners, bureau heads' – who would soon control all the levers of power and dismantle democracy.[20] Burnham's book reflected the rise of proposals for a technocratic elite to take over the reins of government in order to correct the failings of democratic politics, which had not prevented the economic crises of the 1930s. The book had a major influence on George Orwell's vision of dystopian bureaucracy in *Nineteen Eighty-four* (1948).

Burnham's thesis also framed John Donald Kingsley's anxious study of the British Civil Service, *Representative Bureaucracy* (1944). This book began with a memorable description of the organization of the Civil Service: 'Viewed architecturally it remains a strangely rambling structure embodying a miscellany of styles and a bewildering number of wings and annexes.' It was this ramshackle, ad hoc structure that had grown up over the years – rather like the accretions of the sclerotic, half-forgotten rituals of the dying castle in Mervyn Peake's *Gormenghast* (1945) – that now placed democracy at risk. Bureaucracies tended towards autonomy, Kingsley said: 'They become states within states, perfecting elaborate machinery for their governance and reducing to a minimum the area of detailed supervision by political organs.' In 1944, with an 'administrative army' of more than 500,000 that stretched from the National Physics Lab to the cleaners of the 'quiet corridors of Whitehall', Kingsley saw the administrator as 'the representative figure of our times'.[21] At the end of the war, the German thinkers Theodor Adorno and Max Horkheimer published *The Dialectic of Enlightenment*, which excoriated a tradition of Western liberal thought that had only ended up in the bureaucratic administration of mass death. 'There are no longer any hiding places,' Adorno later warned, 'not even any longer the possibility of modestly surviving the winter for a person who loses his position in the administered world.'[22]

World war fostered totalizing bureaucracies, such as the Pentagon, completed in 1943, with its 28 kilometres (17½ mi.) of ring corridors, an enduring emblem of the defensive closed loop of autonomous administration. The post-war era was full of worries about the anti-democratic influence of the 'military-industrial complex', a term first used in 1959 in the anxious outgoing presidential speech by Dwight Eisenhower. Three years later, when C. P. Snow coined the phrase 'corridors of power', he reported that its usage took off immediately. 'The phrase has kept swimming before my eyes,' Snow said, reaching the status of a dead metaphor even before he had published his next novel, called *The Corridors of Power*. It depicted Whitehall machinations around a ministerial scandal, managed in interstitial spaces of corridors rather than in official offices or parliamentary chambers, spaces known as Westminster's 'channels of "closed" politics – the corridors, the committees'.[23] Within weeks of publication, which had been held off until after the general election at the request of the Conservative government, Snow had been given a seat in the unelected House of Lords by the incoming Labour government and the position of Parliamentary Secretary in the Ministry of Technology. It was a bureaucratic position uncannily like his own recurrent alter ego in his novels about Lewis Eliot. Although Snow seemed smugly amused at this turn of events, the phrase 'corridors of power' crystallized the sense that hidden bureaucratic systems increasingly outflanked democratic processes, in the spaces outside accountability.[24]

'All bureaucracies are to a certain degree utopian,' David Graeber argues, 'in the sense that they propose an abstract ideal that real human beings can never live up to.'[25] The typical experience of the structural stupidity of bureaucracy is of course dystopian because laborious processes only become visible when they break down, generate errors, or get stuck in logic loops created purely by their own internal systems.

Satirical fiction has observed this almost as long as modern bureaucracy has existed. In *Bleak House* (1852), Dickens denounced the maddening labyrinths of the Court of Chancery that chewed up and destroyed its petitioners in its interminable machinations. In *Little Dorrit* (1857), a little further into this crucial decade of the bureaucratic expansion of the British state, Dickens attacked the insidious tentacles of the 'Circumlocution Office' and its requirement of 'half a bushel of minutes, several sacks of official memoranda, and a family-vault-full of ungrammatical correspondence' on every matter in the land.[26] Anthony Trollope, writer and suspiciously well-adjusted bureaucrat at the Post Office, where he worked for nearly thirty years under the Benthamite reformer Rowland Hill, wrote *The Three Clerks* (1858) in an explicit riposte to Dickens, setting the action across various Westminster departments, but praising the Office of the Board of Commissioners for Regulating Weights and Measures in particular, which he declared with wounded pride 'exactly antipodistic of the Circumlocution Office'.[27]

It is likely that Herman Melville, himself a deeply reluctant Customs House bureaucrat and failed author, had read *Bleak House* just before composing 'Bartleby, the Scrivener'. This is Melville's seminal portrait of a commercial office of legal copyists undone by its dependence on the unwritten rules of bureaucratic etiquette. Bartleby's passive acts of resistance to the lowliest piecework of copying legal documents, his always politely conditional refusal 'I would prefer not to', leaves him first without money or food, then without lodging, then haunting the stairwells and halls of the Wall Street office, before his final removal as a vagrant to the prison corridors of New York's ominously named 'The Tombs'. Here, his former boss returns again and again 'through the corridors in quest of Bartleby', but it seems inevitable his former employee will simply fade into non-existence, just as the legal copyist Nemo does in his anonymous lodging rooms in *Bleak House*.[28]

The final revelation that Bartleby had been previously dismissed from his privileged job in Washington's Dead Letter Office is richly suggestive: here is the place where letters that never reach their destination go, and are either returned to sender or burnt without remainder, revealing the apocalyptic void that underlies all bureaucratic circulations of paper. The philosopher Jacques Derrida is also obsessed with dead-letter offices in his book *The Post-card*. Derrida suggests that it is structural to signification itself that letters might not arrive at their proper destination but get lost in circulation, and he combines ideas of destiny, destination, error and erring to produce a new concept to underpin all signification: *destinerrance*.[29] This is the secret logic of bureaucracy, too, where rational systems foster their own irrational eruptions, blips and errors. Bartleby behind his screen or haunting the office corridors in Wall Street is the purest expression of the system, not its irrational outside.

In the twentieth century the writer most associated with this illogical logic of bureaucracy was Franz Kafka, the Bohemian avant-garde writer and dutiful clerk of the Workers' Accident Insurance Institute in Prague for much of his working life. Kafka left *The Castle* unfinished, and was more successful professionally writing documents such as 'The Scope of Compulsory Insurance for the Building Trades'.[30] He is also the writer who most insistently associates bureaucracy with labyrinthine spaces and nightmare corridors. In *The Castle* (composed in 1922), K., hoping to keep an appointment with yet another official of the administration, makes his way through the 'waiting hall' and the overspill of petitioners milling about listlessly in the passages running off it, and is led by a servant 'across the courtyard, then through the door and into the low, slightly downhill passage'. This takes K. to a subterranean but brightly lit corridor serving rooms that seem to be at once bedrooms and offices for the secretaries of the higher officials:

> The best possible use was made of space. The passage was just high enough for a person to walk upright. Down the sides, the doors almost touched. The walls on either side stopped short of the ceiling; this was no doubt for ventilation purposes, because in this deep, cellar-like passage the tiny rooms presumably had no windows. The disadvantage of these not quite complete walls was the noise in the passage and inevitably also in the rooms. Many rooms seemed to be occupied, in most people were still awake, you heard voices, hammering, the clink of glasses. Yet there was no impression of any special merriment.[31]

This is one of Kafka's typical oneiric passages, where the description of the space is precise yet the space is impossible to map and all the details are curiously self-cancelling. Any clear purpose of the protagonist, as always, is confounded and confused by the bewildering twists of the architectural volumes he traverses. In the village, things have become 'so interwoven that it sometimes even looked as if officialdom and life had changed places'. There are no clear roads to the Castle above the village, and even its outline is ungraspable in the mist. The unfinished state of the novel feels exactly right to convey the unending passages of bureaucratic processes, 'the ludicrous confusion that may possibly determine the existence of a human being'.[32]

There is a similar moment in *The Trial* (composed in 1914–15) when K. is hurrying for his next opaque yet crucial appointment with one of the officials of the court:

> more or less half-way down the corridor, he saw that it was possible to turn off through an opening without a door on the right. He checked with the usher that it was the right way, the usher nodded, and he took the turn. He found it annoying that he had to walk one or two steps in front of the usher all the time, it could well look, at least in this place, as if he were being taken under escort. K. kept waiting for the usher to catch up, but he immediately dropped back again. Finally, in order to put an end to his discomfort, K. said, 'I've seen what things look like here, so now I'll leave.' 'You haven't seen everything', said the usher in non-committal tones. 'I don't want to see everything', said K., who was genuinely feeling tired, 'I want to leave, how do I get to the way out?' 'You haven't got lost already, have you?' the usher asked in astonishment. 'You go to the corner there, then turn right along the corridor and the door's straight ahead.' 'Come with me', said K., 'and show me the way. There are so many ways here, I'll take the wrong one.'[33]

At other times K. must clamber through attic rooms, or find unlikely back doors in suburbs to make his way to the court, or more often only the next antechamber in an unending chain of waiting rooms. The 'hallway or the corridor' is 'the most striking topography in Kafka's work', Gilles Deleuze and Félix Guattari argue in their study of his fiction, because it is an apparently continuous, logically unfolding space, an 'unlimited straight line', but in Kafka's works hallways always seem to string together completely discontinuous fragments of reality.[34]

More than this, though, the corridor is the space of waiting, of perpetual deferral, the realization that K. will never confront the final authority, either in the castle or the court. Kafka's corridors slyly expand with every step K. takes, any resolution always pushed ahead, receding even as he advances, an unreachable destination. K. is even told this by a priest through the parable 'Before the Law', a text interpolated into *The Trial*, which tells of a countryman summoned before the law, but who is left forever waiting in the hallway outside for the

A cavernous office space in Orson Welles's 1962 adaptation of Franz Kafka's *The Trial*.

right moment to cross the threshold guarded by a doorkeeper. Although K. and the priest typically argue over the many interpretations of this allegory, the tale implies that the Law is an empty authority that can never be directly approached: it exerts itself only through the endless substitutes, the functionaries and underlings who always weirdly proliferate in antechambers and lobbies. Kafka crystallizes bureaucratic dystopia in the waiting rooms and hallways of buildings like hospitals or local government offices or courtrooms where we wait interminably for the right authorities to come to judgements that never seem to arrive. Intensive processes will always tip Rational into Enigmatic Bureaucracy.[35]

Kafka died in 1924, between the end of the sclerotic Austro-Hungarian empire and the Nazi invasion that would bureaucratically process many of his surviving friends and relatives into the concentration camps. During the Cold War, his work was banned by the communist regime of Czechoslovakia because – to writers like Ivan Klima – Kafka's K. was an 'empowered nexus of dissent' against Stalinist bureaucracy.[36] In this way, Kafka fed directly into the absurdist attack on state power in the 1960s.

The Anti-corridic 1960s: Godard, Tati, Nauman

The critique of bureaucracy peaked in the late 1960s and early 1970s, David Graeber argues. The Apollonian language of order and cybernetic control that heralded the beginnings of computerized office systems and global networks of finance was met with the Dionysian protest, situationist agitation and, in the arts, the representation of Beckettian or Kafkaesque absurdity. The leader of the Diggers, one of the earliest agit-prop groups to emerge from San Francisco's counterculture, took aim at the corporate world, suggesting the following political confrontational action: 'Infiltrate the largest corporation office building with life-actors as nymphomaniacal secretaries, clumsy repairmen, berserk executives, sloppy security guards, [and] clerks with animals in their clothes.'[37] Across cinema and conceptual art, instances multiplied where the constricting conformity of bureaucratic life became symbolized by the oppressive corridor.

Jean-Luc Godard's *Alphaville* (1965) sends the weary, trench-coated, hard-boiled detective Lemmy Caution (who had been played by Eddie Constantine in seven previous popular films) across the galaxy from the Outerlands to the cybernetic city of the future, which turns out to be . . . Paris in 1965. This Orpheus in the Underworld was shot without special effects in the hyper-modern architectural spaces where the future seemed immanent in the present. Caution travels across space using the new Paris motorway and checks into a hotel with endless corridors before visiting the Residents' Control Registration offices and the futuristic block that houses Alpha 60, the super-computer that binds every aspect of life to its totalitarian instrumental rationality. This technocratic dystopia is represented by tracking shots along office corridors, sparsely populated by zombified workers who evoke the highly stylized movements through space in Robert Wiene's Expressionist masterpiece *The Cabinet of Dr Caligari* (1920). The electronic rasp of Alpha 60 barks 'Occupé' or 'Libre' as the characters pass each doorway, making the corridors even more menacing.

Godard captured the effects of rapid modernization in Paris from the ebullient *Breathless* (1959) to the dour *Two or Three Things I Know about Her* (1966). The latter captures the building sites and new *grands ensembles* (standardized housing blocks) that create environments for the alienated subjects of modernity the film explores. In *Alphaville* this immanent future was shot at the new Maison de l'ORTF – the vast circular block built as a new radio and television centre in 1963. Godard also used the eleven-storey Esso Tower, also opened in 1963, which featured the signature metal and glass curtain wall of the International Style and was the first of the type to be constructed in France. It announced the arrival of a new business quarter, La Défense, which was created just outside the bounds of the historic centre of Paris and now looms on the horizon as one of those interchangeable business 'downtowns'. 'Alpha 60', the panoptical computer in the film, was named after the Gamma 60, the first multi-programmable office computer, which had been launched by the Compagnie des Machines Bull in 1958 in direct competition with the American corporation IBM (the working title for *Alphaville* was *Tarzan versus IBM*). The references, like the shooting style, are direct and immediate: the utopian future is seemingly cancelled in the dystopian present. It is a terrible shame that the role of Professor Braun, the evil genius of this cybernetic state, was turned down by Godard's first choice of actor, Roland Barthes, already by 1965 the Parisian master of signs.[38]

The French New Wave sought to capture in its *mise en scène* 'the emergence of an American-style modernity organised around consumption and the market'.[39] Alienation is figured in what the critic and fellow New Wave director Eric Rohmer called the 'architecture of apocalypse', the 'entirely fabricated worlds' of a city rapidly being razed and rebuilt around them in the rush for modernization under de Gaulle from 1958.[40] The early dizzy embrace of American popular culture in *Breathless* had cooled by *Alphaville*, however. The film connects the Americanized office and its basement rooms of computer machinery, monitored by bored functionaries (the doctors Heckle

Hard-boiled detective Lemmy Caution arrives in cybernetic utopia, escorted through corridors by Natacha von Braun in Jean-Luc Godard's *Alphaville* (1965). *Below*: Corridor chaos as Lemmy Caution crashes the system in *Alphaville*.

and Jeckle, named after cartoon characters), with the bureaucracy of Nazi totalitarianism. Von Braun, whose name is that of the Nazi rocket scientist who ended up working in America with NASA and making films on space exploration for Disney in the 1950s, oversees executions of those who have 'behaved illogically'. 'The unassimilables were simply killed,' he explains. His daughter Natacha, played by Anna Karina, is tattooed with a serial number, as are many women classed as 'Seductresses' by the state, all of whom move in robotic or zombified shuffles through the corridors.

Presumably Godard's critique was informed by Hannah Arendt's influential reflections on 'the banality of evil' in the Nazi bureaucracy of mass genocide, a phrase prompted by the trial of Adolf Eichmann in Jerusalem after his capture in 1961. 'The essence of totalitarian government, and perhaps the nature of every bureaucracy,' Arendt reflected, 'is to make functionaries and mere cogs out of men' to distance them from the sequence of paperwork that leads, far away, somewhere else, in the camps, to 'administrative massacre'. Arendt's critique became another negative vision of bureaucracy instantly adopted around the world in the early 1960s, deepening the Weberian suspicion of information systems as they were rolled out through business and the state. It is less likely at this stage that Godard knew the actual role of IBM in developing pioneering computerized punchcard systems for the Nazi bureaucracy of genocide.[41]

Alphaville refuses totalitarianism, though, with a resolutely Dionysian critique, also very much of its time. Logic and cybernetic control is refused by the spontaneous irrational act, by love, by the Surrealist poetry of Paul Éluard. Control is figured by the orthogonal grid of the office corridor and the closed loop of bureaucracy (the image of the circle is everywhere, from the flashing round lamp of Alpha 60 in the very first image of the film to the spiral staircases of the office lobbies). The leader of the Surrealists, André Breton, denounced the 'paucity of reality' and opposed the 'unyielding mathematicians' of logic with poetry, collage and jarring juxtaposition, which offered the Surrealist 'eternal act of defiance'.[42] It is the recital of Éluard's forbidden language of love that unfreezes Natacha from the zombie grip of logic, allowing her to rediscover a lost language of desire. When, on a much larger scale, Caution short-circuits Alpha 60, the drone-bureaucrats in the corridor move chaotically, gripping the walls, falling to their deaths. Caution in contrast moves in a straight line behind his gun out of the office complex, climbs into his Citroën, and brings his Eurydice out of the Underworld. The End.

The increasingly radical and Brechtian tactics of Godard's critique in the 1960s is oddly matched by the gentler and ostensibly apolitical comedies of modern life made by Jacques Tati. *Mon Oncle* (1958) is a satire on the open-plan house where 'everything is modern, everything communicates' (no corridors here, until Tati's recurring character Monsieur Hulot returns to his ramshackle old-Paris tenement, still hanging on as a recalcitrant survival). The global success of *Mon Oncle* led to Tati's grandiloquent sets for *Playtime* (1967), which he built at vast and ruinous cost on the outskirts of Paris. This vision of an entirely immersive American modernity of plate-glass offices and non-places of waiting rooms, airport terminals, self-service cafés and slowly collapsing nightclubs, exactly mirrored the construction of La Défense happening across town at the same time. 'Tativille', as it became known, was so large that there was even a notion to build an actual office block to use as a set before renting it out for profit. However, Tati's need to move these giant blocks around on rollers rather precluded that plan. He needed complete control to shoot in 70mm widescreen in his immaculately choreographed, long single takes.

The simple joke of *Playtime* is that the pretensions of cybernetic efficiency of modern planners will always be undone by the chaotic passage of unruly bodies like Monsieur Hulot, who weirdly starts to multiply and produce entropic unravelling in the crowds of these vast sets. The American tourists who arrive at the beginning of the film – in real life, the wives of men who worked at the Supreme Headquarters of the Allied Powers in Europe – never see the historic centre of Paris, the Eiffel Tower being glimpsed only momentarily in the reflection of a closing glass door. A row of posters for tourist destinations around the world features an office block identical to the one in which the travel agent is located. Paris has been replaced by this anonymous, transnational steel-and-glass modernity.

In the office scenes, Monsieur Hulot arrives for a meeting with Giffard and we glimpse his contact turn a corner at the far end of an interminable corridor and advance in real time towards the camera, traversing the whole of the set with gigantic footsteps comically misaligned with his tiny, dwarfed body. This missed connection moves into a cat-and-mouse chase up and down elevators and through closed office cubicles (just in time for the invention of the Action Office). Hulot and Giffard will only meet much later, entirely by accident, in the street. It remains hard to imagine what their meeting is about. As James Harding notes, for all its joys, 'Kafka's sombre shade seems to inhabit the concrete and glass vistas' of the film.[43]

Hulot always confounds the authority of regimented spaces of the post-war consumer world, just as Charlie Chaplin had done in the spaces of the pre-war industrial world of production a generation earlier in *Modern Times* (1936). This bureaucratic world is gridded in straight lines, but Hulot swoops in curves and circles, leaving trails of chaos.

A final example of the investigation of the bureaucratic menace of the corridor in the late 1960s comes from the art world. The artist Bruce Nauman began constructing a series of narrow and constricting corridors in his studio in 1969, initially for video pieces, before turning them into a series of installations that blurred the boundaries between sculpture, performance and installation art. *Live-taped Video Corridor* (1970) was a 12-metre-long (40-ft) corridor, barely the width of the shoulders, restricting any lateral movement, which extended towards two glowing video monitors on the floor at the far dead end. The images came from a camera feed mounted high up at the entrance. One monitor showed a loop of the corridor empty; the

Monsieur Hulot waits for his appointment, dwarfed by the vast office set in Jacques Tati's *Playtime* (1967).

other was a live feed that had the uncanny effect of showing the back of the visitor in the corridor receding into the distance even as they advanced towards the monitor. The effect is to disrupt the mirroring effect of the screen: the viewer is never able to meet their own gaze and either has their own body estranged or erased. Nauman continued to elaborate on this format: multiple widths of corridors, some of which were inaccessible, in *Corridor Installation (Nick Wilder)* (1970), or glimpses of spaces built off the corridor in *Changing Light Corridor with Rooms* (1971). The artist played with perceptions in other ways, sometimes building wedge-shaped or converging walls, as in *Double Wedge Corridor with Mirror* (1970), to further throw the viewer's spatial experience off-balance. To this aggressive visual disorientation was added soundproofing and muffling, so that, Nauman explained, 'as you walk into the V the pressure increases quite a bit, it's very claustrophobic.'[44]

The artist once explained that:

> A number of those corridor pieces came out of a dream. It was about being in a long corridor and there was a room at the end of the corridor. The light was a yellow-grey colour, dim. There

> was a figure on left, unidentified. I had the dream so many times and I kind of figured that it must be part of myself that I hadn't identified.[45]

It is suggestive that this modern architectural space has become so strongly identified with what the critic Anthony Vidler calls the 'warped space' informed by unconscious drives, zones of 'displacement and fracture, torquing and twisting, pressure and release, void and block'.[46] Dreamlike, disorienting corridors have been picked up by other artists, such as in the elaborate installation of Mike Nelson, *The Coral Reef* (2000), now permanently installed in Tate Britain, in which the visitor wanders with a steadily growing sense of panic through the multiple pathways of a labyrinth of uneasy rooms, shabby offices and dusty corridors, rapidly losing the sense of any relation to the exterior space of the gallery. From the opening lobby, 'viewers are able to choose from numerous battered doors and bleak, grimy corridors that seem to endlessly fold back on themselves.'[47] Ryan Gander's *Locked Room Scenario* (2011) took this further by inserting visitors into a large abandoned office space in an anonymous backstreet where uneasy scenarios and encounters with actors in the rooms and along the corridors attempted to amplify a growing sense of dread about what might irrationally erupt from the rational grid of the office.

I would situate these interventions with the rise of Conceptual Art (first named in late 1969), the beginnings of a sustained critique of the institutional complicities of the museum and the market of commercial galleries. 'The working premise is to think in terms of system, the interference with and exposure of such systems,' argued Hans Haacke, one of the most trenchant analysts of art-as-institution. Nauman's performance and video pieces have been explicitly located as a critique of technocracy, 'an increasingly administrative order', in the 1960s.[48] There was a forceful critique of the abstracting of art from any social

Bruce Nauman's *Green Light Corridor*, 1970.

and political context in the 'white cube', with artists taking art out of the museum and into the street or temporary, improvised, non-gallery spaces. Similarly, the focus on the constricting space of the corridor brings light to those unloved or overlooked passageways between pristine white gallery spaces in art institutions. It hints again that, just as corridors were being removed from the open-plan office, other meanings, in excess of the unexamined functionalism of these pieces of infrastructure, were coming into sight at the moment of erasure.

The utopia of corridors in Office Management handbooks, expressed as the efficiency of rational circulation in the 1910s, was not simply succeeded by a later dystopian vision, fully articulated by the 1960s, even if this is one plausible historical trajectory that can be mapped out. As Dickens, Melville, Weber or Kafka attest, the potential madness of bureaucracy was always coiled within the matrix of its administrative reason from the beginnings of the modern mercantile state. Dystopia does not come *after* but inhabits the utopian impulse from the beginning. This view can be further illustrated by going back to the early use of corridors in the utopian projects of Fourier and others in the eighteenth century and observing that they were always shadowed by another emotional tenor to the corridor: dread.

9
The Dystopia of Corridors, II: Dread and the Gothic

Bureaucracy's dream of the frictionless circulation of paperwork and bodies starts to unravel with Bartleby and ends in Kafka's nightmare mazes of passages or the constricting corridors of Bruce Nauman's installations, works inspired by his recurrent dreams. If, as Siegfried Kracauer said, 'spatial images are the dreams of society', then the nightmares of the Gothic promise similar potential for exploring the dystopian imagination.[1]

Horace Walpole's *The Castle of Otranto* (1764), still commonly claimed to be the inaugural Gothic romance, was the product of an author's nightmare, too, 'of which all I could recover', Walpole wrote to a friend, 'was, that I had thought myself in an ancient castle . . . and that on the uppermost bannister of a great staircase I saw a gigantic hand in armour.'[2] As Eino Railo observed in one of the earliest critical studies of this much despised genre, Walpole's book is set in a space of tunnels, dungeons, galleries and 'bewildering vaulted passages'. Ann Radcliffe's melodramas of the 1790s made 'terror novels' a genuinely popular craze, particularly with *The Mysteries of Udolpho* (1794). In this best-selling, labyrinthine novel Railo also observes that we 'pace the rooms and corridors, whose long perspectives display a simple nobility of line' before entering 'passages, which are extremely numerous, winding and narrow, so that they form a veritable labyrinth.'[3] Just as corridors begin to emerge as new spaces in eighteenth-century architecture, so the Gothic imagination begins to haunt them. The symbiosis between corridors and Gothic romance is what I want to explore in this chapter, because this has become the genre that for me best articulates that distinctly modern feeling of spatial dread.

In her study of Gothic fiction, Terry Castle has suggested that the first wave of castles, labyrinths and dungeons provided mobile metaphors for an emergent discourse of depth psychology in the eighteenth century, faltering steps to imagine the novel realm of an inner self.[4] The symbolic reading of space as psychic metaphor has become the default way of reading the Gothic. Stephen King extends the settings of castles or old dark houses to a wider category of the 'Bad Place', those *dys-topoi* that act as 'psychic batteries, absorbing the emotions that had been spent there, absorbing them much as a car battery will store an electric charge.'[5] The haunted house as a 'bad' or 'dark' place of 'unregulated and irrational supplements', as Barry Curtis puts it, has been routinely grasped through the layered topography of Sigmund Freud's model of the psyche.[6] The vertical layering of the house – the basement, the staircase, the attic – map the deep topography of the psyche. Think of Alfred Hitchcock's *Psycho* (1960): the steps up to the mansard-roofed, Carpenter Gothic house on the hill; the fatal staircase up to the landing and Mother's room; the secrets buried below in the basement and the swamp.

This vertical, archaeological model offers rich interpretations, but resolutely ignores the horizontal. The old dark house in *Psycho* is, after all, paired with the modern motel below, twelve single-storey homely cabin-rooms linked along an L-shaped veranda or gallery. This is, as Steven Jacobs notes in his study of Hitchcock's houses, 'a building type [that] is inherently linked with the boring and the ordinary'.[7] It was a banality that was actively sought by Hitchcock to stage the unprecedented horror of Marion Crane's murder in the bathroom. His decision to split the motel away from the house suggests that this new modern space produces its own monsters, its own disturbing emotional affects – brand new motel architecture features as the backdrop for irrational violence in both Orson Welles's *Touch of Evil* (1958) and Louis Malle's *Lift to the Scaffold* (1958).

The unease produced by these soulless, modern, horizontal non-places has never gone away, and they have been most enduringly translated into the corridor spaces of the Overlook Hotel in Stanley Kubrick's *The Shining* (1980). Stephen King's source novel was all about verticality: haunted elevators, basement discoveries, top-floor confrontations, wasps' nests in the attics. Kubrick's film was about the horizontality of the hotel corridors and the hedge maze outside. Each version exploits an entirely different axis for producing dread, which perhaps explains why King so hated Kubrick's adaptation. Attending to these different planes and their emotional resonances can be crucial.

Manuel Aguirre suggests that Gothic fiction:

> manifests itself in haunted buildings, in labyrinths, and prisons, catacombs and caves; in borders and frontiers, thresholds and walls; in the terror of the shuttered room and the protection of the magic circle; in the promise and dread of the closed door . . . The world is defined in horror literature as *space* and, furthermore, as *closed space*.[8]

The associated feeling, I would like to suggest, is often not the heightened states of terror or horror that are usually associated with the Gothic, but a quieter emotional unease: *Angst*. *Angst* is the German word that is 'maddening' and 'tormenting' to so many of its translators, neither quite the concept of dread nor anxiety, but often translated as one or the other, or both, or just stubbornly left in untranslated italics.[9] The etymological root is *angere*, the Latin for constriction or squeezing, the shortness of breath that manifests as a physiological panic, and which underlies the terms *anguish* or *anxiety*. Ernest Jones linked the nightmare to this feeling of suffocation, with recurrent images of the dreamer 'forcing himself through an aperture too small for the reception of his body . . . or he loses his way in a narrow labyrinth, and gets involved in its contracted and inextricable mazes'.[10] This sense of being slowly choked or squeezed is the etymological root for the claustrophobia induced by the modern corridor ('claustrophobia' itself being a term coined in 1879 to describe the anxiousness of feeling closed in by modern city spaces).[11]

I want to establish the case for the existence of a Corridor Gothic, first in fiction and then in horror film, before circling back to use these examples to try to theorize more exactly that quintessential feeling of *Angst* or dread induced by the modern corridor.

Corridor Gothic

Horace Walpole's *The Castle of Otranto* inaugurates the medieval castle as a space whose volumes are confounded by dream-logic, where picture galleries have disturbingly lively portraits and the foundations are riddled with secret passageways and escape tunnels that subvert the patriarch's authority exercised above. Initially passed off as a rediscovered manuscript from the credulous and superstitious sixteenth century, Walpole was being scrupulously accurate in his mock tale to avoid the modernity of a term like 'corridor'.

Walpole is also important for *where* he wrote his feverish hybrid romance: in his folly of a house at Strawberry Hill, on the picturesque banks of the Thames just beyond Richmond. The house, which Walpole worked on for over forty years, was a direct riposte to his father's rigidly symmetrical Palladian mansion Houghton Hall in Norfolk. Houghton had been completed in 1735 and was an expression of Enlightenment order and power in keeping for the country retreat of Britain's first Whig Prime Minister. His son Horace, in contrast, built in miniature from 1749 in a fractured collage of architectural and decorative styles from the eleventh to the fifteenth century, mixing up bits of Rouen and Rheims cathedrals, King's College, Cambridge, Westminster Abbey, medieval stone cloisters, screens and stained glass, with other elements taken from churches across Europe. It was a faked attempt to appear like an organic accretion of the centuries. Walpole appointed a Committee of Taste to ensure that the house maintained its purity of commitment to reviving only the 'venerable barbarism' of the pre-modern Gothic style.[12] Strawberry Hill was much celebrated in its time, so popular that Walpole produced a guidebook *Description of the Villa* for visitors, where everything from the fan-decorated ceiling of the grand Picture Gallery to the smallest bibelots in the Little Corridor was documented.

Gothic Revival architecture was intended to consolidate a certain conception of Protestant England rooted in the deep past to shore up its perilously recent legitimacy. The Whig version of the Gothic announced in its obsession with abbey ruins and ancient cloisters a triumph over the tyranny of Catholic superstition about the past and the new settlement between monarch and state in the Glorious Revolution of 1688. Aristocratic houses even went through a phase of building fake ruins, follies that nevertheless asserted this new settlement. This explains why Charles Barry later elected to rebuild the Palace of Westminster, the parliament building, in Perpendicular Gothic Revival style after the fire of 1834. In *The Stones of Venice* (1851–3) John Ruskin fixed the Gothic for the high Victorian period as a bulwark of pious, artisanal English tradition against modern mass production and the dead hand of mechanistic industry.

Yet the Gothic pile was also an ambiguous symbol of stubborn survival, haunted by a fear of regression to priestcraft and feudal tyranny, or the persistence of superstition. Walpole built Strawberry Hill to anchor his identity in a fabulated genealogy, making himself a scion of the heroic past. Yet, after being humiliated in the Westminster parliament by his enemies – accused of questionable associations with a young man and memorably denounced as a 'hermaphroditic horse' – Walpole retreated from public life to Strawberry Hill and dreamt his uneasy dreams of persecution and tyranny in ancient winding passages. Gothic Revival architecture and Gothic Romance fiction do not always have the same motivations, then, and are complexly intertwined with progressive and regressive tendencies.

It is Ann Radcliffe's resolutely modern novels of the 1790s that show the importance of discriminating between ancient and modern architectural spaces. In *The Romance of the Forest* (1791), the early menace and suspense is located in the ruined Gothic abbey and its 'winding passages', an incoherent space that repeats the paths of the forest beyond that can only 'perplex, with its labyrinths'. These soon enter the heroine's nightmares, where she is first 'bewildered in some winding passages of the abbey; that it was almost dark, and that she wandered about a considerable time without being able to find a door'.[13] Adeline escapes the multiple menaces of the abbey, including a whole subterranean network of passages, tunnels and dungeons below ground, and her return to social order and propriety is marked by her entry to the light-filled chateau of La Luc and its open prospect onto magnificent scenery that might be sublime but can be contained within the gaze rather than overwhelming it with the terrors of the unbounded imagination: 'The chateau was not large, but it was convenient, and was characterised by an air of elegant simplicity and good order.'[14] The precise description of the 'small hall' with its clear distribution of rational spaces to the left and right, the distinction of family parlour and study, suggest that Adeline has been released from superstitious disorder and ushered into enlightened modernity. She has moved from labyrinthine and confounding passages to the logical proportions and distributions of the modern domestic corridor.

The same contrast occurs in *The Mysteries of Udolpho*. Here the castle is internally divided between the incoherent accumulations of its ancient past and more modern sections that provide some kind of relief from tortuous spatial terrors. Emily's extended journey at night through Montoni's castle moves through vaulted galleries, up spiral staircases, down into ruined chapel crypts and into twisting passages 'the walls of which were dropping with unwholesome dews'.[15] These all build towards her famous encounter with the 'terrible spectacle' in a 'recess of the chamber' that causes her to swoon. Precisely what she sees is famously withheld from the reader for several hundred pages. Again, the eventual moral contrast is with the modest domestic scale and rational order of the chateau at La Vallée where Emily will finally settle, freed of the medieval maze of the disordered imagination.[16]

Radcliffe's spatial obsession is specifically mocked by Jane Austen in Catherine Morland's disappointed expectation in *Northanger Abbey* (1817), where she fails to be conducted along any 'gloomy passages' or 'a secret subterraneous communication' when she visits the abbey. Instead, she is bewildered to find eighteenth-century furniture of 'modern taste' and windows with glass 'so large, so clear, so light!' that no sublime obscurity is going to lift her into a state of Radcliffean terror. The older part of Northanger, built around a remodelled cloister, can merely offer her the tortured double negative of 'occasional passages, not wholly unintricate'.[17]

This mockery did not stop Charles Maturin from writing *Melmoth the Wanderer* (1820), one of the most narratively labyrinthine Gothic novels in the language. This complexly nested set of tales about the accursed Melmoth is set in dank convent cloisters, the twisting corridors of aristocratic houses, and the prison dungeons of the dreaded Inquisition. In one sequence, an escape from a monastery involves struggling through a 'terrible passage', 'choking with fear' in the pitch dark, wandering these 'interminable passages . . . amid sepulchral ruins', becoming increasingly claustrophobic and panic-stricken.[18]

The Gothic sensibility thrived on gloomy piles of 'excessive antiquity' long into the nineteenth century. Poe's mouldering manse in 'The Fall of the House of Usher' (1839) sits precariously above the family vaults, 'lying, at great depth, immediately beneath the portion of the building in which was my own sleeping apartment'.[19] The aristocratic pile of the Dedlocks, in Dickens's *Bleak House* (1853), at least has a ghost, but one that strides the terrace outside rather than any interior space. Later, when Lady Dedlock is forced to visit the scheming lawyer Tulkinghorn in his offices near Lincoln's Inn, she peers in at him 'through the glass from the corridor outside', portending her expulsion from the ancestral home.[20] The protagonist of Edward Bulwer-Lytton's horror tale 'The Haunted and the Haunters' (1857) heads into the notoriously haunted house north of Oxford Street with his trusty hound 'fond of prowling about strange ghostly corners and passages at night'.[21] As we have seen, the domestic spaces are much more overtly middle class and domesticated in *Jane Eyre*, Charlotte Brontë's transcription of the Gothic romance, where the 'gallery' that houses the bedrooms at Thornfield Hall conceals a secret above it in 'the dark, low corridor of the fateful third storey' of the servants' quarters, where Bertha Mason is hidden and from where she descends to mount her terrorist attacks on Rochester and Jane below.[22]

Once the corridor had become a common feature of the domestic house by the mid-nineteenth century, it began to feature in 'haunted corridor' stories in the newspapers, with items that hovered uncertainly between reportage, urban folklore and the tall tale. In a typical example, in 1863 the *Kentish Gazette* recycled a story of a seemingly well-known haunting of an old family seat in Somerset: 'The circumstance was, that on almost every night, at twelve o'clock, something that was invisible entered a certain corridor at one end, and passed out at the other', the footsteps accompanied by a sound of swishing silk, suggesting the passing of a female spectre. 'I received . . . ready permission to pass a night, or more, if necessary, in the haunted corridor,' the narrator reports, setting up a table to play cards with a friend so as to 'completely barricade the passage'. When the time comes, the steps approach and recede 'along the dim corridor' with no visible presence: 'I confess I was petrified with amazement,' the account ends, unable to explain away the phenomenon.[23]

By the 1890s possibly an echo of the same story is presented in more overtly fictional terms as the haunting of Ravenhill Castle, a pile reaching back to the Norman Conquest and 'full of nooks and corners, long and crooked passages, galleries and staircases' and also 'a corridor in which there are several suits of armour'. This haunting has modern refurb problems: the suits of armour have been bought up cheaply from an antique dealer in Wardour Street, and the owner 'insisted that there could be no ghost, and that if there ever was one it must have been carried away in the demolition which he effected in the interior of the building'. The ghost of a white lady, seen to 'glide along the passage' turns out to be the cover story to hide from the servants some after-hours shenanigans by the guests. This is a squib of a tale, but in the glide of its ghost from the ancestral hall to the refurbished corridor it traces the passage of the Gothic from ancient to modern spaces.[24] We are in the terrain of Oscar Wilde's wretched, eponymous Canterville ghost (1887), who stomps up and down the passageways clanking chains and 'fled down the corridor, uttering hollow groans, and emitting a ghastly green light' to little effect on the Americans who now own Canterville Chase.[25] Modernity is too vulgar to be haunted in its bland corridors by old-world ghosts.

Corridors were also one of the main sites of haunting in the famous 'real' psychical investigation conducted at Ballechin House in Perthshire in 1897, a controversy that spilled into the letters pages of *The Times*. The Marquess of Bute asked members of the newly formed Society for Psychical Research to investigate an alleged haunting of a house first built in the sixteenth century, then entirely rebuilt in 1803, with a new wing added in 1887. There were specific rooms associated with loud bangs, shrieks and raps, but also a lot of activity in the 'long passage, shut off by a swing-door' that linked the old house to the new rooms. After midnight, many separate visitors 'often heard the swing-door push open and footsteps coming along the corridor', sometimes followed by furious pounding on doors, a terrifying force nearly pulling the wood from the hinges. The investigation, led by the psychic sensitive Ada Goodrich-Freer, was roundly mocked as the shoddy testimony of credulous and predisposed investigators. One explanation was that the house had wood-panelled rooms with

Long shot down the corridor in Robert Wise's *The Haunting* (1963).

passageways behind them, the perfect conditions to trick the easily spooked. The Society for Psychical Research abandoned the case once confidences had been breached in the press, but the book of the investigation by Freer and the Marquess was the source material for Shirley Jackson's classic horror novel *The Haunting of Hill House* (1959), memorably filmed by Robert Wise as *The Haunting* (1963).[26]

These examples rely on buildings where older histories bleed through into modern refurbishments: the classic Gothic fear of return. The golden age of the ghost story (from about 1880 to 1914) presents a number of tales that generate genuine unease from encounters in modern corridor spaces. In Henry James's 'The Jolly Corner' (1908), Spencer Brydon returns to New York to take possession of the mansion he has inherited, only to spend his nights traversing the empty hallways, connecting rooms and corridors with the perverse expectation that 'he might have been met by some strange figure, some unexpected occupant at a turn of one of the dim passages of an empty house.' This enigmatic pursuit carries on through 'gaping rooms and sounding passages'. Brydon corners the double in what seems to be an *enfilade* of connecting rooms that 'gave all three upon a common corridor as well, but there was a fourth, beyond them, without issue save through the preceding' – a dead-end. He is suddenly unwilling to confront the figure behind the door, sinking into what he calls 'vague anguish' and 'with all his resolution, or more exactly with all his dread, he did stop short.' Brydon turns tail and tries to escape the building, only to encounter a deformed spectral other at the bottom of the stairs. He swoons in denial, coming back to consciousness at 'the uttermost end of an interminable grey passage', that 'dark other end of his tunnel'.[27]

James's phrases are exquisitely balanced between the literal and the figurative, the terrain at once an allegorical encounter with a suppressed part of the self, but also an entirely literal traversal of the house. Of course, James advised never taking a straight route through the house of fiction, but always to include an 'ante-chamber or two and the crooked corridor before [the reader] is in the Presence'.[28]

Other examples from the same era might include W. W. Jacobs's 'The Monkey's Paw' (1902), in which the bereaved parents cower in fear in their hall passageway as their son, no longer quite dead, hammers on the outer door. In M. R. James's 'Number 13' (1904), a phantom room appears in a hotel passageway and seems to superimpose itself across the restructured rooms meant to erase it. What happens at the end of the passage in Rudyard Kipling's 'At the End of the Passage' (1890) is so terrifying that the reader is held aloof from it and left only with puzzle pieces about what precisely was seen. Meanwhile, monstrous hybrid creatures slither along the corridors outside interconnected rooms of the only hotel in town in H. P. Lovecraft's horror story 'Shadow over Innsmouth' (1936). The diffident English writer of strange tales Robert Aickman carried this spatial obsession into the post-war era. In 'The Unsettled Dust' there are heaps of the stuff that somehow can't be swept from the rooms and passages of Clamber Court, just taken over by the Historic Structures Fund from its sullen, bankrupt heirs. Dust is what can't be erased in the shift from aristocratic hierarchy to post-war bureaucracy. The hapless protagonist in Aickman's 'The Hospice', marooned in this perplexing guest house overnight, notes that 'the corridors were down to half-illumination . . . and distinctly sinister.' This Kafkaesque place is another of

Aickman's smothering institutions that seem to suck the life from those caught in their machinery.[29]

In contemporary fiction, three novels elevate the corridor to a principal locus of modern hauntedness. Mark Z. Danielewski's *The House of Leaves* (2000) wraps meta-fictional layers around the tale of a mysterious corridor that opens inside the Navidson House. It starts as an anomaly of mismatched internal and external measurements before opening into a 21-metre-long (70-ft) cold, featureless corridor with ominous branches 'sliding on and on, spawning one space after another, a constant stream of corridors and walls', before then unspooling into a vast, unmappable space, measured in one of the last explorations as over 210 kilometres (130 mi.) long. This 'strange spatial violation' remains mutely and maddeningly uninterpretable, a 'hallway [that] offers no answers'.[30] What unnerves the reader is not the ancient mythology of the Minotaur and the labyrinth, which is teasingly evoked throughout, but the steadfast blandness of these corridor spaces. They contain nothing but their own empty modernity.

John Langan's *House of Windows* (2009) centres on an old upstate New York house where the haunting takes the form of portals and corridors opening in impossible places, leaving it 'no longer so much a house as the meeting point for dozens of corridors to who knew where . . . I was seeing the mouths of passages black as emptiness, black and freezing.' They swallow up a diffident professor of English literature who is desperate to contact the spirit of his son killed serving in Afghanistan.[31]

Jeff VanderMeer's Southern Reach trilogy, *Annihilation*, *Authority* and *Acceptance* (all 2014), keeps returning to the space of the institutional corridor, the instrumental rationality of a secret intelligence facility perverted by some contaminating logic of alien otherness that leaks out of the mysterious Area X that has appeared on the shores of Florida and defies any logical causality or spatial fixity. Area X is reached through a tunnel or portal that seems to utterly transform people in their passage. The middle novel, *Authority*, takes place in the

U-shaped Southern Reach building, and tracks how the administered world of the national security state that is meant to contain and control this deluge is invaded by irrational eruptions even in its most apparently rational volumes. The weird border of that zone stretches and flexes: 'Staggering thought: what might come out into the world down a corridor twenty feet tall by three feet wide.'[32] VanderMeer, one of the leading writers of 'New Weird' fiction, had previously set his short story 'Predecessor' in a 'long, straight corridor . . . like the throat of a beast', a simile that typically for this mode cross-fertilizes the architectural and biological.[33]

All of these stories evoke the 'obscene and recessive spaces' concealed behind flimsy partition walls that Joshua Comaroff and Ong Ker-Shing suggest in *Horror in Architecture* lurk behind the apparently functionalist spaces of modern architectural design.[34] In modern horror, the Modernist utopia of creating functionalist 'machines for living in' has instead curdled 'into a potentially psychopathological space . . . where the house surveys its occupants with silent menace'.[35] The Radiant City is replaced with J. G. Ballard's dystopian vision of the violence provoked by the very rationality of architectural volumes.

Horror Film: The Corridor Shot

The corridor is even more important in the visual economy of the horror film, where the corridor shot has become a stock trope since at least the claustrophobic Expressionist spaces of *The Cabinet of Dr Caligari* (1920). It is significant, for example, that the American psychologist John Holden in *Night of the Demon* (1957) – Jacques Tourneur's adaptation of M. R. James's 'Casting of Runes' – has a first inkling of the conjured demon in an otherwise anonymous hotel corridor, just as he reaches his room door. It is a pre-modern invocation in a quintessentially modern space, but also the sudden distorted expansion of that corridor space behind Holden reveals the isolated vulnerability of the psychologist's sceptical rationalism in the face of a supernatural threat.

Shot through classic wide angle, with a shallow focal length, the constrained space of the corridor distorts and expands volumes, disorienting the viewer: 'the edge of the frame becomes skewed, their lines slanting. Empty space within the image is expanded. Distances look greater than they would to the human eye.'[36] This has been used to great effect in the long vistas of the corridors of Hill House in *The Haunting* (1963) or *The Legend of Hell House* (1973), both of which shoot their corridors almost entirely in distorted wide angle.

The corridor is exploited in horror film because as the camera advances through its restrictive space, it multiplies the anticipatory fear from the off-screen space of the doorways and voids that it passes. Dario Argento's *Suspiria* (1977) uses odd pauses and camera drifts from unmotivated points of view in the highly stylized corridors and secret passageways in the space of the dance academy to generate suspense. At the operatic finale, the curve of the hidden corridor, lined with occult invocations that unwind as the camera steadily advances, reveals the coven of witches beyond.

The length of the corridor, whether in straight vista or in angled turns, allows things to advance or recede ominously from the viewer. The constrictive space can contain a threat, turning the corridor into a gauntlet, as has been common in zombie horde films from Romero's *Night of the Living Dead* (1968) and particularly in the shopping mall

Suzy Bannion follows a secret corridor in the dance academy towards the final revelation in Dario Argento's *Suspiria* (1977);

The Baroque dorm corridor in Dario Argento's *Suspiria*.

arcades of *Dawn of the Dead* (1978) to the endless corridors of various Umbrella Corporation research installations in the *Resident Evil* franchise. Or the corridor space itself can become distended, redoubling its role as the space of transition or a portal, as in *Poltergeist* (1982), where the domestic corridor distorts and stretches impossibly. The space of the corridor itself can become the focus of fear, as in an influential film like *Paranormal Activity* (2007), where a considerable portion of screen time is spent waiting for something to emerge from the black void of the landing beyond the half-open bedroom door. In Mike Flanagan's *Absentia* (2011), the underpass at the end of the street is the space for other kinds of occult passage that we can't quite grasp. Constriction unto death in progressively narrowing tunnels ends the British found-footage film *The Borderlands* (2013).

Accumulating examples could be limitless: another way through this material is to point to directors that consistently exploit corridor space. I would nominate three auteurs of the corridor. Roman Polanski uses corridor distortion with Expressionist panache in *Repulsion* (1965), where Carol's madness is expressed in a subjective hallucination of grasping hands pushing through the corridor walls of her apartment. *The Tenant* (1976) uses distorted angles to rove the hallways of the Paris apartment block. Form becomes content in *Rosemary's Baby* (1968), since it is the mysterious blocked corridor in the apartment that holds the clue to the Satanic conspiracy among the tenants of the Dakota building.

David Lynch has continually used corridor spaces to evoke anticipatory fear, from the chiaroscuro of the hallways in *Eraserhead* (1976) to the Deep River apartment block in *Blue Velvet* (1986), vestibules for Jeffrey's entry into adult sexuality. In *Twin Peaks* (1990–91 and 2017), domestic landings, hallways and corridors are transitional domestic spaces freighted with sexual trauma, while violent attacks often come in hotel hallways or institutional corridors. An unmotivated camera drifts through the empty school corridors just before Laura Palmer's death is announced by the principal in the pilot episode. The metaphysical spaces of the Red Room and the White or Black Lodge where Laura later resides are also continually divided up into curtained labyrinths traversed for occulted purpose. Turning the corner of a restrictive alleyway behind the diner in *Mulholland Drive* (2001) reveals a vision so terrifying it kills a man. Lynch even carefully constructed the twisting corridor that leads to the humiliating marriage bed in *Lost Highway* (1997) in one of his own houses on Mulholland Drive. That corridor is a hallucinatory space traversed with mounting fear – at one point the camera itself seems to physically attack Fred there. Richard Martin, who notes Lynch's general obsession with 'the symbolic power of dark corridors, tight channels and claustrophobic spaces' suggests that in *Lost Highway* 'the corridor is a kind of portal, a transformative space into which Fred repeatedly disappears.'[37]

Most influential, though, has been Stanley Kubrick's obsession with perfecting the camera's single-point perspective, making the vanishing lines of the corridor one of his favoured cinematic spaces. The movement of Kubrick's camera, thrusting forwards and backwards to devour space, to master it with absolute technical precision, is his signature gesture, trialled in the linear tracks through rooms in *The Killing* (1956) and further extended in the glides through the trenches in *Paths of Glory* (1957). The architectural volume of the corridor

The camera prowls the empty school corridor as the death of Laura Palmer is announced in *Twin Peaks*'s pilot episode (1990). *Below*: Agent Dale Cooper in the metaphysical corridor spaces of the Black Lodge, from *Twin Peaks: The Return* (2017).

Danny meets the Grady twins in Stanley Kubrick's *The Shining* (1980).

constitutes the path of the movement of the camera itself, the corridor and camera mirroring each other in exact symmetry.

In horror film, it has been impossible to avoid the influence of how the corridors of the Overlook Hotel were shot in *The Shining* (1980). It was one of the first films to use Garrett Brown's new invention, the Steadicam, and certainly the first to invert the device so that the camera prowled only inches above the floor. The film exploits the rigorous horizontality of the corridor, allowing the camera to glide effortlessly along the plane behind Danny's tricycle, the wide angle making the walls loom over him. Jean-Pierre Geuens suggests *The Shining* introduces a 'new scopic regime', the camera liberated from dollies and the hand-held shakes conventionalized as subjective point-of-view, and instead produces a weightless, machinic gaze 'not necessarily of an entity' (as Garrett Brown himself puts it) 'but of something smoother and more eerie'.[38]

Is 'eerie' the right word? What kind of emotion is the space of the corridor meant to evoke? Is it always a space of suspense that builds towards sublime terror, the measure of success for the first wave of the Gothic? When Perec contemplates the 'corridors of the Paris Métro', the spaces suggest to him 'nothingness, the impalpable, the virtually immature' and 'whose mutism is so prolonged that it ends by triggering off something akin to fear'.[39] This quieter emotion, *akin* to fear, is what we need to call dread or *Angst*.

Corridor Dread

Models for the emotional range of the Gothic tend to be limited. The touchstone is Ann Radcliffe's opposition of expansive, cognitive, sublime 'terror' versus the contractive, physiological, grotesque 'horror'.[40] Anything concerning domestic space, though, often gets processed through Freud's discussion of the *Unheimlich* or uncanny, since this is an idea of unhomely coiled inside homeliness, the unfamiliar intrusion leading back to the most familiar. The *Unheimlich* is loaded with the doom of repetition, a space in which prior temporalities soak through and stall in traumatic repetition. This topography has become the default way not just to read the haunted house, but, in some formulations, *every* modern space.[41]

Some of the fiction and film referenced above certainly fits this paradigm – 'The Jolly Corner' is classically uncanny in its doubling. Yet, as I've suggested, the affective range of the corridor is often more focused on the bland, superficial modernity that carries no historical density and resists the temporal layering required of the uncanny. Where Freud offers a psychology of depth, of archaeological strata, the horizon of the corridor is flat. Stepping into one of those infinitely extended modern hotel corridors, what we feel is not the amplified emotions of horror or terror, or some primordial return home. Instead it is the unease of an unhistoried non-place.

In his last book, *The Weird and the Eerie*, Mark Fisher proposed that the eerie is a distinct category of unsettlement, quieter than horror histrionics and operating outside the un/homely dyad. An 'eerie calm' evokes 'something in the calm or the quiet that doesn't belong, or the quietness itself doesn't belong'.[42] The eerie implies an undisclosed extra agency, trembling on the edge of a revelation that need not connect to the supernatural at all but instead hints at the tested or broken limits of human agency. This is why Garrett Brown evokes the 'eerie' for the feeling associated with the corridor shots in *The Shining*, or why it might describe the subjectless camera crawls through corridors in *Suspiria* that imply a malevolent machinic agency at work. For Fisher, though, the eerie is associated with uneasiness in the natural world, or more accurately disquiet at the end of any notion of uncontaminated Nature. It is the mood that portends the arrival of a 'dark ecology'.[43] Dread seems more precise.

In Søren Kierkegaard's distinction between fear and *Angst*, the miserable philosopher argued that fear is generated by determinable objects on specific trajectories, whereas *Angst* is the underlying general predisposition from which these specific fears might emerge, a general anticipatory condition of waiting for something awful to happen. *Angst* is 'the reality of freedom as possibility anterior to possibility'.[44] 'One may liken dread [*Angst*] to dizziness,' Kierkegaard explained, in a famous metaphor:

> He whose eye chances to look down into the yawning abyss becomes dizzy. But the reason for it is just as much his eye as it is the precipice. For suppose he had not looked down. Thus dread [*Angst*] is the dizziness of freedom . . . [when] freedom then gazes down into its own possibility.[45]

Fear comes from an already determined past, legacies doomed to return. Anxiety is tilted towards the undetermined, vertiginous future, producing potential threats with every choice made.

In the 1920s Heidegger transposed this distinction directly into *Being and Time*, but without Kierkegaard's agonized religious framing of original sin and the anticipation of God's punishment. For Heidegger, fear is a lower affect produced by a 'detrimental entity' from 'some definite region' coming close, menacing Being, while *Angst* is the condition of Being-in-the-World as such.[46] 'When something threatening brings itself close, anxiety [*Angst*] does not "see" any definite "here" or "yonder" from which it comes,' Heidegger explained. 'What threatens is *nowhere*. Anxiety [*Angst*] "does not know" what that in the face of which it is anxious is. "Nowhere", however, does not signify nothing: this is where any region lies, and there too lies any disclosedness of the world.'[47]

To be is therefore to be *Angst*-ridden: the dread 'so close that it is oppressive and stifles one's breath, and yet it is nowhere'.[48] Using a slightly different conceptual frame, China Miéville, writer and theorist of weird fiction and cosmic horror, has formulated this dread as 'the surplus value of fear: the accursed share of fear that cannot be reduced'.[49]

In *The Shining*, Danny pedals through the corridors of the Overlook Hotel on his tricycle along routes that unfold continuously yet confound simple mapping. The corridors of the Overlook suggest an 'impossible and illogical structure' that 'converts the stable medium of architecture into a polymorphic language in motion'.[50] It is the *rooms* of the Overlook that contain the stubborn traces of the past, specific 'detrimental entities' that want to tempt the weak beyond the threshold. In the corridors, though, Kubrick's use of the Steadicam invents an unanchored, inhuman point of view – an eerie, veiled agency – that turns the corridor into a space of anticipatory *Angst*. Early reviewers like Pauline Kael complained that *The Shining* was not frightening because it did not understand the Gothic: 'Who wants to see evil in daylight, through a wide-angle lens?'[51] Perhaps she was technically correct, but misunderstood the affect in these scenes. Kubrick certainly employs the Gothic machinery of the 'old dark house' in the conventionalized signs of haunting in the culminating scenes, but the first half of the film reaches after another kind of emotion. In the corridor, and in the choices Danny makes at every junction of the maze, his trajectories embody the dizziness of being angst-ridden. After the loops of the Overlook's labyrinth, the corridor becomes one of the privileged spaces of contemporary cinematic dread.

I think we can now overlay this Gothic dread with the dystopian, anti-corridic turn that was taken in the 1960s. The late Victorian and Edwardian Gothic revival tends to focus on the domestic and the private, the hauntings or intrusions that disturb the differentiating functions of passageways in the private English gentleman's house. The further we move into the twentieth century, this locus of the haunted house is joined by a new sensibility that begins to explore the dread engendered by public or institutional corridors.

I have argued that in housing, the critique of communal or collective living began to turn against socialist dreams in the 1960s, with the demolition of the Pruitt-Igoe estate and Oscar Newman's denunciation of double-loaded corridor apartment blocks as having no 'defensible space'. J. G. Ballard's *High-rise* followed in 1975, the same year as David Cronenberg's first commercial film, *Shivers*, which unleashed frenzied irrationality in a luxury apartment block in Montreal. Bernard Rose's film *Candyman* (1992) is a rich and complex tale of racial violence set (and filmed) in the corridors and abandoned apartments of the notorious Cabrini-Green housing estate, a predominantly African American high-rise complex in Chicago. The corridors and skywalks of the already condemned Heygate Estate in London were used for Joe Cornish's horror-comedy *Attack the Block* (2011), and public corridor gauntlets in high-rise ghettos feature in *The Raid* (2011) and *Dredd* (2012), both with protagonists that have to work their way steadily through the floors to reach their target.

The 1960s also saw the consolidation of a trenchant critique of the 'total institution' of reform, the asylum in particular. Once corridor-plan asylums begin to be decommissioned and abandoned, they become favoured locales for the Gothic sensibility, a modern instance of the ruin that embodies in stone a survival of a superseded system, but one that threatens to return. Horrors of incarceration are intrinsic to asylum texts that have ambitions to be social commentaries, from the sensation fiction of the 1860s to films such as *The Snake Pit* (1948), *Shock Corridor* (1963) or *One Flew over the Cuckoo's Nest* (1975). But the full panoply of asylum tropes are in play by the time we reach the TV series *American Horror Story: Asylum* (2012–13). The series opens with two 'place hackers' breaking into the abandoned Briarcliff Hospital, once a tuberculosis hospital before its conversion to an asylum for the criminally insane. Its ruined corridors, staircases and tunnel in the woods bleed back into the 1960s and the tyrannical double reign of punitive Catholic nuns and Holocaust mad-doctors in a heady brew that tends to consolidate rather than transcend its clichés. Here is the amped-up Gothic rendition of Mayer Spivack's 1967 study of the psychological effects of psychiatric hospital link tunnels: 'One feels victimized here. Something inexplicable is happening as one walks along, disoriented in space and time.'[52]

Asylum Gothic is a subset of what I would call 'biomedical horror', focused on the hospitals and technological environments of the newly intensive medical-industrial complex. Pete Boss observed this shift happening in the middle of the 1980s, with 'the gothic legacy' of the old dark house or madman's laboratory replaced by 'matter-of-fact and routine instances of physical helplessness, frequently at the hands, or rather the tools, of some brightly-lit and hygienic publicly-funded institution'.[53] The pivotal text for this genre is Robin Cook's medical thriller *Coma*, a best-seller in 1977, filmed in 1978. Cook, a doctor, grasped the potential horror of the convergence of the new medical definition of 'brain death', the increasing role of private corporations in medicare, and the burgeoning market in organs for transplant. In *Coma*, a tenacious female medical student unravels a conspiracy between Boston's public hospitals and a private facility where long-term coma patients are kept in a vast hangar to be harvested for organs. She is sent through hospital crawl spaces, hospital corridors and sinister corporate labyrinths to uncover the truth. Cook's novel was reimagined for a TV mini-series in 2012, thirty years on. Now, the healthcare industry is interwoven with insurers, big pharma, venture capitalists and brokerage firms. The reboot also ups the ante on the final horrors exposed. For all the shiny biopolitical terrain of the hall of coma patients, there is a literal underside of this obsessively monitored space, in the dank service tunnels and abject charnel houses beneath, where the bodies are carved up and harvested for saleable body parts.

Since *Coma*, hospital corridors have been a standard locale for the institutional Gothic. The slasher sequel *Halloween II* (1981) is set almost entirely in hospital corridors, using a roving camera to stalk hapless victims in the hallways. In contrast, Lars von Trier's innovative Danish TV series *The Kingdom* (1994) uses service tunnels, basements and elevator shafts to explore the 'obscene and recessive spaces' of modern buildings identified by Cameroff and Ker-Shing in *Horror in Architecture*, to make a tendentious case about the limits of modern medico-technological rationalism.

I could multiply this convergence of the Gothic and institutional critique for virtually every other public corridor space I have examined. For schools, see the Korean shocker by Ki-Hyung Park, *Whispering Corridors* (1998), about a vengeful suicide haunting the halls, or, in a different register, the dreamy temporal and spatial loops of the camera through the school corridors of Gus Van Sant's *Elephant* (2003), his reconstruction of the Columbine school massacre, or, in his subtle reinvention of the stalker genre, the steady pursuit of the heroine through a school corridor in David Robert Mitchell's *It Follows* (2014). Just like the haunted domestic corridor stories of the popular press in the nineteenth century, contemporary tabloids also love such stories: in 2017 Britain's *Daily Mirror* posted footage under the banner headline: 'Secondary School CCTV Camera Capture Terrifying "Ghost" Causing Havoc in Corridors in the Dead of Night.'[54]

But perhaps by now I have more than made my point. In many of these cases it is the bland, horizontal anonymity of the corridor that turns it into a place of unsettlement and unease, the Bad Place or dys-topia of our administered world. The critique of the 'total institution' that began in the 1960s was redoubled by the attack on bureaucracy. With changes to the distribution of office space and the public realm away from the corridor and instead towards open-plan and glass atria, the anti-corridic tendency inverted this building form from its utopian origins into the register of bureaucratic entanglement or Gothic engulfment.

Does that mean we have reached the end of the corridor?

The recently deceased husband wanders the hospital corridors in David Lowery's *A Ghost Story* (2017).

Conclusion: At the End of the Passage

Rudyard Kipling's elliptical short story 'At the End of the Passage' (1890) is the tale of the crack-up and death of an engineer who works at the very limits of the British Empire in India. His friend Spurstow, a doctor, can only travel the vast distance once a week, and tries to treat him for relentless persecutory nightmares, of which we gain only one detail: 'A blind face that cries and can't wipe its eyes, a blind face that chases him down corridors.' As the Doctor departs after another fevered night, the Engineer then sees his own double 'standing in the verandah . . . He approached the figure, which naturally kept at an unvarying distance from him, as is the use of all spectres born of overwork. It slid through the house and dissolved into swimming specks.' The double fulfils its role as the traditional harbinger of death and the Engineer is found dead a week later: 'In the staring eyes was written terror beyond the expression of any pen.' His servants can only say 'my master had descended into the Dark Places.'[1]

Nothing quite makes sense in this tale, hovering in the hyphen between the natural and the supernatural. One of the many odd details is that the Engineer's house is clearly a colonial bungalow, a building type that 'seldom had corridors, as the rooms were entered directly from the verandah . . . or the hall'.[2] The double appears on the verandah, sure enough, but there is actually no passage in 'At the End of the Passage', only the edges of a phantom dream of corridors that must derive from somewhere else.

It has become a standard cinematic trope to figure a crisis or death in a scene where a body on a gurney is rushed through hospital corridors towards the Emergency Room: the subjective point of view of the strip lighting flashing by on the ceiling above; the concerned faces of medics leaning in; forward motion arrested by the doors swinging shut on the bereft relatives left outside. The camera comes to a halt at the end of the passage. It happens in a rush in any medical melodrama; it happens at a more serene pace in the first scenes of haunting in David Lowery's film *A Ghost Story* (2017), where Casey Affleck's white-sheeted ghost comes into bewildering being in a hospital corridor.

Medical dread and the existential angst evoked by office corridors are neatly compounded in John Frankenheimer's extraordinary film *Seconds* (1966), where the secret facility of The Company that stages deaths and replaces the bodies of bored execs is a network of anonymous corporate corridors, banal and featureless until the last white corridor that takes Rock Hudson to his final, gruesome death. Don DeLillo's novel *Zero K* (2016) also repeatedly associates death with corporate corridors. At the billionaire's cryogenic facility, where the embarrassment of death is smoothed over by the language of transitioning, the irritated son

> spent time walking the halls. The halls were nearly empty, three people, at intervals, and I nodded to each, receiving only a single grudging glance. The walls were shades of green. Down one broad hall, turn into another. Blank walls, no windows, doors widely spaced, all doors shut. These were doors of related colours, subdued, and I wondered if there was meaning to be found in these slivers of the spectrum.

His stepmother, being voluntarily prepped for transition into frozen stasis, complains: 'This place, all of it, seems transitional to me. Filled with people coming and going. Then the others, those who are leaving

Tony Wilson is wheeled down the corridor to his surgical death in John Frankenheimer's *Seconds* (1966).
Below: The priest reads last rites over Wilson in *Seconds* (1966).

in one sense, as I am, but staying in another sense, as I am. Staying and waiting.' The facility, called The Convergence, is built in a featureless post-national space in anonymous corporate style: the perfect antechamber for post-modern, post-death death.[3]

In *Zero K*, of course, travelling to the end of the corridor is not intended to end in a black, annihilating dot at the end of a vanishing perspective. The billionaire's investment is in the transcendence of bodily death promised by transhumanists and all those speculative Silicon Valley tech companies that market eternal life to execs outraged that mortality cannot be outbid. What is hoped for is more the trippy corridor of light experienced at the end of Stanley Kubrick's *2001: A Space Odyssey* (1968), which plunges the astronaut into a kind of rebirth, or perhaps the moment at the end of *The Matrix* when Neo finally achieves full consciousness and sees the hallway where he was trapped as pure information, pulsing zeros and ones.

In 1975 Raymond Moody published *Life after Life*, a survey of the experiences of 150 people who had been declared medically dead but had recovered. Moody formulated a generic account of what is now called the Near-Death Experience (NDE): hearing the death pronounced, an out-of-body experience of separation, seeing your own body on the bed below, a harsh buzzing noise, entry into a dark tunnel travelling at rapid speed towards an intense light, the reaching of a border or doorway, a decision or judgement to turn back, and the return into the body, followed by an enduring experience of spiritual enrichment and enhanced life. Although Moody claimed no NDEs are alike, there is a persistence in published accounts of this experience of the Dark Tunnel and the light at the end of the passage. Moody's interviewees described it as 'a cave, a wall, a trough, an enclosure, a tunnel, a funnel, a vacuum, a void, a sewer, a valley, and a cylinder'.[4] Another advocate notes that

> Some refer to this tunnel as long and dark and that they were alone in it throughout the journey. Others say there were bright

> lights that flashed along its walls, or that it was coloured or even transparent, and that other people were there. Almost everyone states that they swooshed through its length at great speed . . . In most cases, a light appears at the end of the tunnel, and experiencers note that is where they are headed – a light described as brighter than the sun.[5]

The experience can be made to conform to many frames of explanation, from the overtly theological via the psychological, whether of death trauma or archetypal symbols of transition, to the hard-wired neurological. Susan Blackmore, for instance, explains the tunnel as an optical illusion produced by cerebral anoxia near death, causing a narrowed tunnel vision effect.[6] Whatever it is, figurations of the approach of death seem to be intensely corridic. They echo the earliest artful conjuration of the feeling of the sacred in the transversal passages of Minoan and Greek temples, but also feel distinctly modern in their evocation of the link hospital corridors where we are wheeled towards death. Interestingly, I have read some accounts that the common phrase 'light at the end of the tunnel', first used in the late nineteenth century, was fixed in general use by Bernard Baruch's celebrated 1946 speech about the need for the international control of nuclear weapons: 'The light at the end of the tunnel is dim, but our path seems to grow brighter as we actually begin our journey. We cannot yet light our way to the end.'[7] The global reach of the bomb leaves us anxious and constricted in a dark tunnel leading towards a wholly other kind of blistering bright light.

The trajectory of this history of the corridor might appear to lead from life to death, utopia to dystopia, the sacred light ahead to the dark dot of the vanishing point. After the 1960s, open-plan offices, vast glass and steel atria, and the lure of loft living reduced the corridor to a shamefaced infrastructural function, hidden and unloved behind service doors. Yet just as the actual corridor seemed to undergo a fatal diminishment, the late 1960s saw the major extension of the metaphor of the corridor to sprawling city spaces and transport systems. The urban corridor was defined in 1969 as 'a linear system of urban places . . . joined by highly developed "bundles" of transport routes'.[8] This seems to be one of the first uses of this metaphor. Increasingly, much of the planet's population lives in urban concentrations that urban planners call corridors. The geopolitical metaphor of protected corridors had started earlier: the 225-kilometre-long (140-mi.) Danzig Corridor, to protect a strategic Polish enclave after the First World War, was first named by Lloyd George in discussions after the Armistice.[9] Since then, there has been a proliferation of humanitarian corridors for civilians during war, ecological corridors for the safe passage of endangered migrant species, or remittance corridors, the invisible financial networks of migrant workers sending money back home. The architectural history might fall away in these extensions of the term, but the more general sense of being immersed or channelled by the built environment of the corridor keeps these usages tied to their source.

This might have seemed like one of those irritating, quirky histories to start with, but the doors along this passage have, I hope, constantly opened into some of the major experiences of modernity itself: the readjustment of the very concept of the private life; the fate of the public sphere; the commodification of everyday life; the possibility of collective living; the chances that built space might reform or rationalize character; bureaucratization and our life as constituted through institutions; the affective tonality of modern feelings of anomie, unease or dread; and our latter-day visions of life after death. 'History,' as T. S. Eliot said in 'Gerontion', 'has many cunning passages, contrived corridors/And issues.' If you press your ear to the door, the void of the corridor beyond is whispering some significant stories about the transformation of our sensibility in the modern world.

References

Introduction

1 Robin Evans, 'Figures, Doors and Passages', in *Translations from Drawing to Building and Other Essays* (London, 1997), p. 55; Paul Olivier, 'Corridor', in *Encyclopedia of Vernacular Architecture of the World*, 3 vols (Cambridge, 1997), vol. I, p. 414; Georges Perec, *Species of Spaces and Other Pieces*, trans. J. Sturrock (London, 2008), p. 5.
2 Steven Morris, Matthew Weaver and Haroon Siddique, 'Three Patients Die at Worcestershire Hospital amid NHS Winter Crisis', *The Guardian*, 6 January 2017.
3 Marc Angélil and Cary Siress, 'Infrastructure Takes Command: Coming out of the Background', in *Infrastructure Space*, ed. Ilka Ruby and Andreas Ruby (Berlin, 2017), p. 14.
4 Gaston Bachelard, *The Poetics of Space*, trans. M. Jolas (London, 2014), pp. 34 and 30.
5 Daniel Jütte, *The Strait Gate: Thresholds and Power in Western History* (New Haven, CT, 2015), pp. 75–6.
6 Christopher Alexander, Sarah Ichikawa and Murray Silverstein, *A Pattern Language Which Generates Multi-service Centers* (Berkeley, CA, 1968), pp. 179–80.
7 Joshua Cameroff and Ker-Shing Ong, *Horror in Architecture* (Novato, CA, 2013), pp. 129–30.

1 Origins

1 Vanbrugh, letters quoted in Jeremy Musson, *The Country Houses of Sir John Vanbrugh, from the Archives of Country Life* (London, 2008), pp. 56 and 65.
2 Charles Saumarez Smith, *The Building of Castle Howard* (London, 1990), p. 54.

3 Entry for 'Covered Way' in the *Encyclopedia Americana* (Philadelphia, PA, 1830), vol. III, p. 604.
4 See Mark Jarzombek, 'Corridor Spaces', *Critical Inquiry*, XXXVI/4 (2010), pp. 728–70. This essay has remained a touchstone for me throughout this project.
5 Christy Anderson, *Renaissance Architecture* (Oxford, 2013), p. 89. See also Kate Marshall, *Corridor: Media Architectures in American Fiction* (Minneapolis, MN, 2013).
6 Musson, *The Country Houses of Sir John Vanbrugh*, p. 19.
7 Stephan Trüby et al., *Corridor* (Venice, 2014), p. 14.
8 R. D. Martienssen, *The Idea of Space in Greek Architecture, with Special Reference to the Doric Temple and Its Setting* (Johannesburg, 1964), p. 146.
9 Mircea Eliade, *The Sacred and the Profane: The Nature of Religion*, trans. W. Trask (New York, 1959), pp. 25–6.
10 Herodotus, *Histories*, cited in Rodney Castleden, *The Knossos Labyrinth: A New View of the 'Palace of Minos' at Knossos* (London, 1990), p. 64.
11 Strabo, cited in Castleden, *The Knossos Labyrinth*, p. 63.
12 Ovid, *Metamorphoses*, trans. A. D. Melville (Oxford, 1986), viii.160–63 and 169–71.
13 Cathy Gere, *Knossos and the Prophets of Modernism* (Chicago, IL, 2009), p. 5.
14 This was W. F. Jackson Knight's speculation in his 1936 book *Cumaean Gates*, cited in Janet Bord, *Mazes and Labyrinths of the World* (Tiptree, 1976), p. 11.
15 See Daniel Jütte, *The Strait Gate: Thresholds and Power in Western History* (New Haven, CT, 2015), p. 36.
16 Frederick E. Winter, *Studies in Hellenistic Architecture* (Toronto, 2006), p. 143.
17 J. B. Greenough, 'The Fauces of the Roman House', *Harvard Studies in Classical Philology*, vol. I (1890), pp. 1–12.
18 Yvon Thébert, Essex, 'Private Life and Domestic Architecture in Roman Africa', in *A History of Private Life*, vol. I: *From Pagan Rome to Byzantium*, ed. P. Veyne (Cambridge, MA, 1987), pp. 313–409.
19 Clive Knights, 'The Spatiality of the Roman Domestic Setting: An Interpretation of Symbolic Content', in *Architecture and Order: Approaches to Social Space*, ed. M. Pearson and C. Richards (London, 1994), p. 133.
20 J. T. Smith, *Roman Villas: A Study in Social Structure* (London, 1997), p. 115.

21 Walter Horn, 'On the Origins of the Medieval Cloister', *Gesta*, XII/1–2 (1973), p. 15.
22 Ibid., p. 19.
23 For a summary of the extensive scholarship on the Plan of St Gall, see Charles B. McClendon, *The Origins of Medieval Architecture: Building in Europe*, AD *600–900* (New Haven, CT, 2005).
24 See Megan Cassidy-Welch, *Monastic Spaces and Their Meanings* (Turnhout, 2001).
25 Cathy Ross, *The Charterhouse: The Guidebook* (London, 2016), p. 50.
26 Michael Thompson, *Cloister, Abbot and Precinct* (Stroud, 2001), p. 55. See also Maximilian Sternberg, *Cistercian Architecture and Medieval Society* (Leiden, 2013).
27 Samuel Pepys, entry for 29 May 1664, *The Diary of Samuel Pepys*, vol. V, ed. R. Latham and W. Matthews (London, 1971), p. 161.
28 Martha Hollander, *An Entrance for the Eyes: Space and Meaning in Seventeenth-century Dutch Art* (Berkeley, CA, 2002), p. 8.
29 Samuel van Hoogstraten, *Introduction to the Noble School of the Art of Painting* (1678), cited in ibid., p. 43.
30 See Orest Ranum, 'The Refuges of Intimacy', in *A History of Private Life*, vol. III: *Passions of the Renaissance*, ed. Roger Chartier (Cambridge, MA, 1989), pp. 207–63. The quotation on closets comes from Angel Day's *The English Secretarie*, as discussed in Alan Stewart, 'The Early Modern Closet Discovered', *Representations*, 50 (1995), pp. 76–100.
31 Roger Chartier, 'Introduction' to *A History of Private Life*, vol. III, p. 7.
32 Mark Girouard, *Robert Smythson and the Elizabethan Country House* (New Haven, CT, 1983).
33 Bryan Jay Wolf, *Vermeer and the Invention of Seeing* (Chicago, IL, 2001), p. 66.
34 Simon Stevin, *Civic Matters* (1590), quoted in Hollander, *An Entrance for the Eyes*, p. 122.
35 Chartier, *A History of Private Life*, vol. III, p. 5.
36 Ranum, 'Refuges of Intimacy', p. 225.

2 The Utopia of Corridors, I: Charles Fourier's Phalanstery

1 Victor Considerant, *Description du phalanstère et considérations sociales sur l'architectonique* (Paris, 1848), p. 39.
2 Charles Fourier, 'An Architectural Innovation: The Street-gallery', in *The Utopian Visions of Charles Fourier: Selected Texts on Work, Love, and Passionate Attraction*, trans. and ed. J. Beecher and P. Bienvenu (Boston, MA, 1971), pp. 243–4.

3 Walter Benjamin, 'Konvolut W: Fourier', *The Arcades Project*, trans. H. Eiland and K. McLaughlin (Cambridge, MA, 1999), p. 629.
4 Thomas More, *The Complete Works of St Thomas More*, vol. IV: *Utopia*, ed. Edward Surtz and J. H. Hexter (New Haven, CT, 1965), p. 121.
5 Plato, *The Republic*, trans. D. Lee (Harmondsworth, 1987), p. 184.
6 Tomasso Companella, *The City of the Sun* (1602), citations from full text translation by Thomas W. Halliday (1885) at Project Gutenberg, www.gutenberg.org.
7 Anthony Vidler, *The Scenes of the Street, and Other Essays* (New York, 2011), p. 21.
8 Anthony Vidler, *Claude-Nicolas Ledoux: Architecture and Social Reform at the End of the Ancien Régime* (Cambridge, MA, 1990), p. 268.
9 Ibid., p. 332. Ledoux's Ideal City is also extensively discussed in Emil Kaufmann, 'Three Revolutionary Architects: Boullée, Ledoux, and Lequeu', *Transactions of the American Philosophical Society*, XLII/3 (1952), pp. 429–564.
10 Hugh Doherty, 'Memoir of Charles Fourier', in *False Association and Its Remedy; or, A Critical Introduction to the Late Charles Fourier's Theory of Attractive Industry, and the Moral Harmony of the Passions* (London, 1841), p. 6.
11 Honoré de Balzac, *Lost Illusions*, cited in 'Palais Royal as Heterotopia' on the Quantum City blog, https://blogs.ethz.ch.
12 Roland Barthes, *Sade Fourier Loyola*, trans. R. Miller (Berkeley, CA, 1989), pp. 104 and 110.
13 See Frederick Engels, *The Development of Socialism from Utopia to Science* (Edinburgh, n.d.), p. 4.
14 See Benjamin, *Arcades Project*, p. 637.
15 Robert Owen, *A New View of Society; or, Essays on the Principle of the Formation of Character, and the Application of the Principle to Practice* (London, 1813), reproduced as Appendix B of *The Life of Robert Owen, Written by Himself* (London, 1857), p. 261.
16 Robert Owen, 'An Address Delivered to the Inhabitants of New Lanark on the First of January 1816', reproduced as Appendix C of *The Life of Robert Owen*, p. 352.
17 Chris Jennings, *Paradise Now: The Story of American Utopianism* (New York, 2016), p. 44.
18 Robert Owen, *Two Discourses on a New System of Society, as Delivered in the Hall of Representatives at Washington* (London, 1825), p. 22. These speeches are also collected by Oakley C. Johnson in *Robert Owen in the United States* (New York, 1970).

19 Owen, *Two Discourses*, p. 22.
20 Ibid., p. 21.
21 Donald F. Carmony and Josephine M. Elliott, 'New Harmony, Indiana: Robert Owen's Seedbed for Utopia', *Indiana Magazine for History*, LXXVI/3 (1980), p. 201.
22 Logie Barrow, *Independent Spirits: Spiritualism and English Plebeians, 1850–1910* (London, 1986), p. 29.
23 Considerant, quoted in Rondel Van Davidson, *Did We Think Victory Great? The Life of Victor Considerant* (Lanham, MD, 1988), p. 56.
24 Considerant, quoted in ibid., p. 248.
25 Ibid., p. 271.
26 Albert Brisbane, *Social Destiny of Man*, reprinted in *London Phalanx*, vol. I (1841–2), p. 411.
27 Ibid., p. 428.
28 'What Is Association? The Edifice – Mode of Living', *The Phalanx: Organ of the Doctrine of Association* (4 May 1844), p. 1.
29 Frederick Law Olmsted, 'The Phalanstery and the Phalansterians', in *Frederick Law Olmsted: Essential Texts*, ed. Robert Twombly (New York, 2010), p. 55.
30 S. M. Pedrick, 'The Wisconsin Phalanx at Ceresco', *Proceedings of the State Historical Society of Wisconsin at its 50th Anniversary Meeting* (1903), p. 203.
31 Dolores Hayden, *Seven American Utopias: The Architecture of Communitarian Socialism, 1790–1975* (Cambridge, MA, 1976), p. 172.
32 Marianne Dwight, Letter (4 March 1846), *Letters from Brook Farm, 1844–1847*, ed. Amy Reed (Poughkeepsie, NY, 1928), p. 148.
33 See Maud Honeyman Greene, 'Raritan Bay Union, Eagleswood, New Jersey', *Proceedings of the New Jersey Historical Society*, LXVIII/1 (1950), pp. 1–20. Quote from Thoreau from 1856 letter, p. 14.
34 See Etienne Cabet, *Travels in Icaria*, trans. L. Roberts, introduction R. Sutton (Syracuse, NY, 2003).
35 [Emilie Dallet], *Twenty Years of Co-partnership at Guise*, trans. Aneurin Williams (London, 1903), p. 18.
36 John Humphrey Noyes, quoted in Ellen Wayland-Smith, *Oneida: From Free Love Utopia to the Well-set Table* (New York, 2016), p. 88.
37 Most of the details in this paragraph come from Janet R. White, 'Designed for Perfection: Intersections between Architecture and Social Program at the Oneida Community', *Utopian Studies*, VII/2 (1996), pp. 113–38. See also chapter on Oneida in Hayden, *Seven American Utopias*.

3 The Utopia of Corridors, II: Social Housing from Petrograd to the Barbican

1 China Miéville, *October: The Story of the Russian Revolution* (London, 2017), pp. 46 and 58.
2 Leon Trotsky, *Literature and Revolution* (Ann Arbor, MI, 1967), pp. 249 and 254.
3 V. Kuzmin, quoted in Richard Stites, *Revolutionary Dreams: Utopian Vision and Experimental Life in the Russian Revolution* (Oxford, 1989), p. 203.
4 Anatole Kopp, *Town and Revolution: Soviet Architecture and City Planning, 1917–35* (New York, 1970), p. 112.
5 El Lissitzky, quoted ibid., p. 120.
6 Owen Hatherley, *Landscapes of Communism: A History through Buildings* (London, 2015), p. 151.
7 For an exhaustive presentation of the buildings and plans for Moscow, see M. Fosso, O. Macel and M. Meriggi, eds, *Konstantin S. Mel'nikov and the Construction of Moscow* (Milan, 2000).
8 For an outline of the history of the OSA, see Stites, *Revolutionary Dreams*, and Kopp, *Town and Revolution*; see also Hugh D. Hudson Jr, '"The Social Condenser of Our Epoch": The Association of Contemporary Architects and the Creation of a New Way of Life in Revolutionary Russia', *Jahrbücher für Geschichte Osteuropas*, XXXIV/4 (1986), pp. 557–78.
9 Moisei Ginzburg, *Style and Epoch* (Cambridge, MA, 1982), pp. 78, 79 and 97.
10 Leonid Sabsovich from *Socialist Cities* (1929), quoted in Christina E. Crawford, 'From the Old Family – to the New', *Harvard Design Magazine*, 41 (2015), www.harvarddesignmagazine.org, accessed 21 May 2018.
11 Zlata Lilana, quoted in Lynne Attwood, *Gender and Housing in Soviet Russia: Private Life in a Public Space* (Manchester, 2010), p. 30.
12 See Stites, *Revolutionary Dreams*, p. 201.
13 Victor Buchli, *An Archaeology of Socialism* (Oxford, 1999), p. 63. Buchli's book results from the year he lived in the Narkomfin in 1991–2, the year of the dissolution of the USSR.
14 Moisei Ginzburg, quoted in Kopp, *Town and Revolution*, pp. 141, 142–3.
15 Hatherley, *Landscapes of Communism*, p. 20.
16 Yevgeny Zamyatin, *We*, trans. C. Brown (London, 1993), p. 94.
17 Svetlana Boym, *Common Places: Mythologies of Everyday Life in Russia* (Cambridge, MA, 1994), pp. 124–5, 140, 141–2.

18 Joseph Brodsky, 'Less Than One', in *Less Than One: Selected Essays* (London, 1987), p. 11.
19 Ilya Kabakov, cited in Kate Fowle, 'On *Labyrinth* (*My Mother's Album*)', in *Not Everyone Will Be Taken into the Future*, exh. cat. by Ilya Kabakov and Emilia Kabakov (London, 2017), p. 43.
20 Le Corbusier, *Towards a New Architecture* (Thousand Oaks, CA, 2008), pp. 263, 227, 229.
21 El Lissitzky, quoted in Nicholas Fox Webber, *Le Corbusier: A Life* (New York, 2008), p. 282.
22 Le Corbusier, *The Radiant City: Elements of a Doctrine of Urbanism as the Basis of Our Machine-age Civilization*, trans. P. Knight et al. (London, 1967), pp. 90 and 9.
23 Le Corbusier, *The Radiant City*, p. 39.
24 Jonathan Meades, *Museum without Walls* (London, 2012), p. 14; Webber, *Le Corbusier*, p. 586.
25 José Baltanás, *Walking through Le Corbusier: A Tour of His Masterworks* (London, 2006), p. 115.
26 David Jenkins, *Unité d'habitation, Marseilles, 1945–52* (London, 1993), n. p.
27 Le Corbusier, *The Marseilles Block*, trans. G. Sainsbury (London, 1953), p. 23.
28 Ibid., p. 12.
29 Le Corbusier, 'Inaugural Speech', in Arthur Rüegg et al., *La Cellule Le Corbusier: L'Unité d'habitation de Marseille* (Marseilles, 2015), p. 101.
30 Le Corbusier, *The Marseilles Block*, p. 23 and p. 28.
31 J. H. Forshaw and Patrick Abercrombie, *County of London Plan, 1943* (London, 1943), p. 1.
32 Owen Hopkins, *Lost Futures: The Disappearing Architecture of Post-war Britain* (London, 2017). The dubious recovery of post-1945 austerity as a retro-style in post-2008 austerity is critiqued in Owen Hatherley, *The Ministry of Nostalgia* (London, 2016).
33 Ian Nairn, 'Subtopia', *Architectural Review* (June 1955), p. 366.
34 Alison Smithson and Peter Smithson, *The Charged Void: Architecture* (New York, 2001), p. 96.
35 Ibid., p. 86.
36 Ibid., p. 84.
37 Helen Webster, in *Modernism without Rhetoric: Essays on the Work of Alison and Peter Smithson*, ed. Helena Webster (London, 1997), p. 84.
38 Smithson and Smithson, *Charged Void*, p. 296.
39 See Alex Powers, ed., *Robin Hood Gardens Re-visions* (London, 2010). Robin Hood Gardens was again denied protected building status in 2015 and demolition of the block finally began in 2017.

40 Geoffrey Moorhouse from 1968, quoted in John Grindrod, *Concretopia: A Journey around the Rebuilding of Postwar Britain* (London, 2014), p. 173.
41 See Irena Murray and Julian Osley, eds, *Le Corbusier and Britain: An Anthology* (London, 2009).
42 Partridge, quoted in Grindrod, *Concretopia*, p. 170.
43 Elain Harwood, *Chamberlin, Powell and Bon: The Barbican and Beyond* (London, 2011), p. vii.
44 Michael Hebbert, 'The City of London Walkway Experiment', *Journal of the American Planning Association*, LIX/4 (1993), pp. 433–50.
45 G. A. Jellicoe, *Motopia: A Study in the Evolution of Urban Landscape* (London, 1961).
46 Reyner Banham, *Megastructure: Urban Futures of the Recent Past* (London, 1976), p. 8.
47 Charles Jencks, *The Language of Post-modern Architecture* (London, 1977).
48 Oscar Newman, *Defensible Space: People and Design in the Violent City* (London, 1972), p. 1.
49 Ibid., p. 27.
50 Alice Coleman, *Utopia on Trial: Vision and Reality in Planned Housing* (London, 1985), pp. 3–4.
51 Ibid., p. 39.
52 Ibid., pp. 67 and 65.
53 Kate Ng, 'David Cameron Pledges to Regenerate "Brutal" and "Dark" Rundown High-rise Estates', *Independent on Sunday* (10 January 2016), www.independent.co.uk.

4 Corridors of Commerce: The Arcade, the Exhibition Hall, the Mall

1 In the Quintin Hoare translation the title is 'Fourier or the Arcades', in Walter Benjamin, *Charles Baudelaire: A Lyric Poet in the Era of High Capitalism* (London, 1983), but in the later Howard Eiland and Kevin McLaughlin translation for *The Arcades Project* (Cambridge, MA, 2002) it is rendered as 'Fourier, or the Arcades'. The comma makes a big difference to the dialectical relation of these terms!
2 Johann Friedrich Geist, *Arcades: The History of a Building Type* (Cambridge, MA, 1983), p. 4.
3 See Bernard Comment, *The Panorama*, trans. A.-M. Glasheen (London, 1999). See also my chapter on London's 'Orientalist' entertainments in Roger Luckhurst, *The Mummy's Curse: The True Story of a Dark Fantasy* (Oxford, 2012), pp. 87–118.

4 *Mogg's New Picture of London* (London, 1838), p. 78.
5 Terence Davis, *The Architecture of John Nash* (London, 1960), p. 102.
6 'Regent-Street Improvements', *The Era* (24 September 1848), p. 8.
7 See Harry Furniss, *Paradise in Piccadilly: The Story of Albany* (London, 1925), p. 6.
8 Prospectus quoted in 'Burlington Arcade', *Survey of London*, vols XXXI–XXXII: *St James Westminster* (London, 1963), available at www.british-history.ac.uk. Last quote is from 'Burlington Arcade', *Morning Post*, 4 January 1819, p. 3, written a matter of days after the Arcade opened.
9 Jane Rendell, 'Arcade', in *Encyclopedia of Urban Studies*, 2 vols (London, 2009), vol. I, p. 35. See also her essay, 'Displaying Sexuality: Gendered Identities and the Early Nineteenth-century Street', in *Images of the Street: Planning, Identity and Control in Public Space*, ed. Nicholas Fyfe (London, 1998), pp. 75–91.
10 Margaret MacKeith, *Shopping Arcades: A Gazetteer of Extant British Arcades, 1817–1939* (London, 1985), for example p. vii or p. 92.
11 Anthony Vidler, *The Scene of the Street, and Other Essays* (New York, 2011), p. 100.
12 Mark Twain, *A Tramp Abroad* [1880] (Oxford, 1996), pp. 555 and 549.
13 *Routledge's (One Shilling) Guide to the Crystal Palace* (London, 1854), p. 11. This is a guide to the Crystal Palace as rebuilt in Sydenham, but opens with this paean to the original.
14 For more commentary, see Paul Young, *Globalization and the Great Exhibition: The Victorian New World Order* (Basingstoke, 2009) and Paul Greenhalgh, *Ephemeral Vistas: The Exposition Universelles, Great Exhibitions and World's Fairs, 1851–1939* (Manchester, 1988).
15 Hippolyte Taine, *Notes on England*, trans. E. Hyams (London, 1957), p. 188 and Le Corbusier, 'The Crystal Palace: A Tribute', in *Le Corbusier in Britain*, ed. I. Murray and J. Osley (London, 2009), p. 106.
16 Paxton's proposal, quoted in George F. Chadwick, *The Works of Sir Joseph Paxton, 1803–65* (London, 1961), p. 209.
17 Douglas Murphy, *The Architecture of Failure* (Winchester, 2012), pp. 1–2.
18 Émile Zola, *Thérèse Raquin*, trans. R. Buss (London, 2004), p. 9.
19 Ibid., pp. 9–10.
20 Siegfried Kracauer, 'Abschied von der Linden Passage', trans. in Geist, *Arcades*, pp. 158–60, quote from p. 158.
21 Louis Aragon, *Paris Peasant*, trans. Simon Watson Taylor (London, 1987), pp. 28, 48, 62.

22 Walter Benjamin, 'Surrealism: The Last Snapshot of the European Intelligentsia' (1929), in *One Way Street and Other Writings*, trans. E. Jephcott and K. Shorter (London, 1985), p. 229.
23 William Severini Kowinski, *The Malling of America: Travels in the United States of Shopping* (Bloomington, IN, 2002), pp. 45–6, and Margaret Crawford, 'The World in a Shopping Mall', in *Variations on a Theme Park: The New American City and the End of Public Space*, ed. M. Sorkin (New York, 1992), p. 30.
24 The best and most detailed survey of Victor Gruen's whole career is Alex Wall, *Victor Gruen: From Urban Shop to New City* (Barcelona, 2005), but see also M. Jeffrey Hardwick, *Mall Maker: Victor Gruen, Architect of an American Dream* (Philadelphia, PA, 2004). I also used Malcolm Gladwell's essay on Gruen, 'The Terrazzo Jungle', *New Yorker* (15 March 2004), www.newyorker.com.
25 Victor Gruen and Larry Smith, *Shopping Towns USA: The Planning of Shopping Centers* (New York, 1960), pp. 149–50.
26 See Jane Jacobs, 'Northland: A New Yardstick for Shopping Center Planning', *Architectural Forum*, 100 (1954), p. 102. Northland limped on to 2015, when it lost its last anchor store.
27 For details, see Wall, *Victor Gruen*, quotes from pp. 97 and 102.
28 Disputes over whether malls can be used for political activity went to the law courts in the 1990s following mall police suppressing anti-war demonstrations. For details, see Lisa Scharoun, *America at the Mall: The Cultural Role of Retail Utopia* (Jefferson, NC, 2012), pp. 89ff.
29 Gruen, quoted in Anne Quilto, 'The Father of the Shopping Mall Hated What He Had Created', *Quartz* (July 2015), www.qz.com.
30 Sanford Kwinter, quoted in Wall, *Victor Gruen*, p. 22.
31 See Vance Packard, *The Hidden Persuaders* (London, 1977) and Rachel Bowlby, *Carried Away: The Invention of Modern Shopping* (London, 2000).
32 Kowinski, *Malling of America*, p. 401.
33 Fredric Jameson, *Postmodernism, or the Cultural Logic of Late Capitalism* (London, 1991), pp. 38 and 43.
34 Tony Dokoupil, 'Is the American Shopping Mall Dead?', *Newsweek* (11 November 2008), www.newsweek.com.
35 Alana Semuels, 'A New Life for Dead Malls', *The Atlantic* (9 March 2015), www.theatlantic.com.

5 The Ecstasy of Communication: The Hotel Corridor

1 For history, see Molly Berger, *Hotel Dreams: Luxury, Technology, and Urban Ambition in America, 1829–1929* (Baltimore, MD, 2011), with a substantial section on Tremont House.
2 Costard Sly, *Sayings and Doings at the Tremont House in the Year 1832*, 2 vols (Boston, 1832), vol. I, p. 9.
3 Anthony Trollope, 'Chapter XXXIV: Hotels', *North America* (New York, 1862), p. 552.
4 William Chambers, *Things as They Are in America* (London, 1854), cited in Berger, *Hotel Dreams*, p. 68.
5 Rufus Jarman, *A Bed for the Night: The Story of the Wheeling Bellboy, E. M. Statler, and His Remarkable Hotels* (New York, 1952), p. 102.
6 *Collier's Weekly* (12 November 1904), cited in Jarman, *A Bed for the Night*, p. 105. Daniel J. Boorstin, *The Americans: The National Experience* (London, 1988), p. 144.
7 W. Sydney Wagner, 'The Statler Idea in Hotel Planning and Equipment II: The Development of the Floor Plan', *Architectural Forum*, XXVII/6 (1917), p. 166.
8 W. Sydney Wagner, 'The Statler Idea in Hotel Planning and Equipment I: Introduction', *Architectural Forum*, XXVII/5 (1917), p. 118.
9 See Anthony Falco, 'Rediscovering the New Yorker Hotel's Underground Tunnel to Penn Station', *Untapped Cities* (22 June 2016), https://untappedcities.com, accessed 24 May 2018.
10 For contemporary discussion, see Edward Earle Purinton, 'The Largest Hotel in the World and Some Reasons for E. M. Statler's Spectacular Success', *The Independent* (8 May 1920), pp. 202–3; (15 May 1920), pp. 237–9.
11 See David Witwer, 'An Incident at the Statler Hotel: A Black Pittsburgh Teamster Demands Fair Treatment during the Second World War', *Pennsylvania History*, LXV/3 (1998), pp. 350–67. This essay concerns the barring of black union member Theodore Johnson from entering a Statler Hotel union meeting in September 1944.
12 Rem Koolhaas, *Delirious New York* (New York, 1994), p. 135.
13 Oscar Tschirky, quoted in James Remington McCarthy, *Peacock-Alley: The Romance of the Waldorf-Astoria* (New York, 1931), pp. 17–18.
14 Albert Stevens Crockett, *Peacocks on Parade: A Narrative of a Unique Period in American Social History and Its Most Colorful Figures* (New York, 1931), pp. 86–7.
15 Ibid., p. 60.
16 Ibid., p. 98.

17 William Marion Reedy, 'A Westerner in the Waldorf', *Reedy's Paper*, vol. XIII (1903), p. 8, quoted in McCarthy, *Peacock-Alley*, p. 62.
18 Crockett, *Peacocks on Parade*, pp. 94 and 96.
19 Henry James, *The American Scene* (New York, 1968), pp. 99, 102–3 and 104.
20 Andreas Bernard, *Lifted: A Cultural History of the Elevator*, trans. D. Dollenmayer (New York, 2014), p. 227.
21 Most of the details here derive from Stephen Watts, *The Ritz* (London, 1963).
22 Ibid., p. 16.
23 Elizabeth Bowen, *The Hotel* (London, 2003), p. 26. See also Vicki Baum, *Grand Hotel*, trans. B. Creighton (New York, 2016).
24 Jarman, *A Bed for the Night*, pp. 114–15.
25 Walter Benjamin, *One Way Street and Other Writings*, trans. E. Jephcott and K. Shorter (London, 1997), p. 49.
26 Raymond Chandler, 'The King in Yellow', in *Stories and Early Novels* (New York, 1995), pp. 418, 427 and 428.
27 Ibid., p. 463.
28 Chandler, 'I'll Be Waiting', *Stories and Early Novels*, pp. 579 and 582.
29 D. J. van Lennep, 'The Hotel Room', in J. J. Kockelmans, *Phenomenological Psychology: The Dutch School* (Dordrecht, 1987), pp. 209–15.
30 On this point, see Gerd Gemünden, *A Foreign Affair: Billy Wilder's American Films* (New York, 2008).
31 Edward Dimendberg, *Film Noir and the Spaces of Modernity* (Cambridge, MA, 2004), p. 15.
32 Andrew Spicer, *Film Noir* (Harlow, 2002), p. 67.
33 Siegfried Kracauer, 'The Hotel Lobby', in *The Mass Ornament*, trans. Thomas Levin (Cambridge, MA, 1995), pp. 179, 183 and 176. For more approaches to the lobby space, see Tom Avermaete and Anne Massey, eds, *Hotel Lobbies and Lounges: The Architecture of Professional Hospitality* (London, 2013).
34 Norman S. Hayner, *Hotel Life* (Chapel Hill, NC, 1936, repr. College Park, MD, 1969), pp. 72, 176 and 182.
35 Ibid., p. 1.
36 Martin Heidegger, 'Building Dwelling Thinking', in *Basic Writings*, ed. David Farrell Kress (London, 1993), p. 363. A useful wider account is Christian Norberg-Schulz, 'Heidegger's Thinking on Architecture', *Perspecta*, 20 (1983), pp. 61–8.
37 See Peter Eli Gordon, *Rosenzweig and Heidegger: Between Judaism and German Philosophy* (Berkeley, CA, 2003), p. 277. There are a couple

of playful, semi-fictional reflections on Heidegger and the existential meaning of the hotel: Wayne Koestenbaum, *Hotel Theory* (New York, 2007) and Joanna Walsh, *Hotel* (London, 2015).

38 Jean-Paul Sartre, *Being and Nothingness: Essay on Phenomenological Ontology*, trans. H. Barnes (London, 1957).

39 Carole Seymour-Jones, *A Dangerous Liaison: A Revelatory Biography of Simone de Beauvoir and Jean-Paul Sartre* (New York, 2009).

40 Thom Gunn, 'The Corridor', *Collected Poems* (London, 1993), p. 85.

41 György Lukács, 'Preface' to *The Theory of the Novel* (1920); cited as the defining metaphor of Stuart Jeffries's *Grand Hotel Abyss: The Lives of the Frankfurt School* (London, 2016), pp. 1–2.

42 Raymond Border and Etienne Chaumerton, *A Panorama of American Film Noir*, trans. P. Hammond (San Francisco, CA, 2002), p. 13.

43 Alain Robbe-Grillet, *Last Year at Marienbad: A Ciné Novel*, trans. R. Howard (London, 1962), p. 17.

44 Erica Ronell, *The Brothers Grim: The Films of Ethan and Joel Coen* (Lanham, MD, 2007), p. 124.

45 Mark T. Conard, 'Heidegger and the Problem of Interpretation in *Barton Fink*', in *The Philosophy of the Coen Brothers*, ed. Conard (Lexington, KY, 2009).

46 Will Wiles, *The Way Inn* (London, 2015), pp. 25–6.

47 Ibid., p. 24.

48 Ibid., p. 95.

49 Ibid., p. 206.

50 Ibid., p. 276.

6 Corridors of Reform: Prison, Workhouse, Asylum, Hospital, School and University

1 Henry Mayhew and John Binny, *The Criminal Prisons of London, and Scenes of Prison Life* (London, 1862), pp. 118–20.

2 Ibid., p. 118.

3 Ernö Goldfinger, 'The Sensation of Space' (1941), in *Ernö Goldfinger: Works 1* (London, 1983), p. 47.

4 Robin Evans, *The Fabrication of Virtue: English Prison Architecture, 750–1850* (Cambridge, 1982), p. 394. See also Thomas A. Markus, *Buildings and Power: Freedom and Control in the Origin of Modern Building Types* (London, 1993).

5 Mary Poovey, *Making a Social Body: British Cultural Formation, 1830–1864* (Chicago, IL, 1995), p. 106.

6 Michel Foucault, *Discipline and Punish: The Birth of the Prison*, trans. Alan Sheridan (New York, 1995), pp. 146 and 172.
7 Ibid., p. 221.
8 Jonas Hanway, *Solitude in Imprisonment*, quoted in Randall McGowen, 'The Well-ordered Prison, England 1780–1865', in *The Oxford History of the Prison: The Practice of Punishment in Western Society*, ed. Norval Morris and David J. Rothman (Oxford, 1995), p. 81.
9 G. O. Paul, *Considerations of the Defects of Prisons*, quoted in Evans, *The Fabrication of Virtue*, pp. 169–70.
10 Jeremy Bentham, *Panopticon; or, The Inspection House* (Dublin, 1791), p. 19.
11 See Norman B. Johnson, 'John Haviland, Jailor to the World', *Journal of the Society of Architectural Historians*, XXIII/2 (1964), p. 105.
12 Norman Johnson et al., *Eastern State Penitentiary: Crucible of Good Intentions* (Philadelphia, PA, 1994), p. 36.
13 Negley K. Teeters and John D. Shearer, *The Prison at Philadelphia, Cherry Hill: The Separate System of Penal Discipline, 1829–1913* (New York, 1957), p. 67.
14 Quotes from George Wilson Pierson, *Tocqueville and Beaumont in America* (Oxford, 1938), p. 471.
15 Charles Dickens, *American Notes, for General Circulation* (London, 2000), pp. 111–12 and 121. Letter to David Colden (10 March 1842), *Letters of Charles Dickens*, vol. III, ed. M. House et al. (Oxford, 1974), p. 111.
16 Mayhew, *Criminal Prisons*, p. 234.
17 J. T. Burt, *Results of the System of Separate Confinement, as Administered at the Pentonville Prison* (London, 1852), p. 47.
18 Mayhew, *Criminal Prisons*, p. 147.
19 Ibid., p. 136.
20 Review of the Second Report of the Pentonville Commissioners, *Pennsylvania Journal of Prison Discipline and Philanthropy*, vol. I (1845), p. 132.
21 Burt, *Results of the System of Separate Confinement*, p. 24.
22 See Sean McConville, 'The Victorian Prison: England, 1865–1965', in *The Oxford History of the Prison*, pp. 117–50.
23 Alan Travis, 'Michael Gove Eyes Pentonville Sale', *The Guardian*, 17 July 2015, www.the guardian.com.
24 Ian Anstruther, *The Scandal of the Andover Workhouse* (London, 1973).
25 The most detailed survey available is Kathryn Morrison, *The Workhouse: A Study of Poor Law Buildings in England* (London, 1999), written to catalogue all the surviving structures for English

Heritage. I have also relied on the exhaustive catalogue, with many supporting documents, on the website www.workhouses.org.uk.

26 Annotation to Head's 'Plan of a Rural Workhouse', cited in Markus, *Buildings and Power*, p. 142.

27 Andrea Tanner, 'The Casual Poor and the City of London Poor Law Union, 1837–64', *Historical Journal*, XLII/1 (1999), p. 200.

28 *Knight's Guide to the Arrangement and Construction of Workhouse Buildings* (London, 1889), p. 7.

29 Ibid., p. 18.

30 Edward Smith, 'Report on the Metropolitan Workhouse Infirmaries and Sick Wards' (1866), quoted in Morrison, *The Workhouse,* p. 98.

31 Florence Nightingale, *Notes on Hospitals: Being Two Papers Read before the National Association for the Promotion of Social Science* (London, 1863), p. 61.

32 See Henry C. Burdett, *Hospitals and Asylums of the World*, vol. IV: *Hospital Construction, with Plans*, 4 vols (London, 1893). Burdett's exhaustive taxonomy divides hospitals into Pavilions, Block Hospitals and Corridor Hospitals, the last to be avoided where at all possible.

33 Michel Foucault, *Psychiatric Power: Lectures at the Collège de France, 1973–74,* trans. G. Burchell (London, 2006), p. 101.

34 Philippe Pinel, *A Treatise on Insanity,* trans. 1806, extracted in *Three Hundred Years of Psychiatry, 1535–1860*, ed. Richard Hunter and Ida MacAlpine (New York, 1982), p. 606.

35 Samuel Tuke, *Description of the Retreat, an Institution near York, for Insane Persons of the Society of Friends* (York, 1813), p. vii.

36 Ibid., p. 106.

37 Ibid., p. 133.

38 Andrew Scull, *The Insanity of Place/The Place of Insanity* (Abingdon, 2006), p. 20. See also Barry Edginton, 'The Design of Moral Architecture at the York Retreat', *Journal of Design History*, XVI/2 (2003), pp. 103–17.

39 Carla Yanni, *The Architecture of Madness: Insane Asylums in the United States* (Minneapolis, MN, 2007), p. 18.

40 C. N. French, *The Story of St Luke's Hospital* (London, 1951), p. 3.

41 Charles Dickens, 'A Curious Dance around a Curious Tree', *Household Words* (17 January 1852), reproduced in French, *Story of St Luke's Hospital*, pp. 61–3.

42 W.A.F. Browne, *What Asylums Were, Are, and Ought to Be* (1837), reprinted in full in *The Asylum as Utopia: W.A.F. Browne and the Mid-nineteenth Century Consolidation of Psychiatry*, ed. Andrew Scull (London, 1991), p. 186.

43 Thomas Kirkbride, quoted in Nancy Tomes, *A Generous Confidence: Thomas Story Kirkbride and the Art of Asylum-keeping, 1840–83* (Cambridge, 1984), pp. 134–5.
44 Thomas Kirkbride, *On the Construction, Organization and General Arrangements of Hospitals for the Insane,* 2nd edn (Philadelphia, PA, 1880), p. 118.
45 Tomes, *A Generous Confidence,* p. 282.
46 Sir James Clark, 'Obituary Notice of Dr. Conolly', *Transactions of the Ethnological Society of London*, v (1867), p. 326. For a revisionist view of his achievements, see Andrew Scull, 'A Brilliant Career? John Conolly and Victorian Psychiatry', *Victorian Studies*, XXVII/2 (1984), pp. 203–35.
47 Maximilian Jacobi, *On the Construction and Management of Hospitals for the Insane,* trans. J. Kitching (London, 1841), pp. 36–7.
48 John Conolly, *The Construction and Government of Lunatic Asylums* (London, 1847), p. 12.
49 Ibid., p. 12.
50 Ibid., p. 19.
51 'Middlesex County Lunatic Asylum, Colney Hatch', *London Daily News* (3 July 1851), p. 6.
52 Ibid.
53 See Jeremy Taylor, *Hospital and Asylum Architecture, 1840–1914: Building for Health Care* (London, 1991), which contains a gazetteer of all those built. This has been updated and completed on the website www.countyasylums.co.uk.
54 See Leslie Topp, 'The Modern Mental Hospital in Late Nineteenth-century Germany and Austria: Psychiatric Space and Images of Freedom and Control', in *Madness, Architecture and the Built Environment: Psychiatric Spaces in Historical Context*, ed. Leslie Topp, James Moran and Jonathan Andrews (London, 2007), pp. 241–61.
55 Erving Goffman, *Asylums: Essays on the Social Situation of Mental Patients and Other Inmates* (London, 1991), pp. 22 and 32. For Basaglia, see John Foot, *The Man Who Closed the Asylums: Franco Basaglia and the Revolution in Mental Health Care* (London, 2015).
56 Goffman, *Asylums,* pp. 211–12.
57 Mayer Spivack, 'Sensory Distortion in Tunnels and Corridors', *Hospital and Community Psychiatry*, XVIII/1 (1967), pp. 14 and 13.
58 Ibid., pp. 18 and 16.
59 See David Charles Sloane and Beverlie Conant Sloane, *Medicine Moves to the Mall* (Baltimore, MD, 2003) and Annmarie Adams, 'Decoding Modern Hospitals', *Architectural Design*, LXXXVII/2 (2017), pp. 16–23.

60 Enoch Powell, cited in 'Enoch Powell's 1961 Speech', www.canehill.org, accessed 25 May 2018.
61 See Mark Davis, *Asylum: Inside the Pauper Lunatic Asylum* (Stroud, 2014); John Gray, *The Abandoned Asylums of New England* (Buffalo, NY, 2011). The quote is from the discussion of derelict asylum photography in Graham Moon, Robin Kearns and Alun Joseph, *The Afterlives of the Psychiatric Asylum* (Farnham, 2015), p. 140.
62 Andreas Huyssen, 'Authentic Ruins: Products of Modernity', in *Ruins of Modernity*, ed. Julia Hell and Andreas Schönle (Durham, NC, 2010), p. 21.
63 Michel Foucault, *The History of Sexuality: An Introduction*, trans. R. Hurley (London, 1987), p. 28.
64 Louis Althusser, *On Ideology*, trans. B. Brewster (London, 2008), p. 184.
65 For details, see Deborah E. B. Weiner, *Architects and Social Reform in Late Victorian London* (Manchester, 1994).
66 Edward Robert Robson, *School Architecture, Being Practical Remarks on the Planning, Designing, Building, and Furnishing of School Houses* (London, 1874), pp. 165–6.
67 Arthur Conan Doyle, 'The Naval Treaty' (1894), *The Memoirs of Sherlock Holmes*, ed. C. Roden (Oxford, 2000), p. 229.
68 See Frank Kelsall, 'The Board Schools: School Building, 1870–1914', in Ron Ringshall, Margaret Miles and Frank Kelsall, *The Urban School: Buildings for Education in London, 1870–1980* (London, 1983), pp. 13–28. See also Mark Girouard, *Sweetness and Light: The Queen Anne Movement, 1860–1900* (New Haven, CT, 1977).
69 W. M. Childs, quoted in William Whyte, *Redbrick: A Social and Architectural History of Britain's Civic Universities* (Oxford, 2015), p. 169.
70 Michael Sadler, 'Preface' to Friedrich Paulsen, *The German Universities and University Study*, trans. F. Thilly and W. Elwang (London, 1906), p. xii.
71 See Debbi Long, Rick Iedema and Bonsan Bonne Lee, 'Corridor Conversations: Clinical Communication in Casual Spaces', in *The Discourse of Hospital Communications: Tracing Complexities in Contemporary Health Care Organizations*, ed. Rick Iedema (Basingstoke, 2007), p. 197. For specifically university corridors, see Rachel Hurdley, 'The Power of Corridors: Connecting Doors, Multiplying Materials, Plotting Openness', *Sociological Review*, LVIII/1 (2010), pp. 45–64.
72 See Mark Jarzombek, *Designing MIT: Bosworth's New Tech* (Boston, MA, 2004). It makes sense that after working at MIT's architecture

department and producing this history, Jarzombek went on to write one of the first sustained studies of the corridor in 2010.

73 Paul Venable Turner, *Campus: An American Planning Tradition* (Boston, MA, 1984).

74 Michael Beloff, *The Plateglass Universities* (London, 1968), p. 113.

75 Ibid., p. 167.

76 Brian Manning, quoted in Whyte, *Redbrick*, pp. 262–3.

77 Quoted in Whyte, *Redbrick*, p. 254. See also the discussion of Leeds University in Elain Harwood, *Chamberlin, Powell and Bon: The Barbican and Beyond* (London, 2011), pp. 83–97.

78 Robert Booth, 'Francis Crick Institute's £700 million building "too noisy to concentrate"', *The Guardian*, 21 November 2017, www.guardian.com.

7 Passages to Privacy: The English Gentleman's House

1 Mervyn Macartney, 'The Home and Its Halls', in *The British Home of To-day: A Book of Modern Domestic Architecture and the Applied Arts*, ed. W. Shaw Sparrow (London, 1904), Section E, p. iii.

2 Orest Ranum, 'The Refuges of Intimacy', in *A History of Private Life*, vol. III: *Passions of the Renaissance*, ed. Roger Chartier (Cambridge, MA, 1989), p. 225. For class differences in terrace housing, see Stefan Muthesius, *The English Terraced House* (New Haven, CT, 1982).

3 Helen C. Long, *The Edwardian House: The Middle-class Home in Britain, 1880–1914* (Manchester, 1993), p. 144.

4 Hermann Muthesius, *The English House* [1904–5], trans. J. Seligman (London, 1979), p. 79.

5 For a full description, see also W. H. St John Hope, *Windsor Castle: An Architectural History*, 2 vols (London, 1913), vol. II, pp. 573ff.

6 Quoted in John Martin Robinson, *Windsor Castle: The Official Illustrated History* (London, 2001), p. 105.

7 For full details, see Derek Lindstrum, *Sir Jeffry Wyatville* (Oxford, 1972).

8 Joseph Nash, *Views of the Interior and Exterior of Windsor Castle* (London, 1848), not paginated. *A Descriptive Catalogue of the Pictures, Busts, Bronzes, etc. in the Corridor of Windsor Castle* was privately printed in 1843.

9 Quote from Sir Lionel Cust, *King Edward VII and His Court: Some Reminiscences* (London, 1930), p. 40.

10 Robert Kerr, *The English Gentleman's House; or, How to Plan English Residences, from the Parsonage to the Palace* (London, 1864), pp. 28, 41, 44, 52 and 53.

11 Ibid., pp. 74, 71 and 76.
12 Ibid., pp. 98, 173 and 184.
13 Ibid., pp. 186–7.
14 Jill Franklin, *The Gentleman's Country House and Its Plan, 1835–1914* (London, 1981), p. 146.
15 J. J. Stevenson, *House Architecture,* 2 vols (London, 1880), vol. II, pp. 116 and 49–50.
16 Muthesius, *The English House,* p. 94.
17 Karen Chase and Michael Levenson, *The Spectacle of Intimacy: A Public Life for the Victorian Family* (Princeton, NJ, 2000), p. 168.
18 Thad Logan, *The Victorian Parlour* (Cambridge, 2001), p. 26.
19 Walter Benjamin, *One Way Street and Other Writings,* trans. E. Jephcott and K. Shorter (London, 1997), p. 70.
20 See the discussion in Chase and Levenson, *Spectacle of Intimacy,* pp. 70ff.
21 Leslie Harris and Jill Banks, 'The Family Corridor at Kedleston Hall', *Georgian Group Journal,* 13 (2003), pp. 108–13.
22 Karen Chase, *Eros and Psyche: The Representation of Personality in Charlotte Brontë, Charles Dickens, and George Eliot* (London, 1984), pp. 59 and 60.
23 Charlotte Brontë, *Jane Eyre: An Autobiography* [1847] (London, 2006), pp. 21 and 52.
24 See Virginia C. Kenny, *The Country-house Ethos in English Literature, 1688–1750* (Brighton, 1984).
25 Brontë, *Jane Eyre*, pp. 126 and 129.
26 Ibid., pp. 346, 380, 407, 396, 413 and 452.
27 Micki Nyman, 'Portals of Desire in Charlotte Brontë's *Jane Eyre* and Fanny Fern's *Ruth Hall*', *Brontë Studies,* XLII/4 (2017), pp. 143–53.
28 Henry James, 'Preface', *The Portrait of a Lady*, ed. R. Luckhurst (Oxford, 2009), p. 7. Henry James, letter to Mrs Humphry Ward, as quoted in Elizabeth Stevenson, *The Crooked Corridor: A Study of Henry James* (London, 1949), p. 142.
29 Henry James, 'Preface', p. 12.
30 Henry James, *Portrait of a Lady*, pp. 36–7.
31 H. G. Wells, *Kipps* [1905] (London, 2005), pp. 150–51. See A. James Hammerton, 'Pooterism or Partnership? Marriage and Masculine Identity in the Lower Middle-class, 1870–1920', *Journal of British Studies*, XXXVIII/3 (1999), pp. 291–321.
32 'Country Homes: Welbeck Abbey', *Country Life* (21 April 1906), p. 564.

33 Llewellynn Jewitt and S. C. Hall, *The Stately Homes of England*, 2nd series (London, 1877), p. 349.
34 Ibid., p. 347.
35 The family history is detailed in A. S. Turberville, *A History of Welbeck Abbey and Its Owners*, 2 vols (London, 1939), with Chapter Eighteen devoted to the fifth Duke.
36 'The Duke of Portland', *Rutland Echo and Leicestershire Advertiser*, 12 July 1875, p. 3.
37 Memoir of Elizabeth Butler, reprinted in Derek Adlam, *Tunnel Vision: The Enigmatic Fifth Duke of Portland* (Welbeck, Nottinghamshire, 2013), p. 25.
38 Lady Ottoline Morrell's recollections, in William Cavendish-Bentinck, 6th Duke of Portland, *Men, Women and Things: Memories of the Duke of Portland* (London, 1937), p. 32.
39 Stefan Trüby, 'Welbeck Abbey's Corridors', *Icon*, 136 (October 2014), www.iconeye.com.
40 See Charles Archard, 'The Eccentric Duke and His Underground Tunnels', *The Portland Peerage Romance* (London, 1907), available at www.nottshistory.org.uk, accessed 28 May 2018.
41 Butler in Adlam, *Tunnel Vision*, p. 24.
42 Morrell in Cavendish-Bentinck, *Men, Women and Things*, p. 36.

8 The Dystopia of Corridors, I: Bureaucracy

1 Russell Barton, *Institutional Neurosis*, 2nd edn (Bristol, 1966), p. 14. From the same year, see also David J. Vail, *Dehumanization and the Institutional Career* (Springfield, IL, 1966).
2 E. M. Forster, 'The Machine Stops', in *New Collected Short Stories* (London, 1987), p. 116.
3 Yevgeny Zamyatin, *We*, trans. G. Zilboorg (New York, 1952), p. 212.
4 Arthur Koestler, *Darkness at Noon* (London, 1982), p. 212.
5 See David Lockwood, *The Blackcoated Worker: A Study in Class Consciousness* (London, 1958).
6 Charles Dickens, *Dombey and Son* (Oxford, 2001), p. 183.
7 Herman Melville, *Bartleby, the Scrivener: A Story of Wall Street* (London, 2010), p. 16.
8 Francis Duffy, 'Office Buildings and Organizational Change', in *Buildings and Society: Essays on the Social Development of the Built Environment*, ed. A. King (London, 1980), p. 262.
9 J. William Shulze, *The American Office: Its Organization, Management and Records* (New York, 1913), p. 88.

10 Quote from Jan Wils, extracted in Jack Quinan, *Frank Lloyd Wright's Larkin Building: Myth and Fact* (New York, 1987), p. 116. Mendelsohn is quoted on p. 117.
11 See Richard Padovan, *Towards Universality: Le Corbusier, Mies and De Stijl* (London, 2002) and Phyllis Lambert, *Building Seagram* (New Haven, CT, 2013).
12 See Christina Henry, 'Preserving Historic Corridors in Open Office Plans', *Bulletin of the Association for Preservation Technology*, XVIII/3 (1986), pp. 75–80.
13 A. Wankum, *Layout Planning in the Landscaped Office* (London, 1969), p. 5.
14 Robert Propst, *The Office: A Facility Based on Change* (Elmhurst, IL, 1968), p. 27.
15 Douglas Coupland, *Generation X: Tales for an Accelerated Culture* (London, 1992), p. 24. Propst's relationship to cubicles in offices fifty years on is examined in Julie Schlosser, 'Cubicles: The Great Mistake', *Fortune Magazine* (22 March 2006), http://archive.fortune.com.
16 Juriaan Van Meel, *The European Office: Office Design and National Context* (Rotterdam, 2000), p. 12.
17 Francis Duffy, *The New Office* (London, 1997), p. 124.
18 Max Weber, 'Bureaucracy', in *Essays in Sociology*, ed. H. H. Gerth and C. W. Mills (London, 1952), pp. 215–16.
19 Ibid., p. 228.
20 James Burnham, *The Managerial Revolution* (London, 1962), p. 81.
21 J. Donald Kingsley, *Representative Bureaucracy: An Interpretation of the British Civil Service* (Yellow Springs, OH, 1944), pp. 7, 186, 10 and 262.
22 Theodor Adorno, 'Culture and Administration', in *The Culture Industry: Selected Essays on Mass Culture,* ed. J. M. Bernstein (London, 1991), p. 104.
23 C. P. Snow, *Corridors of Power* (Harmondsworth, 1964), pp. 7 and 220.
24 See 'Two Cultures in the Corridors', *Time* (20 November 1964), www.timemagazine.com.
25 David Graeber, *The Utopia of Rules: On Technology, Stupidity, and the Secret Joys of Bureaucracy* (London, 2015), pp. 26–7.
26 Charles Dickens, *Little Dorrit* (London, 2003), p. 119.
27 Anthony Trollope, *The Three Clerks* (Oxford, 1978), p. 1. For a study of Trollope as bureaucrat and novelist, see Ceri Sullivan, *Literature in the Public Service: Sublime Bureaucracy* (Basingstoke, 2013).
28 Melville, *Bartleby, the Scrivener*, p. 62. For Melville's life as a bureaucrat, see Stanton Garner, 'Herman Melville and the Customs Service', in *Melville's Evermoving Dawn: Centennial Essays*, ed. J. Bryant (Kent, OH, 1997), pp. 276–93.

29 See Jacques Derrida, *The Post-card: From Socrates to Freud and Beyond*, trans. A. Bass (Chicago, IL, 1987). For a full focus on this notion, see J. Hillis Miller, 'Derrida's *Destinerrance*', MLN, CXXI/4 (2006), pp. 893–910.
30 For Kafka's career in the bureaucratic world of the insurance business, see Howard Caygill, *Kafka: In Light of the Accident* (London, 2017).
31 Franz Kafka, *The Castle*, trans. J. A. Underwood (London, 1997), p. 229.
32 Ibid., pp. 56 and 61.
33 Franz Kafka, *The Trial*, trans. M. Mitchell (Oxford, 2009), p. 52.
34 Gilles Deleuze and Felix Guattari, *Kafka: Towards a Minor Literature*, trans. D. Polan (Minneapolis, MN, 1986), p. 73.
35 Kafka, 'Before the Law', in *The Castle*, pp. 153ff. For the endless deferral of the law in Kafka, see Jacques Derrida, 'Before the Law', trans. A. Ronell and C. Roulston, in *Acts of Literature*, ed. D. Attridge (London, 1992), pp. 181–220. See also Torben Beck Jorgensen, 'Weber and Kafka: The Rational and Enigmatic Bureaucracy', *Public Administration*, XC/1 (2012), pp. 194–210.
36 See Noemi Marin, *After the Fall: Rhetoric in the Aftermath of Dissent in Post-communist Times* (New York, 2007), p. 37.
37 Emmett Grogan, leader of the Diggers, quoted in Howard Brik, *Age of Contradiction: American Thought and Culture in the 1960s* (Ithaca, NY, 1998), p. 135.
38 Details in this paragraph rely on Chris Darke's *Alphaville* (London, 2005) and Alan Woolfolk, 'Disenchantment and Rebellion in *Alphaville*', in *The Philosophy of Science Fiction Film*, ed. Steven M. Sanders (Lexington, KY, 2008), pp. 191–205.
39 James Tweedie, *The Age of New Waves: Art Cinema and the Staging of Globalization* (Oxford, 2013), p. 52.
40 Eric Rohmer, cited ibid., p. 74.
41 Hannah Arendt, *Eichmann in Jerusalem: A Report on the Banality of Evil*, 5th edn (New York, 2006), pp. 288–9. See also Edwin Black, *IBM and the Holocaust* (New York, 2001).
42 André Breton, 'Introduction to the Discourse on the Paucity of Reality', trans. R. Seiburth and J. Gordon, *October*, 69 (1994), pp. 138 and 139.
43 James Harding, *Jacques Tati: Frame by Frame* (London, 1984), p. 124. Details also from David Bellos, *Jacques Tati: His Life and Art* (London, 1999).
44 Bruce Nauman, 'Nauman Interview, 1970', in *Please Pay Attention Please: Bruce Nauman's Words, Writings and Interviews* (Cambridge, MA, 2005), p. 134.

45 Robert Morgan, *Bruce Nauman* (Baltimore, MD, 2002), p. 41.
46 Anthony Vidler, *Warped Space: Art, Architecture, and Anxiety in Modern Culture* (Cambridge, MA, 2000), p. vii.
47 Helen Delaney, in *Mike Nelson: The Coral Reef*, exh. cat., Tate Britain (London, 2010), n.p.
48 Hans Haacke, quoted in Tony Godfrey, *Conceptual Art* (London, 1998), p. 208. Comment on Nauman from Janet Kraynak, 'Dependent Participation: Bruce Nauman's Environments', *Grey Room*, 10 (2003), p. 27.

9 The Dystopia of Corridors, II: Dread and the Gothic

1 Siegfried Kracauer, 'On Employment Agencies', in *The Mass Ornament*, trans. T. Levin (Cambridge, MA, 1995), p. 60.
2 Horace Walpole, letter to William Cole cited in Ruth Mack, 'The Castle of Otranto', in *Horace Walpole's Strawberry Hill* (New Haven, CT, 2009), p. 8.
3 Eino Railo, *The Haunted Castle: A Study of the Elements of English Romanticism* (London, 1927), pp. 7 and 11.
4 Terry Castle, *The Female Thermometer: Eighteenth-century Culture and the Invention of the Uncanny* (Oxford, 1995).
5 Stephen King, *Danse Macabre* (London, 1991), p. 297.
6 Barry Curtis, *Dark Places: The Haunted House in Film* (London, 2008), p. 13.
7 Steven Jacobs, *The Wrong House: The Architecture of Alfred Hitchcock* (Rotterdam, 2013), p. 122.
8 Manuel Aguirre, *The Closed Space: Horror Literature and Western Symbolism* (Manchester, 1990), p. 2.
9 Citations from the translator of Kierkegaard's *The Concept of Dread*, Walter Lourie, who suffered meta-*Angst*: 'I have acquired such a dread of these words, any of which may mean a dozen things'; translator's Preface to *The Concept of Dread* (Princeton, NJ, 1944), p. viii. Another translation of the book in 1980 by Reidar Thomte renders it *The Concept of Anxiety*. There is a lengthy discussion of how to translate *Angst* in the *Standard Edition of the Complete Works of Sigmund Freud*, which comes down on the side of 'anxiety' despite its 'remote connection with any of the uses of the German *Angst*', *Standard Edition*, vol. III (London, 1962), p. 116.
10 Ernest Jones, *On the Nightmare* (New York, 1950), p. 18.
11 See Anthony Vidler, *Warped Space: Art, Architecture and Anxiety in Modern Culture* (Cambridge, MA, 2001).

12 Anna Chalcraft and Judith Viscardi, *Strawberry Hill: Horace Walpole's Gothic Castle* (London, 2007), p. 13.
13 Ann Radcliffe, *The Romance of the Forest*, ed. C. Chard (Oxford, 2009), pp. 21 and 108.
14 Ibid., p. 248.
15 Ann Radcliffe, *The Mysteries of Udolpho*, ed. T. Castle (Oxford, 2008), p. 345.
16 Ibid., p. 348.
17 Jane Austen, *Northanger Abbey*, ed. A. Ehrenpreis (Harmondsworth, 1987), pp. 164, 166, 168 and 187.
18 Charles Maturin, *Melmoth the Wanderer,* ed. C. Baldick (Oxford, 1998), pp. 185 and 191–2.
19 Edgar Allan Poe, 'The Fall of the House of Usher', *Selected Writings,* ed. G. R. Thompson (New York, 2004), p. 211.
20 Charles Dickens, *Bleak House* (London, 1985), p. 631.
21 Edward Bulwer-Lytton, 'The Haunted and the Haunters', in *The Collected Weird and Supernatural Fiction*, vol. I (Beverley, 2011), p. 266.
22 Charlotte Bronte, *Jane Eyre*, ed. Q. D. Leavis (Harmondsworth, 1984), p. 237.
23 See 'A Ghost Story', *Kentish Gazette* (15 September 1863). This is abstracted from Henry Spicer's *Strange Things Among Us* (London, 1863).
24 William Pickering, 'The Ghost's Tryst; or, What These Eyes Saw. A Christmas Tale', *Stanford Mercury* (25 December 1891).
25 Oscar Wilde, 'The Canterville Ghost', in *The Complete Works* (London, 1986), p. 197.
26 A. Goodrich-Freer and John, Marquess of Bute, *The Alleged Haunting of B----- House* (London, 1899), pp. 55 and 66. The investigation is debunked in the bitter account by Trevor Hall, *The Strange Story of Ada Goodrich-Freer* (London, 1980).
27 Henry James, 'The Jolly Corner', in *The New York Stories*, ed. C. Toibin (New York, 2006), pp. 467, 490, 489–90, 495–6.
28 See Elizabeth Stevenson, *The Crooked Corridor: A Study of Henry James* (London, 1961), citing a James letter to Mrs Humphry Ward from 1899, p. 142.
29 Robert Aickman, 'The Unsettled Dust', in *The Unsettled Dust* (London, 2014) and 'The Hospice', in *Cold Hand in Mine* (London, 2008), p. 126.
30 Mark Z. Danielewski, *The House of Leaves* (2000), pp. 64, 24 and 60.
31 John Langan, *House of Windows* (San Francisco, CA, 2010), p. 215.
32 Jeff VanderMeer, *Authority* (London, 2014), p. 139.

33 Jeff VanderMeer, 'Predecessor', in *The Third Bear* (San Francisco, CA, 2010), p. 96.
34 Joshua Cameroff and Ong Ker-Shing, *Horror in Architecture* (Novato, CA, 2013), p. 7.
35 Anthony Vidler, *The Architectural Uncanny: Essays in the Modern Unhomely* (Novato, MA, 1992), p. 161.
36 Thomas M. Sipos, *Horror Film Aesthetics: Creating the Visual Language of Fear* (Jefferson, NC, 2010), p. 107.
37 Richard Martin, *The Architecture of David Lynch* (London, 2014), pp. 181 and 49.
38 Jean-Pierre Geuens, 'Visuality and Power: The Work of the Steadicam', *Film Quarterly*, XLVII/2 (1993–4), p. 14. Garrett Brown quoted from an interview with Danel Olson, in Olson, ed., *Stanley Kubrick's 'The Shining': Studies in the Horror Film* (Lakewood, CO, 2015), p. 569.
39 Georges Perec, *Species of Spaces and Other Pieces*, trans. J. Sturrock (London, 2008), p. 5.
40 See Ann Radcliffe, 'On the Supernatural in Poetry' (1826), reproduced in *Gothic Documents: A Sourcebook, 1700–1820*, ed. E. Clery and R. Miles (Manchester, 2000), pp. 163–72.
41 See Nicholas Royle, *The Uncanny* (Manchester, 2003), p. 24.
42 Mark Fisher, 'Eerie Thanatos: Nigel Kneale and Dark Enlightenment', in *The Twilight Language of Nigel Kneale*, ed. S. Sandhu (Brooklyn, NY, 2012), p. 110. This is expanded in Fisher's *The Weird and the Eerie* (London, 2016).
43 Timothy Morton, *Dark Ecology: For a Logic of Coexistence* (New York, 2016).
44 Kierkegaard, *The Concept of Dread*, p. 38.
45 Ibid., p. 55.
46 Martin Heidegger, *Being and Time*, trans. J. Macquarrie and E. Robinson (Oxford, 1967), p. 230.
47 Ibid., p. 231.
48 Ibid.
49 China Miéville in interview, 'The Surplus Value of Fear', in *Dread: The Dizziness of Freedom*, ed. Juha van 't Zelfde (Amsterdam, 2013), p. 58.
50 Kevin McLeod, 'Corridor Syntax', in *Corridor*, ed. Stephan Trüby et al. (Venice, 2014), p. 98.
51 Pauline Kael, 'Devolution', *Taking It All In* (London, 1986), p. 2.
52 Mayer Spivack, 'Sensory Distortion in Tunnels and Corridors', *Hospital and Community Psychiatry*, XVIII/1 (1967), p. 18.

53 Pete Boss, 'Vile Bodies and Bad Medicine', *Screen*, XXVII/1 (1986), p. 15. I have discussed this genre at more length in my essay, 'Biomedical Horror: The New Death and the New Undead', in *Technologies of the Gothic in Literature and Culture*, ed. J. Edwards (London 2015).
54 See Cormac O'Shea, *Daily Mirror* (4 October 2017), www.mirror.co.uk, accessed 31 May 2018.

Conclusion: At the End of the Passage

1 Rudyard Kipling, 'At the End of the Passage', in *Life's Handicap: Being Stories of Mine Own People* (London, 1923), pp. 204, 206, 207, 208.
2 Madhavi Desai, Mika Desai and Jon Lang, *The Bungalow in Twentieth-century India: The Cultural Expression of Changing Ways of Life and Aspirations in the Domestic Architecture of Colonial and Post-colonial Society* (Abingdon, 2012), p. 42.
3 Don DeLillo, *Zero K* (New York, 2016), pp. 10 and 50.
4 Raymond A. Moody, *Life after Life: The Investigation of a Phenomenon – Survival of Bodily Death* (Atlanta, GA, 1975), p. 29.
5 P.M.H. Atwater, *The Big Book of Near-death Experiences* (Charlottesville, VA, 2007), p. 12.
6 For this range of positions, see Lee W. Bailey and Jenny Yates, Introduction to *The Near-death Experience: A Reader* (London, 1996).
7 Margaret L. Coit, *Mr Baruch* (New York, 1957), p. 585.
8 C.F.J. Whebell, 'Corridors: A Theory of Urban Systems', *Annals of the Association of American Geographers*, LIX/1 (1969), pp. 1 and 4.
9 There were many anxious discussions of the political implications of the Polish Corridor in the 1920s. See, for instance, Sir Robert Donald, *The Polish Corridor and the Consequences* (London, 1929).

Select Bibliography

Adlam, Derek, *Tunnel Vision: The Enigmatic Fifth Duke of Portland* (Welbeck, Nottinghamshire, 2013)

Aguirre, Miguel, *The Closed Space: Horror Literature and Western Symbolism* (Manchester, 1990)

Bachelard, Gaston, *The Poetics of Space*, trans. M. Jolas (London, 2014)

Bailey, Lee W., and Jenny Yates, eds, *The Near-death Experience: A Reader* (London, 1996)

Banham, Reyner, *Megastructure: Urban Futures of the Recent Past* (London, 1976)

Barton, Russell, *Institutional Neurosis*, 2nd edn (Bristol, 1966)

Beloff, Michael, *The Plateglass Universities* (London, 1968)

Benjamin, Walter, *The Arcades Project*, trans. H. Eiland and K. McLaughlin (Cambridge, MA, 1999)

Bentham, Jeremy, *Panopticon; or, The Inspection House* (Dublin, 1791)

Berger, Molly, *Hotel Dreams: Luxury, Technology, and Urban Ambition in America, 1829–1929* (Baltimore, MD, 2011)

Bernard, Andreas, *Lifted: A Cultural History of the Elevator*, trans. D. Dollenmayer (New York, 2014)

Burdett, Henry C., *Hospitals and Asylums of the World*, vol. IV: *Hospital Construction, with Plans*, 4 vols (London, 1893)

Burt, John T., *Results of the System of Separate Confinement, as Administered at the Pentonville Prison* (London, 1852)

Cameroff, Joshua, and Ker-Shing Ong, *Horror in Architecture* (Novato, CA, 2013)

Chartier, Roger, ed., *A History of Private Life*, 3 vols (Cambridge, MA, 1989)

Conolly, John, *The Construction and Government of Lunatic Asylums* (London, 1847)

Curtis, Barry, *Dark Places: The Haunted House in Film* (London, 2008)

Dimendberg, Edward, *Film Noir and the Spaces of Modernity* (Cambridge, MA, 2004)
Duffy, Francis, *The New Office* (London, 1997)
Edginton, Barry, 'The Design of Moral Architecture at the York Retreat', *Journal of Design History*, XVI/2 (2003), pp. 103–17
Evans, Robin, *The Fabrication of Virtue: English Prison Architecture, 1750–1850* (Cambridge, 1982)
—, *Translations from Drawing to Building and Other Essays* (London, 1997)
Fisher, Mark, *The Weird and the Eerie* (London, 2016)
Foucault, Michel, *Discipline and Punish: The Birth of the Prison*, trans. A. Sheridan (New York, 1995)
—, *Psychiatric Power: Lectures at the Collège de France, 1973–74*, trans. G. Burchell (London, 2006)
Fourier, Charles, *The Utopian Visions of Charles Fourier: Selected Texts on Work, Love, and Passionate Attraction*, trans. and ed. J. Beecher and P. Bienvenu (Boston, MA, 1971)
Franklin, Jill, *The Gentleman's Country House and Its Plan, 1835–1914* (London, 1981)
Geist, Johann Friedrich, *Arcades: The History of a Building Type* (Cambridge, MA, 1983)
Goffman, Erving, *Asylums: Essays on the Social Situation of Mental Patients and Other Inmates* (London, 1991)
Graeber, David, *The Utopia of Rules: On Technology, Stupidity, and the Secret Joys of Bureaucracy* (London, 2015)
Greenhalgh, Paul, *Ephemeral Vistas: The Exposition Universelles, Great Exhibitions and World's Fairs, 1851–1939* (Manchester, 1988)
Grindrod, John, *Concretopia: A Journey around the Rebuilding of Postwar Britain* (London, 2014)
Gruen, Victor, and Larry Smith, *Shopping Towns USA: The Planning of Shopping Centers* (New York, 1960)
Hayden, Dolores, *Seven American Utopias: The Architecture of Communitarian Socialism, 1790–1975* (Cambridge, MA, 1976)
Hebbert, Michael, 'The City of London Walkway Experiment', *Journal of the American Planning Association*, LIX/4 (1993), pp. 433–50
Hell, Julia, and Andreas Schönle, eds, *Ruins of Modernity* (Durham, NC, 2010)
Hollander, Martha, *An Entrance for the Eyes: Space and Meaning in Seventeenth-century Dutch Art* (Berkeley, CA, 2002)
Hopkins, Owen, *Lost Futures: The Disappearing Architecture of Post-war Britain* (London, 2017)

Horn, Walter, 'On the Origins of the Medieval Cloister', *Gesta*, XII/1–2 (1973), pp. 13–52

Hurdley, Rachel, 'The Power of Corridors: Connecting Doors, Multiplying Materials, Plotting Openness', *Sociological Review*, LVIII/1 (2010), pp. 45–64

Jarman, Rufus, *A Bed for the Night: The Story of the Wheeling Bellboy, E. M. Statler, and His Remarkable Hotels* (New York, 1952)

Jarzombek, Mark, 'Corridor Spaces', *Critical Inquiry*, XXXVI/4 (2010), pp. 728–70

Jewitt, Llewellynn, and S. C. Hall, *The Stately Homes of England*, 2nd series (London, 1877)

Johnson, Norman, et al., *Eastern State Penitentiary: Crucible of Good Intentions* (Philadelphia, PA, 1994)

Jütte, Daniel, *The Strait Gate: Thresholds and Power in Western History* (New Haven, CT, 2015)

Kerr, Robert, *The English Gentleman's House; or, How to Plan English Residences, from the Parsonage to the Palace* (London, 1864)

Koolhaas, Rem, *Delirious New York* (New York, 1994)

Kopp, Anatole, *Town and Revolution: Soviet Architecture and City Planning, 1917–35* (New York, 1970)

Kowinski, William Severini, *The Malling of America: Travels in the United States of Shopping* (New York, 1985, rev. Bloomington, IN, 2002)

Kracauer, Siegfried, *The Mass Ornament*, trans. Thomas Levin (Cambridge, MA, 1995)

Le Corbusier, *Towards a New Architecture* [1923] (Thousand Oaks, CA, 2008)

—, *The Radiant City: Elements of a Doctrine of Urbanism as the Basis of Our Machine-age Civilization*, trans. P. Knight et al. (London, 1967)

Long, Helen C., *The Edwardian House: The Middle-class Home in Britain, 1880–1914* (Manchester, 1993)

McCarthy, James Remington, *Peacock-Alley: The Romance of the Waldorf-Astoria* (New York, 1931)

MacKeith, Margaret, *Shopping Arcades: A Gazetteer of Extant British Arcades, 1817–1939* (London, 1985)

Markus, Thomas A., *Buildings and Power: Freedom and Control in the Origin of Modern Building Types* (London, 1993)

Mayhew, Henry, and John Binny, *The Criminal Prisons of London, and Scenes of Prison Life* (London, 1862)

Moon, G., R. Kearns and A. Joseph, eds, *The Afterlives of the Psychiatric Asylum* (Farnham, 2015),

Morrison, Kathryn, *The Workhouse: A Study of Poor Law Buildings in England* (London, 1999)

Muthesius, Hermann, *The English House*, trans. J. Seligman (London, 1979)
Owen, Robert, *The Life of Robert Owen, Written by Himself* (London, 1857)
Ringshall, Ron, Margaret Miles and Frank Kelsall et al., eds, *The Urban School: Buildings for Education in London, 1870–1980* (London, 1983)
Robson, Edward Robert, *School Architecture: Being Practical Remarks on the Planning, Designing, Building, and Furnishing of School-houses* (London, 1874)
Rüegg, Arthur, et al., *La Cellule Le Corbusier: L'Unité d'habitation de Marseille* (Marseilles, 2015)
Scull, Andrew, *The Insanity of Place/The Place of Insanity* (Abingdon, 2006)
Shulze, J. William, *The American Office: Its Organization, Management and Records* (New York, 1913)
Smithson, Alison, and Peter Smithson, *The Charged Void: Architecture* (New York, 2001)
Snow, C. P., *Corridors of Power* (Harmondsworth, 1964)
Spivack, Mayer, 'Sensory Distortion in Tunnels and Corridors', *Hospital and Community Psychiatry*, XVIII/1 (1967), pp. 12–18
Stevenson, Elizabeth, *The Crooked Corridor: A Study of Henry James* (London, 1961)
Stevenson, J. J., *House Architecture*, 2 vols (London, 1880)
Stites, Richard, *Revolutionary Dreams: Utopian Vision and Experimental Life in the Russian Revolution* (Oxford, 1989)
Taylor, Jeremy, *Hospital and Asylum Architecture, 1840–1914: Building for Health Care* (London, 1991)
Tomes, Nancy, *A Generous Confidence: Thomas Story Kirkbride and the Art of Asylum-keeping, 1840–83* (Cambridge, 1984)
Trüby, Stephan, et al., *Corridor* (Venice, 2014)
—, 'Welbeck Abbey's Corridors', *Icon*, 136 (October 2014), www.iconeye.com
Tuke, Samuel, *Description of the Retreat, an Institution near York, for Insane Persons of the Society of Friends* (York, 1813)
Van Lennep, D. J., 'The Hotel Room', in *Phenomenological Psychology: The Dutch School*, ed. J. J. Kockelmans (Dordrecht, 1987), pp. 209–15
Van Meel, Juriaan, *The European Office: Office Design and National Context* (Rotterdam, 2000)
Vidler, Anthony, *The Architectural Uncanny: Essays in the Modern Unhomely* (Cambridge, MA, 1992)
—, *Claude-Nicolas Ledoux: Architecture and Social Reform at the End of the Ancien Régime* (Cambridge, MA, 1990)
—, *The Scenes of the Street, and Other Essays* (New York, 2011)
—, *Warped Space: Art, Architecture, and Anxiety in Modern Culture* (Cambridge, MA, 2000)

Wall, Alex, *Victor Gruen: From Urban Shop to New City* (Barcelona, 2005)
Wayland-Smith, Ellen, *Oneida: From Free Love Utopia to the Well-set Table* (New York, 2016)
Weber, Max, *Essays in Sociology*, ed. H. H. Gerth and C. W. Mills (London, 1952)
Weiner, Deborah E. B., *Architects and Social Reform in Late Victorian London* (Manchester, 1994)
Whebell, C.F.J., 'Corridors: A Theory of Urban Systems', *Annals of the Association of American Geographers*, LIX/1 (1969), pp. 1–26
Whyte, William, *Redbrick: A Social and Architectural History of Britain's Civic Universities* (Oxford, 2015)
Yanni, Carla, *The Architecture of Madness: Insane Asylums in the United States* (Minneapolis, MN, 2007)
Zelfde, Juha van 't, ed., *Dread: The Dizziness of Freedom* (Amsterdam, 2013)

Acknowledgements

Thanks to Ben Hayes for commissioning this unlikely project. Thanks also to Michael Leaman for seeing it through, seemingly without a moment's doubt. Susannah Jayes sorted out the pictures and permissions.

For advice and prompts, many thanks to Stacey Abbott, Emily Alder, Simon Barraclough, Mark Blacklock, Mark Bould, Carolyn Burdett, Andy Butler, Amy Butt, Julie Crofts, David Edgar, Catharine Edwards, Jes Fernie, Pawel Frelik, Chris Greenhalgh, Simon Guerrier, Richard Hamblyn, Stephen Hughes, Timothy Jarvis, Mike Jay, Toby Litt, Ross MacFarlane, James Machen, Glyn Morgan, Carol Morley, Victoria Nelson, Michael Newton, Mark Pilkington, Adam Roberts, Laura Salisbury, Andy Sawyer, Alan Stewart, Laura Thomas, Sherryl Vint, Jonathan Wild, Will Wiles, Rhys Williams, Jo Winning. I also want to thank the unknown prisoner in Pentonville Prison who saw me loitering in the street below taking notes and shouted down from one of the windows, 'Oi! What the f*** are you looking at?' This turned out to be a very good question.

Early research was conducted in the wonderful Avebury Library at Columbia University in New York. Many thanks to my hosts there in 2016, Matt Hart and Sarah Cole. Thanks to the Wellcome Trust and Ross MacFarlane in particular for the invitation to give the Roy Porter Lecture in 2017, which forced me to up my game.

Two works came my way in the course of this project that convinced me I was on to something. Will Wiles's *The Way Inn* came as happy early confirmation, and towards the end Chris Greenhalgh sent me unprompted his poem 'Untitled Corridor Project', which uncannily sketches out some of the trajectories of this book. With his permission, this poem forms one of my epigraphs.

This is for Julie, as always, who will now no longer have to explain to the bewildered that her holidays are largely organized around visits to famous corridors. Love and knitting.

Photo Acknowledgements

The author and the publishers wish to express their thanks to the below sources of illustrative material and /or permission to reproduce it.

Alamy: pp. 36 (ArtCollection 2), 75 (ITAR-TAS News Agency), 95 (Anthony Palmer), 188 (Historic Images), 215 (Art Collection); © Crown copyright Historic England Archive: p. 196; Eastern State Penitentiary Image Library: pp. 167, 169; Getty Images: p. 135 (FPG); The Harley Gallery, Welbeck: p. 229; Library of Congress, Washington, DC: pp. 60, 61; Roger Luckhurst: pp. 8, 27, 32, 86 (© FLC/ ADAGP, Paris and DACS, London 2018), 207, 208; Mary Evans Picture Library: p. 96 (© Roger Mayne Archive); Josh Partee: p. 192; Shutterstock: p. 241 (sirtravelalot); © 2018 The Solomon R. Guggenheim Foundation/ Art Resource, NY/Scala Florence: p. 259 (Solomon R. Guggenheim, New York Panza Collection, Gift, 1992 (92.4171) Photo Erika Barahona Ede © SRGF, New York Bruce Nauman/Artists Rights Society (ARS), New York and DACS, London 2018); © Tate, London, 2018: p. 81(©DACS 2018); Topfoto: p. 107; Victoria and Albert Museum, London: p. 115; Wellcome Collection: pp. 174, 184, 186, 187, 195.

Index

Page numbers in *italics* refer to illustrations